Mark Dunn is a public historian and former chair of the Professional Historians Association of NSW and ACT. He is descended from convicts who settled in the Hunter, and he has spent two decades investigating the history, heritage and archaeology of the region.

'Mark Dunn's *The Convict Valley* is a finely detailed and meticulously researched study of the Hunter Valley. Interweaving its Aboriginal, convict and mining past, Dunn reveals the missing and misunderstood complexities of these histories as a gifted storyteller. It is a must read.'
Professor John Maynard, The University of Newcastle

'Deeply researched and beautifully written, *The Convict Valley* tells a new and compelling story about the early colonial Hunter Valley: the forgotten histories of Aboriginal people and convicts and their struggles for Country and survival.'
Professor Grace Karskens, author of *The Colony*

Mark Dunn is a public historian and former chair of the Professional Historians Association of NSW and ACT. He is descended from convicts who settled in the Hunter, and he has spent two decades investigating the history, heritage and archaeology of the region.

'Mark Dunn's The Convict Valley is a finely detailed and meticulously researched study of the Hunter Valley. Interweaving its Aboriginal, convict and mining past, Dunn reveals the missing and misunderstood complexities of these histories as a gifted storyteller. It is a must read.'
Professor John Maynard, The University of Newcastle

'Deeply researched and beautifully written, The Convict Valley tells a new and compelling story about the early colonial Hunter Valley, the forgotten histories of Aboriginal people and convicts and their struggles for Country and survival.'
Professor Grace Karskens, author of The Colony

THE
THE BLOODY STRUGGLE ON AUSTRALIA'S EARLY FRONTIER
CONVICT VALLEY

MARK DUNN

ALLEN&UNWIN
SYDNEY · MELBOURNE · AUCKLAND · LONDON

First published in 2020

Allen & Unwin
83 Alexander Street
Crows Nest NSW 2065
Australia
Phone: (61 2) 8425 0100
Email: info@allenandunwin.com
Web: www.allenandunwin.com

A catalogue record for this
book is available from the
National Library of Australia

ISBN 978 1 76052 864 5

Maps by Cecilie Knowles
Index by Puddingburn
Set in 12/16 pt Baskerville by Midland Typesetters, Australia
Printed and bound in Australia by SOS Print + Media

10 9 8 7 6

The paper in this book is FSC® certified.
FSC® promotes environmentally responsible,
socially beneficial and economically viable
management of the world's forests.

CONTENTS

CONTENTS

TERMINOLOGY AND NAMING

The reader will note that some of the language used to describe Aboriginal people during the period this book covers is often anachronistic and in some cases offensive. It is not the intention of this work to offend, but where direct quotes from documents or manuscripts are used, the original language remains. Individual Aboriginal people are named where possible; however, the groups or clans that they were from are not, as for the most part these were not identified in the historical record. As the book shows, Aboriginal men and women were mobile across the Hunter, moving from the plains to the mountains, visiting the coastal settlements and those inland. For this reason, I have not tied people to particular clans but rather discussed them as individuals in the place they lived and were encountered. And although this book is focused on a time prior to 1850, Aboriginal people survived in and continued to live right across the Hunter Valley after this period. Today, Aboriginal people in the Hunter Valley are represented by seven Local Aboriginal Land Councils: Awabakal, Bahtabah, Biraban, Karuah, Mindaribba, Wonnarua and Worimi. These Councils work in conjunction with other Aboriginal cultural, social and family groups from the coast to the mountains.

I have also chosen to refer to the white population generically as British. In the years that this book covers the majority of the white population were British, albeit with a substantial number of Irish convicts among them. Scottish and Welsh settlers were considered as being British, while there were only small numbers of continental European settlers during this period. The decisions that drove the colonisation of the valley were, however, made by the British: either through the far away Home Office, the colonial governors in Sydney or the military commandants in Newcastle.

ABORIGINAL AND TORRES STRAIT ISLANDER READERS

Aboriginal and Torres Strait Islanders should be aware that this book contains words and descriptions written by non-Indigenous people in official reports, newspapers and letters from the period 1790–1850 that may be confronting and would be considered inappropriate today. It also contains names of deceased people and graphic descriptions of historic and violent events that may be disturbing.

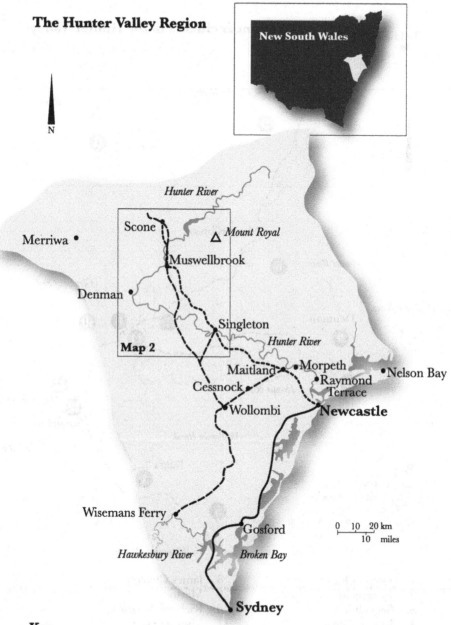

The Hunter Valley Region

New South Wales

N

Hunter River

Scone

△ Mount Royal

Merriwa

Muswellbrook

Denman

Map 2

Singleton

Hunter River

Maitland

Morpeth

Cessnock

Raymond
Terrace

Nelson Bay

Wollombi

Newcastle

Wisemans Ferry

Gosford

0 10 20 km
10 miles

Hawkesbury River

Broken Bay

Sydney

Key

--- convict road into the Hunter from Wisemans Ferry – 1826

----- road through the Hunter from Newcastle to Scone – 1829

── coastal road from Sydney to Newcastle – 1844

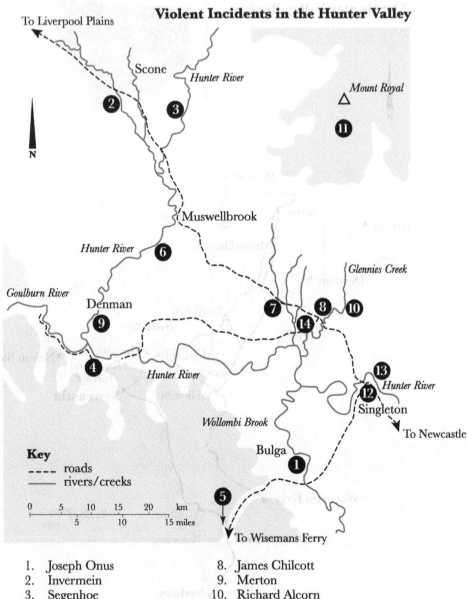

Violent Incidents in the Hunter Valley

To Liverpool Plains

Scone

Hunter River

Mount Royal
△
11

2

3

Muswellbrook

Hunter River

6

Glennies Creek

Goulburn River

Denman

9

7

8

10

14

4

13

Hunter River

12

Singleton

Hunter River

Wollombi Brook

To Newcastle

Key
- - - - roads
——— rivers/creeks

Bulga

1

0   5   10   15   20   km

5   10   15 miles

5

To Wisemans Ferry

N

1. Joseph Onus
2. Invermein
3. Segenhoe
4. Robert Greig
5. Putty
6. Edinglassie
7. Ravensworth (1, 2 & 3)

8. James Chilcott
9. Merton
10. Richard Alcorn
11. Massacre site
12. John Hunt
13. George Claris
14. Ravensworth (4)

INTRODUCTION

A HIDDEN VALLEY

The Hunter Valley is an easy place to like. Newcastle's long, sweeping beaches embrace the city; the harbour is emerging as a new backdrop for restaurants, bars and cafes. The looming coal ships gliding past are one of the few reminders of the city's industrial foundations.

Go inland and you come to the region's famous vineyards. Rolling hills have been landscaped for more than a century with row upon row of well-tended vines. Cellar doors and tasting venues beckon to the thousands of visitors the area attracts every weekend. Horse studs dot the upper reaches of the valley, while rugged mountains hem it in, their stark sandstone flanks reflecting the sun in golden shades of yellow.

The Hunter River, though, is barely seen—maybe glimpsed from the car window scooting along the highway or crossing the Hexham Bridge on a holiday drive north. Few boats ply the watercourse these days, save for those out for some fishing, or perhaps waterskiing around Raymond Terrace. Through the central valley, the rich, thick, black coal seam that sweeps in a wide band from the upper reaches of the valley to the coast is exposed in vast, open-cut mines. These can be a jarring sight when first viewed.

For many, this is the Hunter Valley; this and the historic tourist towns such as Wollombi and Morpeth: heritage buildings and antique centres serving as signposts that hint at a colonial past. But the manicured lawns and ordered landscapes hide the struggles, violence, triumphs and failures of the colonial frontier on which they are built. It has almost been forgotten that this was a convicts' valley; the old convict lumberyard site on the Newcastle Harbour foreshore is one of the few spots to openly acknowledge this past. Other than Sydney and Tasmania, more convicts went through the Hunter Valley in the years between 1801 and 1841 than any other region. Thousands of men and women were banished here or sent to work as assigned labourers.

The valley they entered was not empty, but rich in Aboriginal history, lore and culture. The surrounding mountains have hundreds of art and ceremonial sites, with some of the best examples of rock art on the eastern seaboard. Aboriginal people had worked the land and managed the vegetation and waterways of their Country for generations. They moved across the landscape, occupying every part of it, and formed connections to all the surrounding peoples, from Sydney to the north coast and out to the western plains. Like the convict past, Aboriginal history is barely remembered in the Hunter.

I grew up in the Hunter Valley. I can trace my family back to the early 1820s, when settlers began to pour into what had been a restricted penal station. Our ancestors were not free; rather, they were among the thousands of convicts who came with those settlers, to work the land and build the houses and the roads. I also studied history at school and learnt nothing of these stories. The only convict history I knew was that talked about by my parents, both descended from those first convict workers. Of the region's Aboriginal past, I knew even less.

This, of course, was not unique to the Hunter Valley. Until recently, convicts—and, even more so, Aboriginal people—were largely missing from just about all Australian historical narratives. With a few notable exceptions, they were confined to the first chapters of a book and then pushed aside by a story of triumphant expansionism and settler progress, stuck in a brutal past or 'last of the tribe' narrative.

The same might be said of the Hunter Valley itself. The valley has been sadly overlooked in many of the written histories of colonial Australia, except for the tireless work of local historical societies and family historians. Walter Allan Wood's *Dawn in the Valley*, published in 1972, is one of the few on the subject and was the last comprehensive history of the colonial Hunter Valley published: it is so rare now that it is itself a collector's item. Wood was one of the first to explore at least some of the Aboriginal history of the area, including the terrible violence that swept through the valley in the late 1820s. Convicts, however, are barely mentioned, except in passing. More recently, the work of Cynthia Hunter— much of it written as part of the Maitland City Council Heritage Group—has begun to redress this imbalance. Her fine, detailed work has renewed an interest locally in the convict heritage of the middle valley.

And so it should. Outside of Sydney, the Hunter Valley was the first region to be explored in any detail by the British; it is where the earliest sustained contact with Aboriginal people occurred, and it was occupied by a convict vanguard. There were convicts in the Hunter long before any set foot in Tasmania or crossed the Blue Mountains.

The discovery of coal on the shores of Newcastle Harbour was the catalyst for British occupation. Coal drew them in; cedar held them there. The resources were exploited from the very start, and the extraction of coal, timber and shells to burn for lime had a profound effect on the environment. The legacies of these colonial industries are still obvious throughout the region. Coalmining now has a history of over 215 years in the Hunter Valley, while the red cedar that was once common is now a rarity. Shell middens still line the foreshore of Newcastle Harbour: in some areas they are visible, in others they lie buried under modern development. Their survival is due more to their vastness, built up over millennia by Aboriginal people, rather than to any conservation by the colonial authorities. In the end they were just too big to completely disappear. Many surviving colonial buildings in Sydney and elsewhere remain standing due in part to the mortar made from these shell deposits.

While convicts worked the land, Aboriginal people defended it. From the very first years a complex, interwoven history emerged between the Aboriginal people and the British in the Hunter. In the first decades, a curious coexistence developed. The numbers of convicts and guards were relatively low, and mostly confined to the coast. The few isolated pockets of timber-getters or small experimental farmers did not intrude far into Country. There were skirmishes, and Aboriginal people were employed to track runaway convicts, but, for the most part, contact was limited. However, in the mad scramble for land in the 1820s, as the valley was opened to free settlers, tensions increased and Aboriginal people were placed under enormous pressure. Their Country was being overrun, and violence erupted.

But it was not all violence. Indeed, the violence has for the most part obscured what was a more complex history—one in which friendships and alliances were made, knowledge was shared and traded, and interlocking relationships were formed. Often these relationships existed in parallel to the violence playing out around them.

It is these hidden histories and forgotten stories that this book sets out to capture. It is not a comprehensive history of the Hunter

Valley but, rather, a snapshot, taken from the letters, diaries, journals and memories of those who lived there. It covers a 50-year span, give or take, from the late 1790s to the early 1850s, during which time the land was invaded, a penal station came and went, and the valley was transformed by expansionist land policies as thousands of settlers poured in.

Before the 1850s, the Hunter Valley was a colonial outpost. The large estates granted in the 1820s still dominated the landscape, and the families who owned them still dominated the social and political scene. Convicts and emancipists were still in the majority, and Aboriginal people were maintaining traditions and culture, albeit under increasingly difficult circumstances. Beyond this date, however, everything begins to change and does so quickly. Railways reduce the importance of the river, coal discoveries begin to industrialise the central valley and bankruptcy sweeps through many of the established families. And so it is there that this book leaves off.

But Aboriginal people, convicts and their descendants remained. This book tells some of their early stories.

CHAPTER ONE

THE VALLEY

In the closing years of the eighteenth century, just as Sydney town was finding its feet, a newly discovered harbour some 60 nautical miles or 110 kilometres north began to draw the attention of the colonial authorities. Coal lay scattered on the beaches at the mouth of a wide river; the sandstone cliffs riven through with black seams were fringed by grassy slopes and clustering cedar forests. It was first reported by Lieutenant John Shortland in 1797, who later wrote to his father that he 'dare say in a little time this river will be a great acquisition to this settlement'. Shortland named it Hunter River, after the New South Wales governor, John Hunter.[1]

A VALLEY FORMED

Like much of the east coast of New South Wales, the Hunter Valley—geologically speaking—is both old and new. Parts date back over 400 million years, laid down by ancient volcanoes and fluctuating sea levels. The great coal deposits that underlie much of the valley, popping to the surface around Singleton and in the cliffs

7

at Newcastle, were formed during this era. Other areas show the evidence of the vast, ancient continent of Gondwana, when Australia was linked to New Zealand, Antarctica, South America and India. The high mountain rainforests around the Barrington Tops and Mount Royal Range on the northern fringes of the Hunter stand as some of the last vestiges of the forests from this time. Marine fossils found at Stanhope near Branxton, now 50 kilometres from the ocean, hint at the massive upheavals as the Gondwanan landmass began to break apart 165 million years ago. Alternating saltwater, freshwater and volcanic deposits reveal the fluctuating sea levels and changing conditions across the area.[2]

Some twelve million years ago a great tectonic uplift mashed the ancient layers together, pushing up a mountainous belt that became the Great Dividing Range. Where the ancient, ancestral rivers had once flowed towards the south, they were now forced eastward towards the sea and began the long process of erosion that carved the valley as we see it today. These old fault lines are exposed in the country between Muswellbrook and Wingen, where an older, wider valley can be seen. One of the new rivers was the Hunter. From its headwaters in the high mountains around Mount Royal and the back of the Barrington Ranges, its waters cut through soft sandstone in some parts and were resisted by the basalt outcrops and lava flows in others. The yielding rock and the resistance meant that the waters wandered through the landscape, carving out the valley along the way. Once the waters dropped out of the highlands they began to meander, slowing down, widening out—simultaneously eroding land on their outside curves and depositing alluvium on their inside sweep.

There are four main rivers that flow through the Hunter Valley: the Hunter, Goulburn, Paterson and Williams rivers. So it was that over aeons each formed its respective valley and floodplains, eventually coming together below Raymond Terrace to form the large estuary before entering the sea at Newcastle. It is no coincidence that the land of the central Hunter, through which each of these rivers flows, was heavily utilised in the millennia of Aboriginal occupation and became the most sought-after in the first decades of British occupation.

The valley is fringed with rugged mountains on three sides and the ocean on the fourth. While the sea crashes onto the sandy beaches along the Newcastle coastline, this was not always the case. At the last interglacial period, approximately 120,000 years ago, the sea level was up to five metres higher than now, with waves lapping at the shore near Largs, around Maitland. Fifteen thousand years ago, the sea level along this part of the coast was around 130 metres below the current level, and the shoreline approximately 25 kilometres east of its present position. What is now Newcastle was then far inland, the future Nobbys Island (now Nobbys Head) a prominent feature in a landscape of forest and grassland. As sea levels rose and fell, the mouth of the Hunter shifted up and down the coast. Peat beds discovered some 25 metres underground at Port Stephens are evidence of some of these ancient forests, while remains of trees and coarse gravel 55 metres down at Stockton hint at the buried forests and rivers of the earlier valley.[3]

Around 11,500 years ago, with the ice age retreating, the sea rose once more, flooding into what is now Port Stephens to the north and creating Lake Macquarie in the south. As the waters continued to rise, the shoreline crept in to West Maitland, now 40 kilometres inland. The Williams and Paterson rivers were not yet tributaries of the Hunter, but rather emptied into this great bay independent of each other. The heights of Newcastle and Nobbys Island stood as isolated islands far off the coast. As the geological processes settled and the sea retreated to its present level, the slow silting of the rivers pushed the delta back towards its current position, leaving behind a connected series of swamps and marshlands between Hexham and Seaham and north to Port Stephens, fringed by sand dunes along the coast. The end result was one main river nearly 470 kilometres long, with a collection of major tributaries flowing through a valley almost 180 kilometres inland—further inland than any other coastal catchment in New South Wales—and covering an area of approximately 22,000 square kilometres.[4]

Regular flooding was a feature of this valley. The landscape made it ideal for inundation, with the rivers dropping quickly from high mountains to a very flat valley floor. In big rain events the banks could not cope with the vast amounts of water, and the rivers regularly broke over and spilled across the floodplain. Evidence of flooding during the last 12,000 years shows the slow accumulation of silt and soil that built the alluvial plains. Until flood mitigation works were completed in the 1960s and 1970s, floods were recorded every few decades from soon after the British arrival.

Despite their destructive nature, this long process of flood action made the Hunter one of the most fertile districts in colonial New South Wales. One flood event recorded in 1904 laid down so much soil that the nutrients in it were estimated to be sufficient to support all the crops in the valley at the time for a period of ten years.[5] However, the rugged mountains and gullies that dominate the central and upper valley meant that the rich alluvial soils were confined to a relatively narrow band of ground, hugging the flat lands along the river's course. It was access to this land that fuelled much of the conflict and violence that was to erupt during the 1820s and 1830s throughout the Hunter.

Other resources besides water and good soil were also to be found. The region's variety of landscapes, elevations and climate zones supported a range of vegetation. As elsewhere along the eastern coast, eucalypts had adapted to the Hunter environment: tallowwoods (*Eucalyptus microcorys*), snow gums (*E. pauciflora*) and mountain gums (*E. dalrympleana*) soared up to 60 metres high in the wet forests around

Barrington; Sydney blue gum (*E. saligna*), with its smooth blue-grey trunk, grew throughout the Watagan Mountains that fringe Newcastle; while stringybarks (*E. sparsifolia*), broad-leaved ironbarks (*E. fibrosa*), grey box (*E. moluccana*), yellow box (*E. melliodora*), forest red gums (*E. tereticornis*) and spotted gums (*Corymbia maculata*) intermingled through the lower slopes, the dry-sclerophyll forest, savannah, open woodland and river-flat forest that made up much of the rest of the valley. Along the rivers grew river red gums (*E. camaldulensis*), gnarled and hunched over the waters below. Closer to the coast, swamp mahogany (*E. robusta*) and stands of flooded gum (*E. grandis*) grew in forests near to water. Smooth- and rough-barked apple (*Angophora costata* and *A. floribunda*), kurrajongs (*Brachychiton populneus*), paperbarks (*Melaleuca quinquenervia*) and swamp oaks (*Casuarina glauca*) also grew from the mountains to the sea in the Hunter.[6]

The real prize of the Hunter forests, however, was not eucalyptus but red cedar (*Toona ciliata*). It grew in thick stands along the Hunter River, up the Williams and Paterson, and in isolated stands in the high ranges of the Barrington Tops. A member of the mahogany family, red cedar is a rainforest tree and a survivor of the greater Gondwanan continent. Its relatives grow in Pakistan, India and Southeast Asia, and down the east coast of Australia. They thrive in rich alluvial soil and the rich basalts left over from prehistoric volcanoes. In the Hunter, where both of these soil types are found, they towered to over 60 metres, with wide buttress roots and spreading crowns above. During the years of the penal station at Newcastle they were felled in vast numbers, almost to the point of local extinction.

THE HUNTER'S FIRST PEOPLE

At some point between 20,000 and 45,000 years ago the first people began to arrive in this ancient landscape, moving across the alluvial plains, through the dense rainforest, into the gullies and mountains, following the rivers and creeks. Archaeology in the middle valley around Fal Brook and at Moffats Swamp near Port Stephens suggests dates of 20,000 years for human occupation, with some sites as old as 35,000 years. Evidence around Sydney and the Hawkesbury River points to occupation closer to 45,000 years, suggesting people were settling right through this section of New South Wales, including the Hunter region, around the same time.[7] Shelters, middens, open camp sites, engravings and art, ceremonial sites and bora grounds have all been recorded throughout the Hunter Valley.

Aboriginal people came to know the valley over generations, managing the land to take advantage of the abundant resources. Camp sites and settlements were concentrated around the banks of the rivers, as evidenced in the archaeological record, with the majority of sites within 100 metres of a river or creek.[8] The people in the Hunter Valley then were river people, utilising the waterways as living spaces, food sources and pathways through their Country. Tools were shaped from the large river cobbles that lay in the shallows of the Hunter and its tributaries; bark from stringybark, river gum, kurrajong and other trees was fashioned into canoes from Port Stephens to Newcastle and upriver to Maitland and Singleton; and the long, straight shafts of the grass tree (*Xanthorrhoea australis*) were used for hunting, fishing and fighting spears.[9]

On the coast, nets were fashioned from grasses and plant fibres for fishing, weirs were built as fish traps and oyster shells fashioned into *pirrewuy* (fish hooks).[10] The women around the *yohaaba* (harbour) at Newcastle made *yirrawarn* (fishing line) from the inner strands of kurrajong bark, rolling the strands over and over until the line was fashioned. Women also dived for lobster and collected oysters from the rocks around the shore.[11] Dozens of canoes at a time were observed by the British on the harbour and out to the edge of the ocean, with the women fishing from them. At Lake Macquarie the Reverend Lancelot Threlkeld, who ran a mission there in the 1830s, wrote of the canoes at night with small wisps of smoke from a cooking fire on board looking like a fleet of steamers anchored in the stream.[12] The shell middens built up over generations around the harbour at Newcastle and Lake Macquarie are so large as to point to a pre-contact population in the thousands. The mixture of freshwater and saltwater species together represents the vast range of food types available to, and used by, the people.[13]

Fire was a critical tool in the management of the land; Bill Gammage has called it Aboriginal people's 'closest ally'.[14] The burning regimes in the Hunter created an environment that was both sustaining and sustainable. Burning for pasture and to thin out underbrush represented a deliberate and conscious use of fire to shape the environment to the needs of the people who lived in and depended on it.[15] Land was fired using a rotating mosaic system that controlled intensity and allowed plants and animals to survive in refuges. The fires were lit depending on the time of year to suit the area and condition of the bush, with the prevailing weather crucial to the timing. During fire season, neighbouring clans would be advised so that adjoining areas could be managed properly, while burning during the growing seasons of particular plants would be avoided at all costs.[16]

Grass, in particular, benefited from this systematic approach, with controlled burning encouraging new growth that, in turn, attracted grazing game. Other vegetation types and animals required different approaches, hence the mosaic effect. Mallee fowl, for example, could withstand only small, patchy fires, while possums and gliders thrived in forests burnt more frequently.[17] The open, parklike appearance enthusiastically noted by the British in the Hunter Valley from the earliest days of contact was a direct result of this management. But not everywhere was burnt. The thick, jungle-like brush that fronted the rivers, areas where food resources (such as yams) or medicinal plants grew, and areas around certain ceremonial sites were closely managed to avoid damage.

Some archaeologists and anthropologists have argued that trading contact between Aboriginal people in the Hunter Valley was based on a north–south axis. Coastal people, such as the Awabakal around Newcastle and Lake Macquarie, appear to have had more contact with groups to the north, such as the Worimi at Port Stephens and the Biripi/Birpai around the Manning River, and south to the Wanangine/Guringai at Broken Bay. Further inland, the Wonnarua were in closer contact with the Darkinjung, occupying the mountains to the south stretching towards the Hawkesbury, and the Kamilaroi, whose vast Country extended west through the gap in the range near Merriwa and stretched north towards the Queensland border.[18] The Gringai clan around the Allyn and Paterson rivers, and the Geawegal in the foothills of the Mount Royal and Liverpool ranges, also had connections to their larger neighbouring groups. Many reasons, such as topography, impenetrable forests acting as a barrier or different patterns of occupation between coastal and upper valley areas, have been put forward as possible explanations for these patterns of interaction.

The archaeology suggests that tool-making material, for example, differs significantly between inland and coastal peoples. Evidence of the materials used supports this pattern. Sites in the middle and upper valley commonly include local red or yellow cherts, mudstones or quartzite taken from river stones to make spear points, scrapers and other items, whereas towards the coast and in the river estuary nearly all sites show a preponderance of Merewether white or grey chert from the cliffs around Newcastle.[19]

While some form of separation may have existed, historical accounts from the first years of contact suggest a complex web of connections through trade, marriage and religion. The existence of Hunter Valley materials—such as cherts and quartzites—in tool assemblages in the Hawkesbury points to inter-area trading, while the similarity of rock-art sites, both painted and engraved, in the middle Hunter and the Hawkesbury suggests a commonality in spiritual belief and story tradition.

Coastal people traded *Xanthorrhoea* stems to be used as spear shafts for possum fur belts and cloaks from inland, and for the red clay gathered at *Ko-pur-ra-ba*—a smouldering coal seam known as Burning Mountain in the far inland reaches of the valley—which was used to mark bodies for ceremony around Newcastle.[20] There are many tracks that crisscross the mountains linking adjoining territories and groups, some known by or shown to the British. The Boree Track, for example, runs from near St Albans on the Macdonald River in Darkinjung Country north towards Wonnarua Country around Wollombi and Bulga. Another started in Wonnarua Country close to Denman in the valley's west and pushed through the Cassilis Gap towards the western plains around Mudgee and the Kamilaroi nation.[21] Another pathway led south from Newcastle along the edge of Lake Macquarie and on to Broken Bay, where it joined a second from Pittwater down to Sydney, linking Awabakal and Worimi to Wanangine/Guringai and into Gayamaygal Country. Add to these land tracks the use of the Hunter and other rivers in the valley, and a complex web of connections begins to appear.

With deep connections to the land and Country came both physical and spiritual knowledge of the Hunter Valley. As well as trade items, stories and ceremony moved back and forth across the landscape. The Boree Track was likely an important ceremonial route, passing close by Mount Yengo and other important sites. A series of interrelated art sites along its route and around Mount Yengo shows links from the Hawkesbury all the way to the Hunter Valley.

The Wonnarua people, across the floodplains of the middle and upper valley, told of sky spirits that interacted with each other to create the valley. When finished, they opened the valley floor and let the waters run to form the rivers and creeks, bringing life to the land.[22] Around the coast a significant number of stories relate to the geology and geography of the valley. *Whibayganba* (Nobbys Island), at the entrance to Newcastle Harbour, was the resting place of a giant kangaroo who occasionally shook himself, causing the ground to shake and rocks to fall from the cliffs. Nearby, above what is now Newcastle Beach, a sacred place in the high cliff known as *Yi-ran-na-li* demands that anyone who passes by not speak, otherwise rocks will crash down upon them.[23] Inland, another story relates how a giant lizard wandered across the land, its tail carving out the valley as it passed. The lizard remains in the mountains, his head making up Yellow Rock sited prominently near Broke, his body making the ridgeline behind.[24]

The Reverend Lancelot Threlkeld recorded a number of these stories in the 1820s and 1830s, related to him by Biraban—also known as McGill—who acted as a translator, interpreter and intermediary for Threlkeld. He noted that local Aboriginal people at Lake Macquarie told how all the land and the mountains around the lake had once been covered by a big flood, with only one family escaping in a canoe to the highest point. Cockle shells found on high ground were evidence of the story. This story, coupled with those of the giant kangaroo of Nobbys Island and *Yi-ran-na-li* at Newcastle Beach, offers a tantalising hint of a long-held environmental memory of higher sea levels, distant earthquakes and experience of place passed through generations.

Of these stories and sites, the most significant was that of Baiame. The great Ground Spirit Baiame, as described by anthropologist R.H. Mathews in 1893 and represented in at least one major art site on the edge of the Broken Back Range, was the dominant spiritual figure of the Hunter Valley and beyond. Baiame and his half-brother or kinsman Daramulan were central to initiation and ceremony, with rock art, engravings and ceremonial sites from the Sydney and Blue Mountains areas, through the Hunter Valley, west and north to Brewarrina and into southern Queensland.[25] Mount Yengo, halfway between Windsor and the Hunter Valley, is considered to be the site from which, when finished on earth, Baiame stepped into the sky. The stories, lore and traditions shaped the way that the people interacted with the Country around them, with their neighbours and with those beyond.

It was into this ancient landscape, with its interconnected trading societies and complex spiritual rituals and beliefs, that British people began to arrive in the 1790s. With close trading, familial and spiritual connections stretching from the shores of Sydney Harbour through the mountains and along the coast to the Hunter Valley, word of these new arrivals at Sydney had likely already reached Awabakal, Worimi and Wonnarua people well before any appeared on their shores.

The fertile valley, which sustained thriving Aboriginal communities from the sea to the far mountains for tens of thousands of years, had been shaped over millions of years by a series of dynamic and at times cataclysmic geological events. The future success of the Hunter Valley as an agricultural and farming settlement was as much a product of this process, of the land, the soil and the river, as it was the hard work, forced or otherwise, of the convicts, farmers and settlers who were to come.

CHAPTER TWO

FIRST CONTACT

It is not difficult to imagine the British arrivals' first views of the Newcastle coastline. The long stretches of sandy beaches interrupted by sharp sandstone cliffs are still there. The thin seams of coal seen from the ocean for the first time by James Cook on board the *Endeavour* in May 1770 are also still obvious. Sailing eleven kilometres out to sea, Cook noted a 'small round rock or Island laying close under the land'—the first description we have of Nobbys Island.[1] It was to be another twenty years before anyone from England took another look.

In September 1790, while the settlement at Sydney was still finding its feet, five convicts from Rose Hill slipped out of the harbour in an open boat in an audacious, if ill-considered, escape.[2] Although assumed lost at sea by the authorities, John Tarwood, Joseph Sutton, George Lee, George Conoway and John Watson had instead come ashore on the beaches north of Newcastle near Port Stephens. Taken in by the Worimi people, the five had been given Aboriginal names, taken wives and had children. In August 1795, the four survivors—Sutton having died at Port Stephens—were discovered living among Aboriginal people at Port Stephens and were returned to Sydney.[3]

In his account of the colony, David Collins, the Judge Advocate and Secretary of the Colony, wrote that on arrival back in Sydney, the four men 'passed their time in detailing to crowds both of black and white people which attended them their adventures in Port Stephens'. The men spoke in glowing terms about those among whom they had lived. The language they had learnt, it seemed, was different to that spoken around Sydney; Collins noted that Aboriginal people in Sydney did not understand all of what was said—except one, a young man named Wur-gan.[4] He was the son of a woman from beyond the mountains to the north who knew multiple languages and had taught Wur-gan. His 'roving disposition' meant that he knew all the dialects from Botany Bay to Port Stephens. He may have been a *buntimai*, a messenger or ambassador, which would enable him to move between territories.[5] Wur-gan and his mother are the first mentioned Aboriginal people who had connections between Sydney and the Hunter Valley.

So while Aboriginal people moved back and forth across the country, it is these convict runaways who can be credited with being the first of the British colonists to set foot in the Hunter Valley.

The British were next at Newcastle in June 1796. Collins recorded that a fishing boat had returned to Sydney having entered an unnamed bay near to Port Stephens and collected a number of large pieces of coal. The bay, although not named, was most likely Newcastle Harbour. In contrast to Tarwood and his companions, these unnamed fishermen 'conducted themselves improperly', according to Collins. Two were severely wounded by Aboriginal spears, one later dying from his wounds in Sydney Hospital.[6] Still, no real interest was shown in this bay, for its coal or anything else. It took another, more audacious escape to finally set the British to exploring.

THE *CUMBERLAND* ESCAPE

In September 1797, convicts at Broken Bay seized a government boat, the *Cumberland*, with the intention of escaping the colony. Some of the *Cumberland*'s crew were also keen to leave and joined the convicts. Four men who wanted no part in the venture were allowed to depart in a small boat. These men landed at Pittwater and made their way to Sydney, where they raised the alarm. Governor Hunter immediately dispatched two boats in pursuit, one to go north and the other south. In charge of the northbound pursuit was Lieutenant John Shortland. He had been master's mate on the *Sirius* in 1788. In 1792, Shortland had returned to England; he was promoted and came back to the colony two years later. Shortland searched in vain for the *Cumberland* as far as Port Stephens. On his return voyage, to escape a rising gale, he entered what was the mouth of the Hunter River, running his whaleboat between Nobbys Island and the headland. A strong current running later in the day made him realise that he had discovered a new river as well as the harbour in which he was sheltering.[7] In a letter to his father in September 1798, Shortland described how he had discovered the new river and named it Hunter River in honour of the governor. He thought ships as large as 250 tons (254 tonnes) could safely load there and was confident that 'in a little time this river will be a great acquisition to this settlement'.[8] Although it is Shortland's arrival in 1798 that Newcastle takes as its founding date, escaping convicts had been there at least eight years earlier and Aboriginal people had occupied the area for millennia.

The cargo that Shortland envisaged ships would be able to load so easily was coal. It was the abundance of coal visible in the cliff seams and lying around on the shore that caught the attention of the colonial authorities. Coal was to be found in such quantities that the area was given the unofficial name Coal River. Coal had also been spotted almost simultaneously in the cliffs south of Sydney in the Illawarra, but the apparent ease with which it could be gathered at Hunter River made this site, in the eyes of the authorities, a more viable prospect. Governor Hunter was himself keen to visit, expressing this desire in letters to England, but never did. Instead, he gave permission to local merchants and emancipist traders, including Simeon Lord, James Underwood and Hugh Meehan, to go there, kickstarting a coal industry that continues to this day.

ENTERING AN OCCUPIED VALLEY

It was the Worimi around Port Stephens and the Awabakal around Newcastle who had the first contact with escaped convicts and fishermen. Inland were the Wonnarua, whose Country spread across the alluvial river flats of the Hunter and into the foothills of the mountains north and south. The Biripi/Birpai lived around the Barrington and Gloucester region and Manning Valley to the north, while the Kamilaroi occupied the top end of the valley, around the Goulburn River and Liverpool Plains. For the Kamilaroi, the Hunter Valley was at the southern end of their Country, which stretched out north and west over the ranges towards Tamworth and the Queensland border.[9] Each Aboriginal group identified with a particular area, connecting to their own Country through ritual, ceremony and management of the land, but their connections and travels extended much further. The Reverend Lancelot Threlkeld, who established a mission station first at Newcastle and later on the shore of Lake Macquarie, observed in 1825 that Aboriginal people around Newcastle had connections from the Hawkesbury to Port Stephens, with their boundary being the southern shore of Lake Macquarie, north to Newcastle and the Hunter River, and west approximately sixteen kilometres inland from his mission.[10] Historian Paul Irish has described these broader connections as an 'affiliated coastal zone', an area along the coast between the Shoalhaven, Sydney and Port Stephens in which a consistent pattern of family connections and movements can be seen from the first days of British settlement right through the nineteenth century.[11]

Within these main groups were smaller clans, linked through marriage and family across the entire region and beyond. The interwoven kinship encouraged a commonality of language, with local dialects, as well as linkages through trade and ceremony. The result was a certain amount of fluidity across boundaries and borders, with transition zones and areas of common passage such as trade routes or pathways to ceremonial grounds. This connectivity linked people to a broader Aboriginal economy and cultural knowledge bank stretching from Sydney, through the Central Coast and Hawkesbury, up the northern coast, into the Gloucester Valley and New England, to the Bathurst Plains in the west and up towards the Queensland border.

The colonists referred to the groups by generic names such as 'bush natives' or in relation to where they were first encountered. Those along the coast, the Awabakal and Worimi, were not afforded any such distinction; instead, it was those they came across away from the coast that were differentiated in such ways. Those Aboriginal people they called 'bush natives' in truth could equally have been described as river people, for all the inland groups were reliant on the *Coquun* (Hunter), *Doorribang* (Williams), *Yimmang* (Paterson) and Goulburn river systems as well as the multitude of creeks and streams that fed them.

As we have seen, the archaeological and historical evidence illustrates interconnectedness: through the Hunter Valley, beyond the mountains towards Mudgee and Bathurst, and up and down the coast from Botany Bay to Port Stephens and beyond. It was no doubt this connectivity that assisted in spreading word of the arrival of the British in Sydney in 1788, and it is conceivable that some from the Hunter, both the coastal and inland people, heard this news and may have travelled towards Sydney to see the new arrivals in the years prior to any British appearing at Newcastle. There is plenty of evidence of movement across the country between the two settlements in the years to come.

THE MERCHANT TRADERS

Simeon Lord began the run regularly to Newcastle from 1799, including from 1801, in his ship the *Anna Josepha* named after the wife of the new governor, Philip King. The other merchants soon followed and spearheaded sustained British contact with the Hunter Valley. Their ships' crews discovered there were more resources to exploit than the coal lying on the shore, and it was not long before the red cedar that grew in thick stands along the riverbanks was also being logged. Parties stayed for long periods, with Meehan staying at least one month in May 1801 and others staying up to two months by 1803. These groups dug sawpits on the edge of the harbour to mill the timber, bringing back between fifteen and 70 milled logs per trip. The men took some rations but procured what else they needed, such as fresh water, fish and game, while at Newcastle.[12] This was not an empty valley they were entering, but one occupied by Aboriginal people from the coast to the mountains in the far distance. While there had previously been reports of clashes between Aboriginal people and fishermen, the increasing numbers of British people coming into the area also increased the likelihood of trouble. It was not long before word reached Sydney of violent encounters.

The crews on these ships were armed but not accompanied by soldiers or officials. The harbour and river were outside the limits of the influence of the colonial authorities, largely uncharted and unknown. For the first time, but not the last, the Hunter was the frontier of the colony. There was a certain amount of nervous vigilance to these parties, as any number of things could go wrong, but also a freedom of movement and action given their operations were beyond official eyes. Their small craft were vulnerable to the vagaries of the weather, and to the rushing tide and unpredictable surf that funnelled through the harbour mouth between the shoreline and Nobbys Island. Men could easily get lost in the uncharted bushland or the myriad channels and waterways that led away from the main harbour, while swampy ground and the river itself were treacherous places for men who could not swim. But it was encounters with Aboriginal people that caused the most concern. As the number of trading ships began to increase, so too did reported incidents of violence between ships' crews and Aboriginal people.

The first serious incident took place in April 1799. Reports reached Sydney that two boats authorised to go to the Hunter River for a load of coal had been 'cut off by the natives'. Governor Hunter immediately dispatched an armed whaleboat to investigate, with Henry Hacking, former quartermaster of the First Fleet's *Sirius*, in command. Hacking was trusted by the governor and was confident in his own abilities, having already survived an ambush by Aboriginal people close to Sydney.[13] On his arrival, Hacking saw one of the two boats on shore—burnt—with its sails and crew missing. Searching the area, he encountered a large body of Aboriginal men, all armed with spears, who (Hacking reported) told him that the men from the boat had left the area and returned to Sydney. Suspicion guided Hacking's actions from here. Not believing them, Hacking threatened to shoot if they did not tell him where the missing men were; in what must have been an unnerving moment for Hacking, the Aboriginal men laughed at him. They poised as if to launch their spears and countered that if he did not give them the small two-oared boat plus a whaleboat he brought with him and leave immediately, they would kill him and all his men.[14]

Attempting to regain control of an increasingly tense situation, Hacking levelled his musket and snapped it without priming, firing the powder with no shot in an attempt to scare them. These men were not easily frightened, however, and instead advanced. Hacking quickly primed his weapon and fired buckshot into the assembled group, knocking four down. When only one man got up, Hacking, figuring that the other three were mortally wounded, retreated, packed his boat and left. As it turned out, the warriors had not been lying. The missing boat crew later turned up in Sydney, having apparently travelled overland.

David Collins wondered what had caused the sudden show of hostility, putting it down to the tendency of Aboriginal warriors to attack on impulse, making it difficult to trust them. He noted in his *Account of the English Colony*, without a hint of irony, that the British visiting the Hunter River had always treated Aboriginal people with kindness and civility, apparently forgetting his very own reporting of the improper conduct of the stranded fishermen back in 1796.[15]

We cannot know for sure what happened that day with Hacking. It is worth considering, though, that it could have been the warriors themselves who were on guard against Hacking and moved to defend themselves. Hacking had form in this type of encounter. In 1789, he had reported being followed by up to 40 men while he was hunting in the bush around Sydney. Feeling threatened, he presented his weapon to scare them, firing birdshot and then buckshot, wounding some men and scattering the rest.[16]

The year after Hacking's aggressive encounter, another group—this time unauthorised—made landfall at Newcastle. In November 1800, the government ship *Norfolk* was seized by fifteen convicts at Broken Bay and taken north. Driven by bad weather into Newcastle, the ship ran aground on the northern shore of the harbour at a spot thereafter called Pirate Point. Nine of the fifteen convicts seized another boat belonging to a merchant crew there gathering coal and cedar, before once again making for the open sea. While the nine who sailed on were later captured by an armed cutter sent from Sydney in pursuit, the six who remained behind crossed the harbour to the southern side and made a camp around what is now Throsbys Creek. The men survived on fish and meat supplied by Aboriginal groups, as well as maize and pumpkins grown from seed. It was the first settlement of any duration established by the British in the region. The group would be joined over the coming months by other convicts bolting from visiting merchant boats.

Nothing more would have been known of this group had not three of the men, tired of the bush life, decided to leave and return to Sydney. Two of them survived the overland trip south, being picked up in Broken Bay by Lieutenant James Grant, who was on an exploratory expedition in the area. Grant returned the escapees to Sydney, where they were put on trial. One of the captured convicts told Grant that he had come overland from Newcastle, crossing the Hawkesbury River after bargaining a lift in a canoe with an Aboriginal man. None of those who remained at Newcastle were heard from again, but at least some evidence of their interactions survived. A woven grass fishing net thought to be of British origin was found with Aboriginal people at Throsbys Creek by the first official survey party in 1801. Later, on the same expedition, the escaped convict leader, a man named Grace, was seen in the far distance dressed in a jacket and trousers. An Aboriginal man told Grant that Grace was the only man left of the escapees.[17]

These few examples provide tantalising glimpses of life on the edge of the colonial world in the years prior to 1801. Convicts moving through the bush, clashing with or living peacefully beside Aboriginal people, crossing major rivers via canoe or making permanent camps speak of a convict population growing increasingly familiar with the margins of the known settlement. As Grace

Karskens has noted in *The Colony*, while some convicts became lost or were killed in the bush, more 'were learning about the country, journey after journey, until topography, paths, creeks, rivers and vegetation were familiar'.[18]

A SURVEY OF THE RIVER

In June 1801, with increasing numbers of private vessels visiting the area, Governor King instructed Lieutenant James Grant, master of the survey ship *Lady Nelson*, to proceed to the Hunter River and undertake an official survey. Grant, sailing on 10 June, was joined by Lieutenant Governor Colonel William Paterson, surgeon John Harris, surveyor Francis Barrallier, artist John Lewin, six soldiers, two sawyers, a pilot, a miner, labourers and workmen and an Aboriginal envoy, Bungaree. Barrallier was tasked with completing a survey of the harbour and the course of the Hunter River. A second ship, the schooner *Francis*, accompanied the expedition with orders to collect specimens of flora and fauna and, if weather permitted, to continue to Port Stephens and make further observations.

Bungaree was already a well-known Aboriginal man in Sydney when he accompanied Grant on the Hunter survey. He was identified with Broken Bay, although the exact area is unknown, but may have also had existing connections with the Hunter when he joined the party. He was familiar with British exploration, having sailed with Matthew Flinders in May 1798 on board HMS *Reliance* to Norfolk Island. Bungaree accompanied two other Aboriginal men on that voyage, Nanberry from Sydney and Wingal from Port Stephens. Wingal's presence in Sydney when he joined the *Reliance* demonstrates the connections between the Hunter and Sydney even at this early stage. In 1799, Bungaree travelled with Flinders for a second time, acting as an intermediary for Flinders' survey of Glass House Bay (Moreton Bay) and Hervey Bay. Flinders later recorded that Bungaree's 'good disposition and open manly conduct' had won his esteem.[19]

The role of envoy or guide was vital for British people entering into unknown territory and was already an established practice by the time Grant headed towards Newcastle. A man such as Bungaree could assist with the sometimes delicate negotiations involved in entering another group's territory, interpret language and gesture or help with identifying potentially dangerous situations. Bungaree was what historian Henry Reynolds has described as a 'professional guide', someone who was already familiar with, or had lived in or around, the British settlements and was regularly employed to join expeditions. He could apply a combination of traditional skill and knowledge and an understanding of British culture and language to act as an on-the-ground diplomat.[20]

It was not far into the voyage of the *Lady Nelson* that Bungaree was called on to serve as an interpreter. When the ships were off the heads of Lake Macquarie, a crew member (employed for having recently been to Coal River), mistook the entrance to Lake Macquarie for Newcastle and the boats set towards it. The entrance was already known as Reids Mistake, so called when William Reid, the captain of the coastal trader *Martha* heading to Newcastle for coal, also mistook the entrance for that of the Coal River in July 1800.[21] Although the *Lady Nelson* did not enter the lake, a ship's boat was lowered and took surgeon Harris to reconnoitre the shore. On his return, he was accompanied by an Aboriginal man who had run down to meet him, calling in broken English 'Whale Boat' and 'Budgerie Dick', or Good Dick, a name Grant assumed had been given him by earlier sailors in the area. Grant directed Bungaree to question Dick. Before Bungaree started the interview he motioned for Dick to sit, which Grant had witnessed before used as a friendly gesture, after which the two men sat in silence for twenty minutes, again an important part of the etiquette in meeting a stranger.

After this the two men entered into a conversation, drawing closer to each other as they spoke. Despite this, Bungaree gave Grant little information, which Grant assumed was due to the men not understanding each other, as 'some of our people, who were best acquainted with the language spoken by the natives round Sydney, were at the same loss'.[22] Of course, Bungaree was not from Sydney, but Broken Bay, which was close to Lake Macquarie and within the circle of language that Reverend Threlkeld later identified as stretching from Sydney to Port Stephens. Bungaree was thus likely to have understood Dick perfectly well.

Why he did not pass on what he heard to Grant is unknown and for Grant there was no opportunity to find out for, on arrival at Newcastle, Bungaree left the ship and slipped off into the surrounding bush.[23] Bungaree's departure suggests a closer connection to the Hunter region than previously thought by historians. It would be a bold move for an Aboriginal man to walk off alone through someone else's Country without having gained the proper permissions. Bungaree clearly knew the country and had connections. Bungaree's desertion does, however, raise the interesting possibility of a strong motive in his volunteering: perhaps he joined the voyage for his own purposes rather than to assist Grant. Bungaree would have walked between Broken Bay and Newcastle or indeed the Hunter district and Sydney before. His voyaging with Flinders would have shown him an easier option, and he may have volunteered to join Grant's survey crew as a way of cutting down his own travel time. If this was the case, Bungaree was not simply the interpreter there to do Grant's bidding, but may have calculated the benefits to himself before even joining them. Bungaree had scored himself a free ride. Budgerie Dick also left the party at Newcastle soon after.

AN ABUNDANCE OF RESOURCES

Grant and his party stayed for six weeks exploring the harbour and river. Their survey confirmed the ready accessibility of coal, with the miner, assisted by convict labourers, soon at work extracting it and loading the *Francis* from the base of a small hill that Colonel Paterson had named Colliers Point. With an eye for future use, Grant and Paterson noted the forest timbers, the open grassland and the areas that were subject to flooding. As the survey progressed, the abundance of resources became increasingly clear. Paterson wrote enthusiastically in his journal of the future he saw for the settlement of the valley:

> From the several excursions I made during the time the *Lady Nelson*
> lay in Freshwater Bay I am of opinion that Government might
> derive many advantages by forming a small settlement at this place.
> In the 1st instance, the coals are a principal object. 2nd Boiling salt
> which could be done with little labour. 3rd Burning shells that are
> here in great abundance. Besides, salting fish might be carried on
> with considerable benefit if some industrious fisherman could be
> found for that purpose, as the fish are plentiful and good. There is
> excellent pasture for cattle, but until where the rivers meet is not fit
> for cultivation.[24]

The shells formed vast middens that surrounded the harbour and the estuary at Newcastle. Harris wrote to Governor King, 'such quantities of oyster shells I never in my life beheld. The schooner [*Francis*] might be loaded in a day, and a hundred vessels her size.'[25] Paterson was equally amazed: 'the quantity of oyster shells on the beaches inland is beyond conception; they are in some places for miles. These are four feet deep, without either sand or earth.'[26]

Grant's timber-getters began working on Ash Island in the harbour and quickly headed further upriver. They came across sawpits dug by Meehan's earlier expeditions still in place on the northern shore of the harbour, while enough cedar had been reported along the Hunter River above its confluence with the Williams River for it to be named the Cedar Arm. Barrallier reported that the Paterson River (as the Williams River was then known) 'has the advantage to have on its banks the finest cedars ever seen which may be transported on rafts with ease'.[27] At other places, imposing stands of fine timber dominated the landscape. On the river in the mid-valley, Grant noted in his journal:

> Cedar grows along the banks of the river in great abundance and great magnitude. The ash, gum-trees of all sorts, the swamp oak and tea tree is also in great plenty and very large, together with various other woods.[28]

Paterson noted the grass-covered slopes and fields with all the appearance of sheep pasture in England, so much so that he named the hills on the southern side of the harbour Sheep Pasture Hills, though the name did not survive the later settlement. Grant also wrote of the luxurious grass that he encountered further up the river.[29] The grasslands were intersected by valleys in which timber grew, sheltered from the winds.

Grant and Paterson also found the fishing net made of grass that they supposed was left by the *Norfolk* runaways, although it could well have been Aboriginal in origin. Nearby in a stream the remains of a stone weir or fish trap were also seen, 'the work of the native inhabitants, this being one of their principal devices for taking fish'.[30]

The fish trap, the grassy slopes and the sheltered timber all pointed to long years of Aboriginal land management. Bill Gammage has identified the interchange of grassy fields and stands of trees as a template created by Aboriginal people across Australia. The association of grass and forest was closely managed to give ready feed to the herds of kangaroo and other grazing animals they relied on, while maintaining areas of forest for shelter, plants and smaller mammals to thrive. Similarly, the fish trap seen by Grant was an indicator of a complex and engineered aquaculture system and, as Bruce Pascoe has argued, furnishes evidence of an Aboriginal economy that allowed populations to sustain themselves in one area.[31] Evidence of Aboriginal occupation was all around. Smoke from fires was seen in the area beyond Ash Island, canoes were pulled up on the banks, and middens of oyster shells of great depth lined the harbour foreshore, enough that Harris thought they might fill 100 ships (which is exactly what they did when convicts were sent to burn lime in the years to come).

CONTACT

Budgerie Dick, who had left the party previously, reappeared after two days, bringing with him two other men, one of whom was someone Paterson already knew from Sydney. Paterson and the man talked together. Could this have been merely a coincidence? Or was it a cross-cultural catch-up initiated by the Aboriginal man on hearing Paterson was in his neighbourhood? Once again we can discern evidence of connections between Sydney and the Hunter region.

Grant and his party continued to move upriver, noting stands of usable timber, taking depths, hauling fish and collecting birds and animals, all the while observed by Aboriginal people. The evidence of recent flood was seen by Grant as he moved upstream. He noted that the debris was almost 50 feet (15 metres) off the ground, with marks on the trees showing the water level and evidence of over-flowing of the riverbanks.

Their encounters with Aboriginal people mounted. Grant had warned his sawyers to be aware of any surprise by Aboriginal people, but to act with prudence and avoid clashes. Paterson had come across a camp site approximately 40 miles (64 kilometres) upriver at a place he named Shanks Forest Plains (Shank was a shipbuilder and the designer of the *Lady Nelson*'s unique shifting keel system, which allowed the ship to proceed in very shallow waters up the river). The camp had been abandoned, and all they found were the ashes of the fires and footprints of children. While many Aboriginal family groups were wary and watched from a distance, some individuals approached the British with interest. At another point, Paterson heard Aboriginal voices without seeing anyone, came across a canoe recently pulled on shore and saw trees felled by them. He reasoned that their shyness was due to there being runaways from the *Norfolk* among them.[32]

Barrallier and the second mate, meanwhile, met an older man in the bush who they took on board the ship. Describing him as a 'bush native', Grant noted that he had all his front teeth in contrast to those around Port Jackson, for whom tooth evulsion was a sign of initiation. The man remained cautious, refusing to eat with the crew until a dead crow was offered, which he took and warmed on the galley fire before eating. A tomahawk was also given him, although Grant was disappointed the older man offered no name for it.

When the man was returned to shore, the ship's crew indicated that they wanted a demonstration of his dexterity and use of the tomahawk by pointing at a nearby tree and making the signs as if to climb it. The man readily began making notches in the bark, placed his foot into one and continuing the technique he 'very nimbly ascended to the top' nearly 12 metres above the ground. In the branches above he moved to an adjacent tree, descended and disappeared into the bush. Grant noted notched trees all around the river.[33] Nearly twenty years later, convict artist Joseph Lycett painted Aboriginal men at Newcastle climbing trees in the same manner.

The further upriver the party went, the more encounters were had. Grant passed several groups in canoes on the river, the canoes with small cooking fires in them, a practice already observed on Sydney Harbour. Another man, who at first appeared to hide from the British, was enticed into one of the ship's boats via an exchange of gifts: a pocket handkerchief from Grant, a possum fur headband net from the man. As the man boarded, a chorus of voices called from onshore and the man called back, quietening them. Grant, surprised by the number of voices, assumed those onshore were calling to see if the man was alright and that his return call told them there was nothing to fear. The man was taken downstream to the *Lady Nelson* where he spent the night, apparently in amazement of all he saw. The following morning he was presented with a tomahawk, a gift Grant soon realised was highly prized. The man used the word *mogo* for the tomahawk, which Grant took to be the name for it. *Mogo* was the word recorded by Collins for tomahawks in Sydney. However, the Reverend Lancelot Threlkeld in his study of the language published in 1834 identified *mogo* as what he called a barbarism, a word that had been introduced by the British and which replaced the local word, which Threlkeld recorded as *bai-bai*, meaning axe or tomahawk.[34] Clutching his prized gift, the man was returned by boat to the exact place he had been picked up.

The word was now out about the distribution of tomahawks. On returning from the drop-off, the boatmen were surprised to see the old man from the previous day, who had displayed his climbing prowess on the riverbank, accompanied by a man approximately seventeen years old. Expressing a desire to return to the *Lady Nelson*, both were taken aboard where the young man asked for a tomahawk for himself. On being given one, the two men agreed to sit for their portrait, which, Grant records, was sketched by artist John Lewin.[35] Sadly, no known portrait from this expedition survives. Some of Lewin's artwork from the survey party does survive. He sketched the *Lady Nelson* at anchor in Newcastle Harbour, close to the northern shore near present-day Stockton. He also sketched the imagined vision of the two survey ships rounding Nobbys Island and entering the harbour, a scene no doubt witnessed by Aboriginal people on shore. His most evocative work, though, is of Paterson and himself under the cover of a tent on the banks of the Paterson River, named by Paterson after himself. The two men sit relaxed on the ground, muskets and hunting rifles propped against the tent poles, birds hanging from the cross bar, with a fire burning out front. Other men in the party sit partly obscured in the billowing smoke. This watercolour, kept by Paterson in his personal collection, is the first image of the British in the Hunter and captures a moment on the cusp, before everything changed for the region and the Aboriginal people who lived there.[36]

The contact reported by Grant up the river shows some com-prehension by the Aboriginal groups of the opportunities for trade with the British. Curiously, though, other than the exchange of the fur headband, there is no other mention of trade. For Grant, the ship was a safe and controlled space from which to operate, but the willingness of all these men to board the *Lady Nelson* suggests that they previously had some contact with ships. The regular visits of the ships of Underwood, Lord, Meehan and other traders would have brought with them a growing familiarity with these types of exchanges; for, although Grant's was the first official party, he was not the first to visit, as we have seen. Indeed, he was not even the first to venture so far upriver. Grant encountered a party of nine private sawyers several miles upriver while on his survey. Sent by Commissary John Palmer to collect timber, the men were prepar-ing to walk overland to Sydney as their provisions were running low when they saw Grant's ships from the top of a hill. As Grant only had two sawyers with him, he commandeered the men into his own party to assist.[37]

During their six weeks on the river between 10 June and 22 July 1801, Grant's survey party went at least as far as modern-day Dalwood, where they named a small mountain Mount Elizabeth (now Mount Hudson) after Paterson's wife, and another nearby Mount Ann after the governor's wife.[38] However, with their provisions running low and a deadline to return to Sydney before August, Grant's party was forced to turn back and prepare to depart.

ESTABLISHING A PERMANENT FOOTHOLD

Before leaving the Hunter River, Grant established a camp near two small freshwater streams on the southern edge of the harbour close to Colliers Point. He built a hut for the use of the miners he intended to leave there. A small boat was also left, along with provisions, arms, ammunition and tools. This was the first attempt at a permanent camp at Newcastle and signalled the administration's intention to begin full-scale exploitation of the valley's resources.

The main party sailed for Sydney on 22 July 1801, by which time Governor King had dispatched two men, a Mr Broadbent and John Platt, the colony's only qualified coalminer, to the Coal River to advise Paterson on where the best place for a mine would be, before he, too, returned to Sydney. A small detachment of five soldiers also arrived from Sydney under the command of Corporal John Wixtead, whose orders were to supervise the mining operations, clear and cultivate some ground and report on the movement of any vessels that came and went. The governor declared the coal and timber to be the exclusive property of the Crown. No vessel was to proceed to the harbour without the governor's permission, nor were they to load any coal or timber that was procured using public or convict labour. This did not preclude private traders from utilising their own labour, but as the government camp was situated around the most accessible deposits of coal, it meant that nominally the river and its resources were now in the firm hand of the government.[39]

Mining was soon underway. Two government vessels had already visited by August 1801 and taken out 45 tons (45.7 tonnes) of coal in total, which were traded to the master of the ship *Cornwallis* at Sydney, 'the first natural produce of the colony that has tended to any advantages'.[40] Another private ship was also at the river loading coal and timber bound for the Cape of Good Hope, representing the first export of coal from New South Wales.

In October, magistrate Martin Mason was sent to administer the small mining camp, taking over command from Wixtead, who struggled to control the soldiers and the prisoners. Wixtead remained at the settlement as part of the military guard. With the arrival of Mason, the settlement—for which the name 'Kings Town', after the governor, had been mooted—was given the official name Newcastle, although Coal River also remained in common usage for almost twenty years.[41] Mason worked on the efficiency of the mining, as well as assigning two or three convicts to engage in fishing in the harbour, the object being to obtain as many fish as possible for salting and transport to Sydney. Soon after arriving, Mason wrote to Governor King that mine tunnels had been dug and reported promisingly that the coal was better the further in they went. The coal was dug by hand and removed from the mine by convict carriers, who took it to a stockpile on the beach, from where it was hand-loaded into boats. Mason requested that timber slabs be made available to line the mine floor. If this improvement were made, wheelbarrows could be employed to move the coal out of the mine, freeing up men to dig. He also suggested a wharf be built for coal loading, eliminating the need for the convicts to load small boats on shore and row the coal to the waiting ships. By November, four mines had been dug, the longest tunnel being just over 31 metres. From these, 190 tons (193.1 tonnes) of coal were extracted.[42]

The settlement was predominantly male, although a few women were there: wives or girlfriends of the soldiers. Two women, Jane McFee and Harriet Willards, were at the settlement at the end of October but left soon after. McFee went of her own accord, while Willards' behaviour was 'such that even the soldiers have drummed her out of their society'.[43] What she did or why she was there is not recorded. At least two other women were also there, one with Wixtead and another who was employed washing the soldiers' uniforms. They were among the population in November when the settlement consisted of Mason, Corporal Wixtead, five privates and sixteen convicts (including those in the mines), a black-smith and a carpenter.[44]

With an eye to a permanent settlement, Governor King sent Surveyor General Charles Grimes and surveyor Francis Barrallier once again to undertake a more detailed survey than that carried out by Barrallier on the *Lady Nelson*. In December 1801, Grimes retraced the route of Grant and Paterson as far as Shanks Forest Plains, examining suitable spots for cultivation and stands of timber in particular. Grimes' report was not glowing, noting areas of extensive swamp, low-lying land underwater before the banks of the river had even overflowed and clear evidence of recent heavy flooding. He did manage to explore another river running into the Hunter, remarking upon the blue gum and apple trees (angophoras) growing on the low ground and the plentiful stands of cedar and kurrajong along its banks. Grimes named this the Paterson River, but he was in fact on the Hunter itself above the present-day town of Raymond Terrace, while the upper reaches of what Grimes thought was the Hunter River was instead the Williams River.[45]

The naming of the rivers and natural features observed during this second survey, as well as by those earlier expeditions, conveyed a mix of official patronage and descriptive, almost experiential, naming practices, as had occurred around the Hawkesbury settlements. The Williams and Paterson rivers were named after the lieutenant governor. Other places, such as Freshwater Bay, Pirate Point (Stockton), Colliers Point (Fort Scratchley), Sheep Pasture Hills (east Newcastle) and Shanks Forest Plains (near Maitland) were named informally, the colloquial expression of those on the survey party or the sawyers, fishers and miners who preceded them.[46]

None of these names survive formally in the modern Hunter Valley. Of course, all these features already had names: Aboriginal names. The process of Aboriginal naming across their Country was intense, with almost every landscape feature named wherever Aboriginal people lived.[47] In and around Newcastle, the names were also there, although in these first forays the British showed little to no interest in them. *Muloobinbah* is Newcastle's original name; *Coquun* is the name of the Hunter River, *Tahlbihn* that for Colliers Point, *Burrabihngarn* for Pirate Point, the *Doorribang* is the Williams River and the *Yimmang* the Paterson River.[48] In recent years, the Geographical Names Board in New South Wales has recognised some of these via its dual naming policy: Nobbys Head/*Whibayganba*, Flagstaff Hill/*Tahlbihn*, Pirate Point/*Burrabihngarn*, Port Hunter/*Yohaaba*, Hunter River (South Channel)/*Coquun*, Shepherds Hill/*Khanterin*, Ironbark Creek/*Toohrnbing* and Hexham Swamp/*Burraghihnbihng*.

During Grimes' survey, according to Mason, he encountered hostile Aboriginal groups along the river. However, the descriptions of those around the camp suggest otherwise. A party of between 60 and 70 men, women and children came into the settlement 'without spears and manifested the most friendly manner' according to Mason, with another group further upriver who, after appearing to challenge Mason landing in his boat, sent two men out in a canoe to paddle ahead of him and show him the way through the deep water channel and help him to push his boat when it struck a mudflat.[49]

The canoes reported by Grant and Mason were a common form of transport among Aboriginal people, from the harbour all the way up the river to at least present-day Singleton. They were similar in design and construction across the Hunter: commonly a sheet of bark tied at either end with bark strips (the same style as those in the Sydney area, the Hawkesbury and the Nepean). The means of propulsion, however, differed depending on the part of the river on which they were used. On the harbour and deeper sections of the river, small paddles were employed, one in each hand, while further upriver the canoe was guided by a long pole, much like an English punt.[50]

Mason's settlement did not last long. Within two months of his taking over, the convicts were in open mutiny, which was only resolved through the intercession of Wixtead and another soldier.[51] In December 1801, he was recalled to Sydney, leaving under a cloud of poor management and harsh treatment. His appointment raised some eyebrows from the start, with Judge Advocate Richard Atkins and magistrate the Reverend Samuel Marsden both refusing to serve on the bench with him due to his treatment of a convict woman in Sydney. With Mason gone, Corporal Wixtead was left in charge of dismantling the camp. By February 1802, the first attempt at settlement was over.

CHAPTER THREE

A CONVICT OUTPOST

NEWCASTLE

Since 1797, when Shortland made his report on the newly discovered harbour, the coal and timber resources of the Hunter had been exploited by the British. Even after the failure of the 1801 settlement, government and private ships continued to make the journey to the river. It is probable that a permanent settlement would eventually have been re-established at some future point to secure the coal for the government, but in the end it was an uprising by Irish convicts in Castle Hill that made it happen.

On the evening of 4 March 1804, Irish convicts on the government farm at Castle Hill, north-west of Sydney, set in motion a plan worked out over months to overpower their guards and march to Parramatta in a desperate bid for freedom. Although nearly 300 rebels were mustered from Castle Hill and Parramatta, with more expected from the Hawkesbury, the uprising was doomed from the start by informers, poor communications and overwhelming force of arms. Following a brief battle on the road to Windsor between the Irish and a party of soldiers and armed civilians, fifteen rebels lay dead, with many wounded and the rest captured or scattered.[1] The shock of the uprising prompted Governor King to move quickly to isolate the ringleaders. Nine of the captured leaders were summarily tried and executed while a further 34 were transported to re-establish the coalmines on the Hunter River.

Command of the new settlement at Newcastle was given to First Lieutenant Charles Menzies of the Royal Marines, then on board HMS *Calcutta*. On 18 March 1804, Menzies, having resigned from the Marines, took command of the party to reopen the coalmines with a sergeant, nine rank and file of the New South Wales Corps, a marine from the ship *Buffalo*, a superintendent, a surgeon, an overseer and three experienced miners assigned to him.[2] Of the 34 Irish rebels, there were two carpenters, three sawyers, a gardener and a salt-maker included, who were to form the first labour force. The small contingent left Sydney on 27 March in the ship *Lady Nelson*, the very same that had surveyed the harbour in 1801, accompanied by the colonial vessel *Resource* and the sloop *James*. The party was joined by artist Ferdinand Bauer and botanist George Caley, with the fleet seen off by Governor King.[3]

The re-established settlement was to serve as a place of secondary punishment for convicts: a penal station within a penal colony. Its isolation from Sydney, surrounded by bush and rugged mountains, served to keep the convicts in place, while their labour supported the economy of the colony through the getting of coal and timber, the burning of shells for lime and the making of salt. This dual purpose of punishment and commerce, however, created a problem with the operation of the station.

There were a number of ways a convict could end up in Newcastle but for the most part it was for an offence committed in the colony. Sentences were imposed by a magistrate, the criminal court or by order of the governor. Free settlers or those convicts free by servitude could only be sent to Newcastle after conviction by the criminal court. Those sent on the governor's pleasure, with the length of sentence not specified, were often recommended to be allowed to return to Sydney after one year if their behaviour merited it.[4] However, as most convicts lacked the experience needed for the type of work required—an issue not peculiar to the Newcastle outpost—some convicts were sent to Newcastle because of their skill rather than for any particular crime they had committed. This was the case for Benjamin Grainger, transported for life, who was sent to Newcastle in 1810 because he was a miner. He remained as supervisor of the coalmines until he retired in 1822.[5] This style of arbitrary exile was one of the more unfortunate ways of ending up at Newcastle. Confusion over sentencing was a perennial feature of the place, with regular pleas from convicts and inquiries from commandants about when sentences had expired.

On arrival at Newcastle, Menzies, commandant in 1804–5, put the convicts to work with a camp re-established on the southern shore of the harbour, close to the 1801 site. The camp was clustered around the base of the hill at Colliers Point, near the first mine adits dug in 1801 and two small freshwater springs that ran down from the sandhills behind. By April 1804, Menzies reported that he was under shelter and in May a further twenty English convicts, who had misbehaved on their transport from England, had been added to the workforce to balance the otherwise overwhelming Irishness of the place. By the end of 1804, the population at Newcastle had risen to 128.[6] A painting by Bauer completed soon after the settlement was established shows Menzies' house on a rise overlooking the camp, with a scattering of tents down the hill towards the harbour. A signal flag (sent in May) flies on a point above the ocean, with scattered trees and open grasslands dominating. This landscape, ideal for the new camp, was the work of thousands of years of Aboriginal management and labour.

In October 1804, just eight months after the camp's establishment, botanist Robert Brown, who spent two weeks collecting plant specimens in the neighbourhood, described the fledgling town:

> In the morning I took a short walk in the neighbourhood of the town which occupies the gentle slope of a grassy hill. At present it consists of two rows of small houses or huts, that nearest the sea inhabited by the prisoners, the other parallel to it occupied by the detachment of the NS Wales Corp. The Commandant's house is situated at the upper end of the town and faces the landing place. The Military officer's house and store house on the right, the surgeon's and superintendent's on the left form with it a semicircle.
>
> A row of houses parallel to the other two and nearer the sea is begun. It is intended to erect the permanent store house on a little rising ground near the landing place.
>
> Mr Menzies has already built a very sufficient stone wharf alongside of which small vessels may take in their cargoes whether coal or cedar.[7]

With the mines at work, Governor King reaffirmed that all the coal and timber was government property and instructed Menzies that no one was to cut timber or take coal without written permission from the governor. Ships that attempted to do so without official sanction were to have their crews seized and then be scuttled.[8] Fees charged for the loading of private vessels with coal and the sale of cedar in Sydney were used to offset at least some of the costs of the settlement.

Newcastle operated exclusively as a penal station from 1804 until 1821, during which time around 3000 convicts came and went, some staying for short periods, others for many years.[9] Port Macquarie replaced Newcastle from mid-1821 and convicts were gradually transferred north to this new penal outpost. Newcastle developed a reputation as a place of harsh punishment, with savage and sometimes brutal commandants. During this phase eight ruled—Charles Menzies (1804–5), Charles Throsby (1805–6), William Lawson (1806–10), John Purcell (1810–11), Thomas Skottowe (1811–14), Thomas Thompson (1814–16), James Wallis (1816–18) and James Morisset (1818–23). Hemmed in by an unforgiving bush, the convicts were worked hard; punishment was often severe and those who dared to run would likely starve, wander lost in the bush or be ruthlessly hunted down by pursuing soldiers, bands of Aboriginal warriors or both. In the narrative of New South Wales's early history as a convict nightmare, Newcastle strove to be the perfect model.[10]

Magistrates considered sending convicts to Newcastle a harsh option reserved for the most 'troublesome' characters. Convicts, already dislocated from their families and companions in the old country, were once more uprooted from whatever normality they may have been able to create for themselves in Sydney and sent further into the wilderness of Australia's bush. Indeed, the breaking of convicts' connections with other persons of improper character was one of the benefits as far as the authorities were concerned. However, these men and women were also the vanguard of settlement in the Hunter Valley and established the frontier, particularly the cedar and timber gangs. It was these convicts who had the first prolonged contact with Aboriginal people, who came to know the bush and the landscape, and who were among those that, when given the option, actually chose to stay.

Although the coal at Newcastle had been a major factor in the re-establishment of the penal station, the methods of extraction were rudimentary and remained so until 1817. Coal was accessed via horizontal adits driven into the side of the hill at Colliers Point, under what is now Fort Scratchley in Newcastle's east end. At first the coal was mined by hand and carried by convicts to waiting ships, wading out over the rocks and sand. By the close of 1804, a wharf had been constructed to enable more efficient loading.[11] By 1810, the coal was being taken to ships in two 1-ton (1.02 tonne) tip-carts along a slab path to the wharf. The mines were beset with issues, including poor ventilation and the constant influx of water, which was captured underground in a series of dams and then either bailed out or diverted to other adits to escape the mine. The poor infrastructure was coupled with a critical lack of experienced miners throughout the years of the penal station. Those who were there were often employed on other tasks such as quarrying or, from 1818, building the breakwater between Colliers Point and Coal Island (Nobbys Island). All these factors hampered the production of coal. In the first year of production only 150 tons (152.5 tonnes) of coal were raised, but this rose steadily each year until 3915 tons (3978.9 tonnes) were mined in 1820, the highest tonnage of any year.[12]

Although the work was difficult, with conditions underground hot, dark and dangerous, the specialist miners did enjoy privileges not offered to other convicts at Newcastle. Expected to cut two-and-a-half tons (2.54 tonnes) per day, the mining gangs often completed their work within the allotted work time of ten hours and, once finished, were permitted to rest. At the same time, they received double rations due to the arduous nature of the work; as the rations constituted their wages, from the beginning of the industry miners were at the top end of the wage structure in the colony. This was further entrenched in the years after 1811, as the British coal industry was also expanding and fewer miners were being transported to the colony, making professional miners increasingly scarce. The skilled miners were assisted by a gang of labouring convicts who were employed bailing water, hauling coal and loading boats. Unlike their skilled companions, these men received only the standard ration.[13]

The other main employment for the station was timber-getting. The timber resources around Newcastle and along the banks of the Hunter, Williams and Paterson rivers and their tributaries were vast and varied. Great stands of cedar, red gum, ash and other timbers grew within easy reach of the rivers, upon which the logs could be transported after felling. Timber was a valuable resource in the expanding colony, used for construction, shipping and even trade, and the timber gangs were sent further and further into the valley to procure it.

Initially the timber gangs were small, a reflection of the limited number of men available. The first gang sent out consisted of just five men. Working close to the station, they managed to cut more than 488 cubic metres of timber over three days in June 1804. These men were the station's frontiersmen, the front line of expansion into the valley: exploring the hinterland, reporting on good land and pastures, and encountering the Aboriginal people who lived along the river. Their camps became semipermanent outposts. Within five months of the establishment of the station, timber was being felled almost 112 kilometres upriver from Newcastle, around the junction of the Hunter and Paterson rivers near present-day Morpeth.[14] Venturing further and further in the quest for cedar and other species, the gangs and their military guard were required to stay in the bush for longer and longer periods, with most being out for four to five weeks, but by 1815 some were away from Newcastle for up to six months at a time.[15]

The river was central to the operation. Trees, once felled, were brought to the edge of the river, where they were then lashed together, fastened with iron staples to form a raft and floated towards the Newcastle settlement. A small hut erected upon the raft gave shelter to the rafting crew on their way down. The method employed for cutting timber differed depending on the timber required, for it was not only cedar that was sought but also rosewood (*Dysoxylum fraserianum*), red honeysuckle (*Banksia serrata*), grey ironbark (*Eucalyptus paniculata*) and Sydney blue gum (*E. saligna*), among others.[16]

Each gang was set a quota of logs to procure, with the overseer choosing the trees once they were on site. Cedar gangs were expected to retrieve up to 100 logs per month, but the amount could differ depending on how far the logs had to be dragged to the river. Different gangs were allocated different trees to cut, and different trees required more or fewer men to fell and transport. By 1820, eighteen men were normally assigned to get cedar, but up to 30 could be in an ironbark gang. The higher number of men allocated to ironbark gangs acknowledged the increased difficulty of cutting those trees, a reality further illustrated by the fact that cedar gangs often reached their monthly quota within three weeks.[17] Timber parties venturing upriver were issued rations depending on how far they were going from the settlement, sometimes carrying a month's provisions, as well as iron pots, frying pans and grinding mills, on top of their equipment load. At their camps, they built shelters and small thatched huts in which to live. In 1817, the chief engineer of New South Wales, Major George Druitt, believed the work of the timber gangs to be the hardest of any in the colony.[18]

Despite the general orders proclaiming all timbers to be the property of the government in 1804, private tenders continued to come to Newcastle with permission from the governor to cut timbers. The ships of merchant Thomas Reiby and emancipists James Underwood and Henry Kable were regular visitors to Newcastle in the first months after the station was established.

It was determined early that although the ground around the camp was not ideal for cultivation, as it was primarily sand dunes or marshland, it was too dangerous to establish any farms far from the camp without a military guard. Although Menzies had worked to establish a peaceful coexistence with Aboriginal groups, the numbers of Aboriginal people upriver made him wary of establishing any isolated outposts. He reported on his efforts in July 1804, saying 'we have always been and still continue on the most-friendly terms with numerous Natives here', a situation on which Governor King congratulated him.[19] With the prospect of eventually establishing farms close to the station, Menzies had travelled upriver with one of the timber gangs to inspect the soil. He reported:

> I do not think, as the Natives of that part frequently pay visits here on account of the Fishery, that they would be found at all troublesome, and even if they were, the means to prevent them could soon be sent from the settlement. Should your Excellency approve of it, the ground shall be cleared, which with very little trouble can be done, as it is thinly clad with trees.[20]

While Menzies was confident that any potential trouble was preventable, relations with Aboriginal people were being tested by actors beyond his control. Menzies was made aware that Aboriginal people had frequently 'been very ill used by some who are neither guided by principle or humanity'.[21] Menzies suspected that there had already been a number of incidents upriver involving commercial timber gangs from Sydney, but there were three events in particular that finally ended the operations of private, unaccompanied gangs in the Hunter.

In July 1804, a gang of sawyers from the ship *George* working 113 kilometres upriver from Newcastle was attacked by a group of men 'who differ much in disposition from those down the river'. Sensationally reported in *The Sydney Gazette*, a party of Aboriginal men had approached the crew, who, suspecting they were not entirely friendly, reportedly treated them with 'civility and caution'. Without warning, one of the Aboriginal men grabbed at a musket,

wrestling with the timber-getter for it. The rest of the group threw
their spears at the sawyers, who responded with musketry. One
warrior was killed before the British retreated in their boat to a
distance beyond the reach of the spear throwers. The crew of the
George did nevertheless manage to get over 70 logs of cedar for
their trouble.[22] This was the first report of an Aboriginal group on
the Hunter attempting to seize a musket. Whether they sought to
include one in their own arsenal or were just trying to disarm the
sawyers is not known.

This incident was followed by two more in November. First the
boat of botanist Robert Brown was attacked on the river near Ash
Island; shortly afterwards, a sawyer employed by Messrs Underwood
and Kable was beaten, his musket and other arms stolen.[23] *The
Sydney Gazette* again reported the incident as the action of 'troublesome natives'. Menzies, however, placed the blame squarely on the
sawyers, referring to it as a trifling misunderstanding, which he
regarded as a matter of course when people acted so imprudently.
Although he did not elaborate on the matter, he did hint at a disparity in treatment: 'it is somewhat strange to remark as often as
our boats are up the river that they never attempted to molest any
person belonging to the settlement'.[24]

Apparently, only strangers were clashing with local Aboriginal
groups at this time. Why would this be the case? It could be that
under Menzies' directions, and with the regular need to venture
from the relative safety of the station, the convict gangs had come
to an understanding with the local Aboriginal people, enabling
them to work unmolested. More likely it was that as the convict
gangs were overseen and protected by armed soldiers, Aboriginal
people avoided any conflict in fear of being shot or the possibility
of reprisals. While both private and government timber gangs were
armed, the private gangs were not as heavily defended and maybe
presented a more tempting target to Aboriginal warriors. Another

possibility is that the relative discipline under which the Newcastle gangs worked reduced the potential for conflict. The gangs coming from Sydney were working unsupervised and, Menzies suspected, had been involved in a number of incidents prior to the two attacks.

The tussle for the musket in both instances is of note. Interactions in Sydney by this time had already shown that Aboriginal men were well aware of both the power and the limitations of the musket. In capable hands it was a weapon to be respected, especially if deployed in numbers by well-drilled soldiers; however, in the hands of an untrained sawyer, after it was fired once there was ample opportunity for a fast attack before it could be primed again.[25] Following the attack on Underwood's men in November 1804, Governor King wrote to Menzies saying that in light of the 'misunderstandings that happened with the Natives and Underwood's sawyers', no sawyers would be allowed to fell cedar up the river or its branches. Menzies suggested instead that some trustworthy men be sent upriver with the station's boats to avoid any ill consequences.[26] And so it was that, for the next sixteen years, the timber trade in the Hunter Valley was exclusively managed by the colonial authorities.

For the convict timber gangs, the search for stands of timber took them further and further upriver. Once the timber was felled and rafted back to Newcastle, the logs were gathered on the shore of the harbour for processing. A lumberyard was eventually established close to the wharf on the harbour's edge, where the logs were sawn into planks for dispatch to Sydney on a quarterly basis or as special orders were made. Special orders of planks were made for boatbuilding as early as 1805 and later for specific pieces of furniture. In 1810, the then-commandant, John Purcell, ordered two logs for a dining table to be shipped to Sydney; in 1814, 8000 feet (2438.4 metres) of cedar was required for the construction of the colonial secretary's house in Sydney; and in 1816, 588 feet (179.2 metres) of cedar was wanted for Government House at Parramatta.[27] Sometimes it was more than just planks and logs that were needed. In 1815, Governor Macquarie instructed Commandant Thompson to employ someone to collect cedar and rosewood plants, as well as any other tree or shrub growing at Newcastle and possessing particular beauty, for transplanting into the Governor's Domain. They were to be carefully packed so as to arrive in Sydney safely.[28]

Over the life of the penal station, more than 7164 cedar logs alone were shipped to Sydney. Year on year the value of the timber outstripped that of the coal, making timber the settlement's most precious resource. At the closure of the station in 1821, the total value of the cedar alone was nearly two-and-a-half times that of all the coal extracted.[29]

Two other extractive industries were also carried out at Newcastle: salt-making and the production of lime. Salt-making, through a combination of solar evaporation and gentle boiling of sea water, was short-lived, only occurring between 1805 and 1808. Lime burning began in 1808 and continued until the closing of the penal station. Although large shell middens had been noticed in 1801, the mining of these shells commenced only in 1808, probably to make lime mortar for the construction of the local gaol in the same year.[30] Production varied depending on demand but, by 1820, 70 men were employed at Limeburners Bay on the foreshore of Fullerton Cove, with most of their output contributing to Governor Macquarie's building boom in Sydney. It was hard, dangerous work, made all the more so by regular harrying from Aboriginal groups, described by Commandant Morisset in 1820 as being 'both troublesome and formidable'.[31]

BOLTING

During the years of the penal station, the discipline and relative privation of convicts were often harsher than for those in Sydney.

In May 1804, six of the Irish convicts who were part of the original Castle Hill group were caught planning another uprising in Newcastle. Two were returned to Sydney for punishment; in Newcastle, three received 200 lashes each, and the fourth, a convict named Tierney, was set 500 'or as many as he can take without endangering his life'.[32] A second plot was uncovered among a cedar gang in September. Thomas Desmond, a recaptured convict, told the authorities that they planned to murder the superintendent and the soldiers and then escape.[33]

Absconding, or bolting, from the timber gangs was rife throughout the station's operation, only starting to ease around 1818. The relative isolation and small number of guards made the temptation to run difficult to resist. It was most often individual convicts or small groups who bolted, although in 1810 eight convicts ran from the cedar gang, with some being repeat offenders. The same year, the commandant at the time, John Purcell, reported that he sent his best convicts almost 100 miles (161 kilometres) upriver to collect timber, suggesting a level of trust not seen in other work environments. In 1818, Commandant James Morisset reported that the timber gangs recorded fewer runaways than operations in the town. Morisset put this down to his having selected his most trustworthy convicts for the task. By Morisset's time, the timber-getters were operating from semipermanent camps established along the river close to the present towns of Morpeth and Maitland, with gangs roaming as far inland as Branxton on the Hunter and into the foothills of the Barrington Ranges along the Williams and Paterson rivers.

When Governor Macquarie inspected the penal station in 1818, he noted that the cedar gang had a 'military guard of a Corporal and three privates to protect them from the natives'.[34] Although the timber gangs were reported as having contact with Aboriginal people, we do not have much in the way of detail. In contrast,

contact between Aboriginal people and runaways from the settlement was regularly reported. From the earliest days, convicts had
been taking to the bush to escape, most attempting to make it back
to Sydney or to the Hawkesbury settlements.

Curiously, one of the first runaways brought in was not from
Newcastle at all, but was the sole survivor of a failed escape
from Sydney. In August 1804, James Field came into the station,
starved, stripped and speared. He reported that his two companions
were killed by Aboriginal warriors when their boat was wrecked on
the coast some 100 miles (161 kilometres) north of Newcastle. Field
had himself been speared, stripped and then left, but, surviving the
attack, he had made his way south towards Newcastle. As he got
near, he found that the Aboriginal people closer to the station were
friendlier and fed him with fish and fern roots. Field was the perfect
propaganda opportunity for Menzies to illustrate what convicts
could expect if they decided to run, and he was paraded in front
of the mustered men, his spear wounds and contusions offering a
graphic illustration of the danger.[35]

While most absconders were caught or came back of their
own accord, the lack of success did not stop others from trying.[36]
Aboriginal trackers were employed by the colonial authorities
from the earliest days of the penal station to bring in absconders and often accompanied soldiers in pursuit of them. They were
the most effective way to pursue runaways and struck a primeval
fear into those who ran. Bungaree, the interpreter and intermediary on Grant's original survey, was one of the first to catch
a runaway convict, in October 1804.[37] Bungaree was a regular
visitor to Newcastle at this time. In June 1804, he had escorted
six Aboriginal men back to Newcastle from Sydney aboard
the *Resource*. Governor King was of the belief that the men had
come to Sydney soon after the Newcastle station was founded to
examine the growing town. Menzies, who considered Bungaree

a peacemaker and go-between, was so pleased with his conduct generally that he supplied food and clothing to him from the penal station stores. He was 'the most intelligent of that race I have as yet seen and should a misunderstanding unfortunately take place he will be sure to reconcile them'.[38]

The reliance on Aboriginal trackers inevitably created a dangerous situation for all involved. Convict runaways often resorted to violence to avoid recapture, and Aboriginal men used their spears to subdue them. Bungaree's own father was murdered by three convict runaways on their way towards Sydney from Newcastle late in 1804. It was reported at the time that Bungaree's father was 'advising' them to return when he was killed. The men were captured and returned to Newcastle, but there was not enough evidence to convict them for the murder.[39]

While the risk of spearing was a real possibility in the minds of escaping convicts, it is difficult to know how great a risk it was. The colonial secretary's correspondence details a range of cases where convicts were returned by Aboriginal warriors or came back themselves after suffering a spear attack, although more came back of their own volition, hungry and exhausted.

That is not to say that spearings did not occur. Charles McMahon and Thomas Cowan, runaways picked up at Broken Bay in 1807, had both been speared. Roger Farrell, sent to Newcastle accused of being 'one of Bligh's mob', witnessed a companion killed by Aboriginal spears in 1810. Herbert Stiles and Ed Edwards were returned from an escape attempt stripped and beaten in 1813. Five men—Jack Coleman, Thomas Keernan, John Law, Isaac Walker and a man named George—were all speared in the space of four days, from 20 to 23 August 1816; George Little was speared by a group of five Aboriginal men with whom he had camped the night in 1817; and John McDonald was speared to death while looking after the government tobacco crop in 1820.[40]

Following the spearing of the five runaways in 1816, Colonial Secretary John Campbell agreed with Commandant James Wallis, writing 'I fully agree with you that the Natives having speared so many runaways from Newcastle as mentioned by you, will have the good effect of deterring others from deserting for the future'.[41] However, taken as a whole, the reported incidents appear to have occurred only a few times a year.[42] The fear of a violent death in the wilderness is more likely to have been propagated by authorities, as shown by the case of James Field, than the reality of the situation.

A STIRRING OF VIOLENCE

Aboriginal people were also the victims of violence. Many were well known at Newcastle and some had close connections to the penal station. One such was Burigon, an elder at Newcastle and companion of Commandant James Wallis. They hunted and fished together, and Wallis painted Burigon in one of three group portraits he completed of Aboriginal people around Newcastle. In 1818, at Wallis's request, Burigon and 40 others entertained Governor Macquarie with a corroboree. Wallis wrote of Burigon:

'There are scenes in all our lives to which we turn back to with pleasurable, tho perhaps, with a tinge of melancholy feelings and I now remember poor Jack [Burigon] the black savage ministering to my pleasures, fishing, kangaroo hunting, guiding me thro track-less forests with more kindly feelings that I do many of my own colour, kindred and nation.'[43]

In October 1820, Burigon was fatally stabbed by John Kirby, an absconding convict. The incident occurred on the edge of the settlement, behind the Christ Church overlooking the town. Kirby and another man, John Thompson, had escaped a few days earlier but were captured by Burigon on the outskirts of the station. Burigon and his group, including Biraban/McGill (another well-known Aboriginal man), were bringing Kirby to meet a party of soldiers coming out of Newcastle to arrest the men. Kirby, on seeing the approaching troops, made a desperate attempt to flee once more. Producing a knife that had been hidden in his clothes, he stabbed Burigon before being struck down with a blow from a waddy wielded by one of Burigon's companions. Although Burigon was attended to by the station's surgeon, he died of his wounds the following week. Kirby was taken to Sydney, tried and found guilty of murder, and subsequently hanged in December 1820.[44]

Although this was the first time a British person was executed for the murder of an Aboriginal person, it was not the first punishment for an attack on an Aboriginal man in Newcastle. The same month Kirby attacked Burigon, Robert Davis and William Page received 50 and 25 lashes respectively for cutting, abusing and threatening an Aboriginal man against bringing in bushrangers.[45]

While most of the spearings were of convicts, not all were. A series of incidents involving soldiers and sailors also occurred, as did collaborative attacks between absconders and Aboriginal men. In 1808, John Spillers and John Bosh, two seamen from the ship *Halcyon*, as well as a young boy of eleven, were attacked by an Aboriginal man known as Port Stephens Robert. The three had gone to a beach across the harbour from the station to look at the remains of a shipwreck. Spillers and the boy were both killed; Bosh escaped and raised the alarm. Port Stephens Robert was known in the station and had recently been in a fight with Bungaree, leaving him with a distinctive divot in his forehead.[46]

Soldiers were also occasionally targeted. In 1814, a soldier returning from chasing an absconder was speared, stripped and had his arms and ammunition taken. More seriously, in April 1817 Peter Connachton, a private in the 46th Regiment, was killed in a skirmish with six Aboriginal men, two of whom he had been hunting with. Connachton had spent four days with convict George Little, hunting around Mount Sugarloaf, west of Newcastle. The two men had been joined on the second day by two Aboriginal men, Babalou and Obeio, and several more the day after. By day three, the Aboriginal party consisted of Babalou, Obeio, Gorman, Young Crudgie, David Lowe and Tanirairo. The names of each man, later reported by Little, were a mix of traditional names and names likely given them by convicts or soldiers, showing some familiarity. These were not men totally unknown to each other. Still, Connachton and Little were wary, Little later reporting their suspicions of the men's intentions and that he and Connachton stayed awake all night. Why? He did not say.

It can get cold around Newcastle in April, and in the morning Connachton invited the men to warm themselves in front of the fire. He offered his jacket to Gorman, and Little did the same to Babalou. In a sudden movement, Obeio, Gorman, Young Crudgie, David Lowe and Tanirairo all launched spears at the two men, striking Little in the left arm and breast, and Connachton in the chest. Connachton managed to fire his musket, pre-primed and loaded, before falling to the ground dead. The warriors gathered up the jackets and a kangaroo that had been caught by Connachton and left.

While commandants were never happy with convicts being speared, there appears to have been no retaliation around Newcastle against Aboriginal people for doing so. It was a convenient, if unofficial, method of containing and dissuading absconders. Spearings of soldiers were another matter. In response to the death of Connachton, Wallis took hostages, including the wife and five children of an Aboriginal man who eventually brought Gorman into the settlement in exchange for his family. Eventually, David Lowe and Obeio were also captured. Wallis let the man's family go, but kept the three men, a woman and a child confined in the gaol. What became of Gorman and the others is unknown.[47]

NEWCASTLE TOWN

During the first twelve years of the station, Newcastle remained a fairly small, isolated outpost. Run by six different commandants over this time, the day-to-day operations precluded any particular development. Violence between Aboriginal people and the station was limited, confined to absconders, the odd daring attack on a soldier and some clashes with timber-getters. In part this was due to the small footprint of the station, confined as it was to the edges of the harbour and a few timber camps upriver. Before 1812, the population hovered around 100, with convicts coming and going depending on their sentence. By 1816, the numbers were around 300, with enough children for a small schoolhouse to be established in May of that year. Seventeen children, aged from three to thirteen years, mostly with convict parents, were taught the basics of reading, writing, arithmetic and religion by convict teacher Henry Wrensford, sent to Newcastle in 1815. The school, still teaching in Newcastle and now Australia's longest-running school, was established as one of Governor Macquarie's public charity schools, whose purpose was to educate the children of convicts in particular in the principles of a moral and useful life in the colony.[48] By 1821, about 1000 people lived in and around the town, of whom 51 were female convicts and another twenty or so the wives and children of soldiers, administrators and some convicts.[49] The increased population brought with it the outlines of the town that would become Newcastle. The small grid of streets clustered around the harbour would later be formalised by surveyor Henry Dangar into the town grid of the future city of Newcastle. Watt Street, for example, runs directly on top of the first street of the penal establishment, then known as George Street.

There are few images of the station during its first twenty years and fewer maps or plans, but enough to show the gradual formalisation of the station. In 1807, artist John Lewin painted the station for Governor Bligh, showing a neat row of huts running back from the waterfront towards the commandant's house on the ridge behind. The government wharf juts into the harbour, and the whole place looks much as botanist Robert Brown had described it in 1804. Just over ten years later, convict artist Joseph Lycett painted the next series. Lycett, transported to New South Wales in 1813 for forgery and then sent to Newcastle for the same offence in 1815, painted a series of scenes in and around the town between 1816 and 1818 under the patronage of Commandant James Wallis. Lycett's works depict the growing town, the landscape surrounding it, including the river and Lake Macquarie, and a series of studies of the day-to-day life of Aboriginal people showing ceremony, corroboree, hunting, fishing, burial and ritual punishment: evidence of a continuing traditional life undisturbed by the British. Burigon, Wallis's friend and companion, is shown in at least one, possibly two, of the paintings, and it is thought that he may have acted as a guide and intermediary for Lycett at Wallis's behest, allowing him to observe and record such intimate scenes of Aboriginal life.[50]

Two of his paintings done in circa 1818 show the town: one from almost the same vantage point as Lewin in 1804, near the church looking towards the sea, the other looking back from the signal hill, now Fort Scratchley, towards the church on the hill behind the settlement. Both show the orderly, military town as developed by Wallis: whitewashed huts and buildings in neat rows enclosed with low paling fences. In his *Inner View of Newcastle*, looking across from Lewin's vantage point, a hunting party of two white men and an Aboriginal man are shown returning to the settlement with their dogs and a catch of kangaroo. Maybe this is Wallis and Burigon, included by Lycett to acknowledge their patronage.

Lycett is also credited with painting a cedar collector's chest for Governor Macquarie depicting scenes of Newcastle and containing specimens of birds, fish and animals collected in the region. He also helped with plans for the settlement's church built by Wallis and the painting of scenes inside.[51] Wallis was himself an accomplished amateur artist, painting Aboriginal people around Newcastle. Wallis, who some consider the first patron of the arts in Newcastle, also encouraged convict artist Richard Browne, who was transported to Newcastle from 1811 to 1817, and convict engraver Walter Preston to capture scenes of Newcastle and the surrounds. Browne, who had also painted for an earlier commandant, Thomas Skottowe, painted a series of individual portraits of Aboriginal people, including Burigon, during his time in Newcastle. For his engravings, Preston used copper sheeting requested by Wallis on the pretext of coppering the bottom of ships at the settlement.[52] To add to the artistic pool, Edward Charles Close, a lieutenant in the 48th Regiment stationed at Newcastle from 1819, painted a series of townscapes and panoramas of Newcastle, capturing the development of the town in the later years of the convict station. All four captured the natural beauty of what was ostensibly a hellhole of convict punishment and misery.[53]

Art was not the only creative output. In 1812, convict James Hardy Vaux published *A New and Comprehensive Vocabulary of the Flash Language*: a convict dictionary. Sent to Newcastle in 1811, Vaux dedicated his work to Thomas Skottowe, whom he considered to exercise enough 'liberality of sentiment' to appreciate the dictionary's worth. No doubt with an eye to his future, he thanked Skottowe for his 'very humane and equitable treatment' and his 'temperate and judicious government', and assured him that Vaux's chequered and dissolute past was behind him. Sadly for Vaux, after returning to Sydney he reoffended and came back to Newcastle in 1814 for another four years. Vaux's immersion in the language of the convicts would be a handy reference for those in the administration who had to deal with them. Vaux introduced into print such terms as 'bolt', meaning to run or leave suddenly; 'fence', a receiver of stolen goods; 'finger-smith', a midwife; 'flash-man', a dissolute character who subsisted on the liberality of unfortunate women; 'rump'd', to be flogged; 'scrag'd', hanged; 'up-in-the-stirrups', to be flush with money; and 'whiddler', a person not to be trusted with a secret.[54]

Wallis may well have used Lycett to show off his achievements in Newcastle. Upon gaining command, Wallis was given specific instructions by Governor Macquarie on the administration and development of the station. During this period, he issued 50 Government and General Orders covering harbour regulations and signals, work efficiency, punishments, sale of government items, fraternisation between convicts and soldiers, and other day-to-day directions. When he left Newcastle, he was commended by Macquarie for his humane treatment of the 700-plus prisoners, as well as his work in the building of the settlement—including a very handsome church with an elegant spire and capacity for 500 people; an excellent hospital constructed of stone and enclosed with a paling fence; a large, commodious gaol of stone; a barrack built using brick for two subalterns; a brick barrack for the assistant surgeon; a large, comfortable barrack for the convicts; a guardhouse, watch house, boathouse, lime house and new lumberyard with the necessary workshops; and an enlargement of the old wharf.[55]

He also made a start on a strong stone pier from the mainland towards Nobbys Island and promoted the reform of his convicts and their children by opening a school for the children of convicts. Much of this infrastructure was captured in Lycett's and Close's paintings.

Wallis's achievements as commandant from 1816 to 1818 contrasted with earlier commandants. He is the best-remembered commandant, and the one who left the most lasting impression.

Christ Church, for example, remained standing on the hill overlooking the growing city until replaced in 1884 (although its 'elegant spire' was short-lived). His predecessors often found themselves struggling with the station's management, juggling control of the convict population in Newcastle with management of the outposts, including small farms along the Hunter and Paterson rivers from 1812. Additional responsibilities included the discipline of the soldiers, keeping an eye on visiting ships for possible smuggling, and dealing with the personalities of the other government officials, such as the surgeons and chaplains. Some commandants were tainted by colonial politics as well. William Lawson, commandant from 1806 to 1810, was relieved of his command by Governor Macquarie under a cloud, with claims of personal violence towards prisoners and the detention of convicts sent to Newcastle for their support of Governor Bligh. Macquarie ordered the release of those 'who had been sentenced from Party factions, political or other partial causes', of which there were at least five. The relief of Roger Farrell on being released was evident in his missive to Bligh saying: 'May you live long triumphant over your enemies—May the laws of Great Britain soon convince the treacherous usurpers that they were not so far out of reach as they imagined on the 26 Jan 1808.'[56]

John Purcell, commandant in 1810–11, had an ongoing disagreement with Assistant Surgeon William Evans, whom he considered a snob and an interferer at Newcastle. His predecessor, William Lawson (1806–10), complained of similar problems. Lawson and Purcell also harboured a deep distrust of the master of the government vessel *Lady Nelson*, which visited Newcastle regularly. Purcell suspected the master, Bryan Overhand, of, among other things, smuggling cedar, allowing convicts in his care to escape, and arranging liaisons between his sailors and the female convicts at Newcastle, and noted that Lawson had struck Overhand with a

cane on one occasion.[57] Although Purcell was relieved as commandant under a cloud of suspicion, he expressed his frustrations to the
governor, noting that 'I have abundance of Enemies but if a Saint
from Heaven was sent to the Coal mines to command he would so
soon have the same if he does his duty'.[58]

AN EXPANDING FOOTPRINT

From 1812, the permanence of the station was consolidated by
the establishment of a series of farms along the Paterson River.
The first farms, at Patersons Plains, were experimental, given
out to four well-behaved convicts under the orders of Governor
Macquarie. In 1818, more farms were allocated at Wallis Plains—
now known as Maitland—on the Hunter River. The area was
named by Macquarie in 1818 in honour of Wallis, erasing the
Aboriginal name for the place: *Bu-on*.[59] Macquarie also named
the nearby creek Wallis Creek, while Wallis reciprocated by suggesting that a large freshwater lagoon be called Lachlan Lagoon
after the governor's son.[60]

The benefit of the farms was twofold: first, they provided some
incentive to well-behaved convicts to gain a foothold in the colony,
and, second, they boosted the penal station's food supply, most of
which came from Sydney or the Hawkesbury.[61] By 1814, there were
at least five farms, including a grant to Assistant Surgeon William
Evans, and by 1818, when Governor Macquarie visited a second
time (he had inspected the station in 1812), there were eight: six
run by convicts and two by free settlers.[62] Macquarie was satisfied
enough with their progress by 1814 to order those settlers—as he
referred to them—their families and servants to be taken off the
government stores and for them to be allowed to send small quantities of excess wheat and maize to the Sydney markets.[63] This was the
first small step towards agricultural commerce in the Hunter Valley.

Initially these farms were not land grants but, rather, official permission to use the land, which could be rescinded if the convicts harboured runaways or broke the law. Most, however, were later formalised as small grants. John Swan, the first convict settler, who was farming by 1813, was still in the district in 1828 with his wife Margaret and three children. Benjamin Davis, given a farm in 1814, remained there with his wife until 1823, when he exchanged it with William Evans for another of 200 acres (81 hectares) at Wallis Plains, where he stayed until his death in 1840.[64] Of the fourteen convicts eventually given farms, twelve were still on those farms or other nearby properties in 1828, including former coalmine supervisor Benjamin Grainger. The two who were not had died.

The farmers faced constant challenges. One of these was the river and its many moods. The river was a dangerous place: after rain, sudden freshets could raise its level rapidly, and hidden snags could upturn a boat on the calmest stretch. For convicts who were not strong swimmers, either of these events could be fatal. In July 1815, George Pell, one of Macquarie's well-behaved convict farmers, was drowned along with Daniel Brown, William Gudgeon and Katherine Flynn when their boat capsized as they were returning to the farms from Newcastle. Two of the bodies were never recovered. In 1821, another five people drowned on the river when their boat was capsized in a storm. This time two convict workers, Thomas Trainer and Jeremiah O'Neil, two settlers' wives, Elizabeth Allen (wife of convict settler John Allen) and Mary Swan (wife of John Swan) and her son Stephen were the victims.[65]

Living in proximity to the river also brought with it the threat of floods. From the earliest British survey, evidence of floods and flooding was noted. In 1801, James Grant saw debris in cedar trees 12–15 metres above the river. In 1809, William Lawson reported a large freshet at the mouth of the river extending some distance out to sea and went upriver to check on any inundation.[66]

Actual flood damage was first recorded in 1811 when a great flood took a large quantity of cedar logs away, carrying them in all directions. The first farm went under in 1819 when a settler, Thomas Boardman, lost his whole crop and the whole of Wallis Plains was submerged.[67]

The farms were initially managed more as appendages to the penal station than as an independent settlement area. Convict farmers were still under the control and management of the station commandant and liable to punishment for any misdemeanour or transgression, with penalties including the loss of assigned labour, confiscation of crops, a return to the work gangs or even loss of the farm property altogether.[68] Still, the presence of farms gave runaways a target to plunder or a safe place to hide. Benjamin Davis was suspected of harbouring George Stone and Samuel Brooks, who had been living in the bush for nine months when apprehended in April 1816. Stone and Brooks supplied Davis with kangaroo skins in return for corn, iron pots, arms and other conveniences. It was recommended that Davis be returned to government service to discourage other settlers from helping runaways, although as noted earlier he appears to have escaped permanent sanction, remaining on farms in the district until his death in 1840.[69]

Davis no doubt knew that there was money to be made out of kangaroos in this period, as the settlement, short on beef and pork, had turned to kangaroo as an alternative food source. Commandant Thomas Thompson informed the governor in November 1815 that it was impossible to procure kangaroos as there were not enough dogs to hunt them, and besides, kangaroos were found so far from the settlement that they were putrid before they could be brought in.[70] Dogs were crucial to the hunt: they chased the kangaroos, exhausted them, cornered them and brought them down. As such, dogs were a prized animal in the settlement, especially for those convicts wanting to escape and live in the bush.

From 1816, increasing numbers of runaways were staying in the area and living off the land as bushrangers, stealing where they could; hunting dogs were an essential part of this lifestyle. The problem was widespread enough that, in 1818–19, Commandant James Morisset ordered that kangaroo-hunting dogs should be destroyed. The killing of the dogs had the desired effect, with escapes subsequently dropping off.[71]

THE BEGINNING OF THE END

The bushrangers and the farms began to erode the impression of isolation that the penal settlement had fostered as part of its harsh reputation. This isolation had always been more an illusion than a reality. Aboriginal people moved back and forth from Newcastle to Sydney regularly, as did the more determined runaways. By 1818, Governor Macquarie, recognising this fact and the benefits of using the fertile land to settle the increasing numbers of free emigrants, began scouting for a new site for a more isolated penal station. He eventually settled on the Hastings River further north, at what is now Port Macquarie.

As if to confirm Macquarie's plans, in March 1820 John Howe, the chief constable at Windsor, arrived at Wallis Plains after an overland expedition from the Hawkesbury.[72] Howe blazed the trees to mark his way back, and by July runaway convicts were following Howe's road out of the valley. Howe was followed in July 1821 by the Reverend George Augustus Middleton, who travelled on foot directly from the Hawkesbury to Newcastle. Middleton also blazed the trees to allow his cattle and men to follow him. Like Howe's road, escaping convicts found the Parson's Road, as it became known, very useful, and by December twelve prisoners had escaped along that path.[73]

With two clearly marked paths through the bush, the usefulness of the penal station as an isolated place of terror was effectively over.

The valley was now more valuable for its rich, fertile soil, grassy plains and fresh water, and so the convict station was marked for closure.

The years of the penal station laid the foundations for British expansion in the Hunter, precipitating the profound impacts on the environment and the invasion of Aboriginal Country that were to follow. The lessons learnt by the authorities with regard to convict management, punishment and discipline were also adapted for future penal stations such as Port Macquarie and Moreton Bay. Newcastle's isolation, harsh labour regime and punitive punishment model were replicated across the future penal stations.[74] The resentment, fear and violence that had been features of convict and Aboriginal relations during the penal station era were to increase rapidly through the 1820s and 1830s. The exploitation of the natural resources, especially the coal, cedar and other timbers, that had underpinned the convict economy of Newcastle continued to be a driving force in the years following the penal station's closure. The mining of coal in the Hunter Valley to this day is a direct and lasting legacy of this first twenty years of the penal station.

CHAPTER FOUR

AS FINE A COUNTRY AS IMAGINATION CAN FORM

On 17 November 1819, John Howe, chief constable at Windsor, wrote to Governor Macquarie after a three-week expedition through the mountains north of the Hawkesbury River. He had discovered 'a fine tract of land for cultivation and grazing . . . situated on the banks of a fine fresh water river'. For 21 days he had trekked through the rugged mountains and narrow valleys north of Windsor, thinking he was heading in the direction of the Bathurst Plains. The quest to find alternative routes over the Blue Mountains to Bathurst drove a number of early attempts from Windsor, but it appeared that Howe was the first to make it a reality. And, in a way he was, although he was not near Bathurst but instead on the banks of the middle reaches of the Hunter River, near the modern village of Jerrys Plains.

Howe was the first British person to make it through the wild, mountainous landscape, but not the first to try. His success was built on three earlier known attempts, and probably countless short expeditions, explorations and probes into unknown country of which we know nothing. They were all part of a broader quest out of the Cumberland Plain by those farmers and settlers along the Hawkesbury–Nepean in the search for better grasslands and the potential rewards of discovery.

THE FIRST ATTEMPTS: SINGLETON, PARR, SINGLETON

Benjamin Singleton, the son of a convict farmer on the Hawkesbury, made the earliest attempt to find a pathway north from the river. Singleton had arrived in New South Wales in 1792 on board the *Pitt*, a young boy with his brother Joseph, his mother Hannah and convict father William. The family took up a grant of 90 acres (36 hectares) at Mulgrave Place on the Hawkesbury in 1797 and eventually constructed a series of watermills at Kurrajong and Lower Portland Head. In 1808, older brother James arrived from England as a free settler and built a third mill on the river nearby. Around September 1817, Benjamin made his first attempt to head through the mountains that enclosed this part of the Hawkesbury. He headed into the uncharted area between the Colo and Macdonald rivers, known to the Hawkesbury settlers as the First and Second Branch. The expedition followed the Macdonald River to the south and west of Mount Yengo, which rises prominently above the surrounding peaks, but made it no further. He may have had an Aboriginal guide accompany him and likely another Hawkesbury settler, George Loder, but no written account has survived; the route was merely sketched out on a later map drawn by Surveyor General John Oxley, also in 1817.[1]

In late October 1817, Singleton's attempt was followed by Thomas William Parr, a ticket-of-leave convict surveyor and draughtsman. Parr, known as William, had recently accompanied Oxley on a five-month expedition beyond the Blue Mountains in search of an inland sea, getting as far south as present-day Griffith before returning via the Macquarie River north-west of Bathurst.

It was Parr who prepared the map showing Oxley's expedition, which included the route Singleton had taken. It was likely this addition that convinced authorities to allow Parr to explore further, although no official orders appear to have been issued.[2]

Parr left Windsor on 30 October 1817. His aim was to discover a new route north-west over the mountains to the grass plains north of Bathurst. Leaving with enough food for five men and two horses, his party included Singleton, convict Robert Frances and two other unnamed convicts, one assigned to him and the other to Singleton. Although meticulously planned and plotted, his adventure was thwarted by treacherous country, storms and heavy rain, encounters with a series of bushfires and his eventual shortage of food. He did get further than Singleton had though, reaching the headwaters of the Macdonald River before returning to Windsor on 29 November.

Parr faced difficulties from the very start. It rained heavily for the first few days and nights, slowing his progress. Despite this, his journal is full of high praise for the country he made his way through. He notes the excellent pasturage, the hills covered in fine grass and the valleys well-watered with creeks and streams. Nine days in, he declared that up to that point 'there is not better Land to Graze Cattle, in the Colony'. Three days later, Parr, with small grassfires burning on both the flats and hills, supposed that they were 'evidently done by natives but we could not see them'.[3] Further inland, Parr entered into a valley, close to the modern town of Putty, which had been managed by Aboriginal people through fire. He noted: 'All the whole surface to this place appears to have been burnt about Two Months ago so that the face of the Country is like Land covered with fine young wheat.'[4] While Parr was witnessing the benefits of controlled fire management by Aboriginal people, he was about to encounter the danger of a large bushfire that would scuttle his plans altogether.

On 14 November 1817, two days after seeing the wheat-like pastures, Parr noted that the country in all directions, the hills and valleys on each side, were covered in smoke and 'the sun was the colour of Blood'; in the distance, the horizon was all in flames.[5] Singleton announced his intention to turn back the next day, having been in low spirits for some days. Although Parr convinced him to stay on, the following day his mind was set and he turned back towards Windsor, taking Robert Frances and a packhorse with him. He also took the best part of the rations, leaving Parr and the rest short of food.

In spite of the lack of food and an increasingly dangerous bushfire situation, Parr pushed further into the mountains. He was rewarded with more pasture land and was convinced he would make it through to Bathurst. Again he described the country in ebullient terms. On 18 November he wrote 'I cannot avoid stateing [*sic*] that I never saw anything so picturesque & fine in all my travels. The surface is as if covered with fine young wheat and not a Bush nor a bough of a tree to be seen upon it', while the hills, he noted, were 'covered with the same verdure up to the very ridge', and the apple (angophora) and gum trees were the largest he had ever seen. He saw mobs of kangaroos in the valleys and, passing a lake, witnessed a great flock of 50 black swans, as well as hundreds of ducks and other birds.[6]

Only once did he see any Aboriginal people. They were in a valley in the distance 'generally about the skirts of the flames'. Parr sent out one of his men hoping to get some information from them, 'but on his hailing about Twelve of them, all the notice they took of him was coo,ee'.[7] He had suspected that the fires had been lit by Aboriginal groups, and yet their scale suggests something more. Bill Gammage has examined the fire management of Aboriginal people across Australia. It was a controlled process, as it still is where it is practised. Gammage argues that rarely did these fires burn into the night, as this represented a loss of control, and that they were most often set before rain as opposed to after it.[8] Parr may have both been seeing the effects of a controlled burn, as illustrated in his descriptions of fresh green shoots and grasslike fields of wheat, and been in the midst of a bushfire. He grew increasingly concerned as each path was cut, the fire raged 'with the greatest fury' and burning trees dropped branches in one place and rolling down the hills ablaze in another. The noise of the 'burning trees from the hills, I could compare to nothing more like, than a siege with heavy Artillery'.[9] The next day, 22 November, he wrote:

> This morng [sic] I tried if it were possible to effect a passage over the Hills which had been burnt the preceding Night but the danger was too great. Standing Trees were on fire in every direction, & at short intervals either a Burning Limb fell, or a tree, so that the ground was literally covered with fire.[10]

It was all too much. Low on food and surrounded by fire, Parr decided to turn back and head for Windsor. The return journey was made all the easier as the fires had swept through the country they had already traversed, leaving it bare and open. Although Parr added to the knowledge of the surrounding country, his expedition was largely a failure. He was not heading towards Bathurst as he thought but, instead, deep into a mountainous country, riven with rivers and creeks sided by steep cliffs and ravines. He illustrated part of his journal, sketching the country that stretched before him. A sketch, from 15 November, drawn near Putty, shows a distant Mount Wareng and Mount Yengo standing as waypoints in what appears to be an endless sea of mountains and ridgelines.

Five months later, on 25 April 1818, Benjamin Singleton decided to give it another try and, like Parr, set off to find a new way to Bathurst from Windsor. Singleton had the advantage of having now covered some of this ground twice, and was no doubt confident of success. His desire was to move fast and light. With him were four unidentified white men and an Aboriginal guide, again unnamed. He appears to have had no horse to carry supplies, and so must have had each of the party carry something instead. For extra food they probably relied on hunting and gathering along the way.

Although nowhere recorded, it is likely that on his first trip out, and on Parr's, the routes had been marked, possibly by cutting a blaze in the trees as they went. This would account for Singleton's rapid progress. He reached Colo in a day, a journey Parr had taken five days to complete, and got to Putty in three-and-a-half days, compared to Parr's eight.[11]

Unlike his first attempt, Singleton kept a journal on this trip. Lacking the detailed survey information of Parr's, the account is not clear on the route taken beyond Putty; however, his party headed north-west, running parallel to the Hunter Valley and into increasingly mountainous country. It reads as if they were lost. Perhaps their guide was beyond the limits of his knowledge as well, for their path was soon barred by thick vines and brush forest. On the night of 5 May 1818, Singleton's camp was harassed by a party of Aboriginal men. Around eight o'clock, the group heard voices in the darkness, followed by the cracking of sticks and then the noise of large rocks rolling towards them from the heights above. Rolling or throwing rocks down was a tactic that had been successfully employed by Aboriginal people in skirmishes with the British around the Hawkesbury already, and one that Singleton and the others may have been aware of.[12] The effect was to spread panic among the party. Singleton wrote in his journal that as the stones crashed down towards them,

every man of us arose and fled from the fire secreting ourselves behind trees with our guns and ammunition where we could have a view of the fire Doubting if we staid by the fire every Man was lost spent the Whole of the Night in that Condition Raining very Hard the Native whom we had with us was timid than any of us saying he was sure we should be killed.[13]

Although an attack appeared imminent, none came. The following morning, as the party set off, they encountered a group of more than 200 Aboriginal men, clothed in skins and armed with spears. One man, named Mawby, spoke some English and claimed that the rest had never seen a white man before. Through his Aboriginal guide, Singleton encouraged Mawby and four others to come forward, and he asked them if his party could continue west. They told him it was impossible due to rocky country and there being no water.[14]

Mawby asked Singleton's purpose. He responded, via his guide, that it was to get to Bathurst or find good grazing land. Mawby told Singleton that good grass was two days to the north-east beside a wide river that flowed in both directions. It could not be swum across nor could the water be drunk, according to Mawby. Singleton surmised the river was tidal and probably ran into Port Stephens. Mawby was instead talking about the Hunter River, but this was as far as Singleton would get. Despite the directions to the grazing land he was seeking, the encounter with 200 men after an attack in the night convinced him, and his party, to abandon the expedition and return to Windsor. Singleton wrote of his fear that if they went towards the river, the men would follow them and betray them for the provisions on account of him having only five others in his party. Further, his own guide 'was more in dread' than themselves, and so the decision to turn back was taken.[15]

As is so often the case with colonial accounts, a brief account of a fleeting encounter poses more questions than answers. On the face of it, it is not hard to understand why Singleton and his party chose to turn back. They had been out for just over a week, they appeared lost, their guide was in apparent fear for his and the others' safety, they had been attacked in the night and they were now confronted by a large group of armed Aboriginal men. It is not clear whether they would be in less danger from the 200 going towards the grazing lands or returning to Windsor, but the encounter poses some questions. On the night of 5 May, when the party was attacked, Singleton had recorded that they camped close to the base of the largest mountain he had ever seen. Thanks to historian and bushwalker Andrew Macqueen, we now know that mountain is Mount Monundilla, a highly significant place for Aboriginal people from the Hunter and beyond. Rock art and other ceremonial sites have been identified on and around Mount Monundilla. This could explain the large group of men he encountered, possibly men from a number of different areas converging for ceremony. The rolling of rocks and breaking of sticks may itself have been a warning to stay away rather than a dedicated attack on the group. An armed group of 200 could easily have overwhelmed Singleton's small party in the darkness if they had so desired.

Mawby's knowledge of the tidal river and his English skills suggest that he had had contact with or lived around the Hunter, probably around Morpeth where the effect of the tide wanes. Possibly he came from further down towards Newcastle, where the river is wide and salty at its mouth. Maybe he picked up English through contact with the convict timber-getters or the soldiers at Newcastle. His knowledge of Country, the good grass and wide river also illustrates the connections that crisscrossed the Hunter and the ranges that surrounded it.

Despite three failed attempts to find a route over the mountains from Windsor, it was not long before a fourth expedition was undertaken. The desire to find a way was driven by a combination of a series of prolonged droughts and the overgrazing of the

Cumberland Plain in the Sydney basin. A drought from 1813 to 1815 put added pressure on the grasslands of the Cumberland Plain; a second drought in 1818–19 intensified the deterioration of the natural pastures. Stock losses were amplified by the halving of the wheat harvest in 1814–15 and the failure of maize crops in the same period. Although rain fell in 1817, drought recurred in the summer of 1818 and floods along the Hawkesbury added to the misery.[16] All these factors combined to encourage explorations beyond the mountains for better, more reliable pastures, and it was in these conditions that John Howe set off from Windsor in October 1819.

JOHN HOWE: 1819

John Howe arrived in New South Wales as a free settler in 1802, receiving a grant of 100 acres (40 hectares) at Portland Head, near Sackville on the Hawkesbury. In late May 1804, he was wounded by a spear in an Aboriginal raid on his property, one of a number of farms attacked along the river at Portland Head in May and June.[17] In 1809, he became secretary to the local constable Andrew Thompson and in 1810, on Thompson's death, Howe administered the estate. In 1812, he was appointed chief constable for Windsor and from 1813, with his partner James McGrath, Howe won a number of civil construction contracts, including the building of the new road from Sydney to Windsor via Parramatta, the toll bridge over South Creek and the enlargement of the wharf at Windsor. He was also grazing cattle on his grants at Kurrajong and Richmond Hill, supplying beef to the Sydney markets and working in his capacity as a licensed auctioneer.[18]

Leaving Windsor on or about 22 October, Howe's party moved quickly, reaching Putty in four days by following in the footsteps of Parr and Singleton. His group consisted of eight men: John Howe as leader, his son-in-law George Loder, settler John Milward, convicts John Eggleton, Charles Berry and Nicholas Connelly, and two Aboriginal guides: Myles and an unnamed man. He had two packhorses and provisions for three weeks, with each man also armed with a gun.[19] For George Loder, this was perhaps his second, possibly third time out, having maybe accompanied Singleton on his first two attempts.[20]

The choice of Myles as his guide was an interesting one for Howe to have made. As chief constable, Howe would have already known Myles as a leader of men and a warrior. They may have crossed paths already. Three years earlier, in July 1816, William Cox, former soldier, road builder and now magistrate for the Hawkesbury, wrote to Governor Macquarie as violence raged in his district. Cox outlined a series of recent violent clashes and urged action from Macquarie, proposing that there should be no friend-ships or connections between settlers and Aboriginal people.[21] Cox provided Macquarie with the names of eight Aboriginal men he considered dangerous, four of them notorious. At the top of his list was a man named Miles [sic].[22]

Acting on Cox's recommendations, Macquarie made it known that following attacks along the Hawkesbury and Nepean rivers, and despite the offer of clemency to those Aboriginal men who would surrender, ten leaders were still urging their followers to commit attacks. Macquarie issued a proclamation urging settlers, convicts and even friendly Aboriginal men to capture the ten or, if they could not be captured, 'by such means as may be within their power to kill and utterly destroy them as outlaws and murder-ers'. A reward of £10 was offered to anyone who could capture or produce evidence of the death of any of the ten men. Number two on the list was Myles, spelt as Howe spelt it.[23]

Warfare had been a regular occurrence on the frontier around Sydney since 1788. Flare-ups, clashes and campaigns had marked the Cumberland Plain, with military parties, militia and individual settlers all involved. The close and tight-knit nature of the settlement, especially along the Hawkesbury, meant that the Aboriginal warriors involved were often known by name, and the British involved in reprisals were equally well-known among the Aboriginal groups. It was a war between neighbours. The year 1816 had marked a high point in the conflict, with a massacre of fourteen Aboriginal men, women and children at Appin by soldiers under the command of James Wallis, who was made commandant at Newcastle in recognition of his leadership during this period.[24]

Macquarie's proclamations served as an effective banishment of Aboriginal people from the settlements, harking back to tactics used by earlier administrations in the colony. Men with spears and groups of six or more Aboriginal people were forbidden from approaching farms or settled areas. This method appears to have worked; in November a second proclamation was issued, lifting the warrant on those surviving Aboriginal men listed in July. Several had already been killed or captured. The remainder were encouraged to give themselves up before 28 December, when a 'General Meeting of Friendly Natives' was to be held at Parramatta. If they did so they would be forgiven, pardoned and taken under protection of the government.[25] William Cox contacted Howe to arrange escorts for those Aboriginal men heading into Parramatta to take part.[26]

Myles' inclusion in Howe's party three years later identifies him as one of the survivors and suggests that he was reconciled with, and had been accepted by, the British. Presumably he had come into the settlements sometime after Macquarie's proclamation, and his bush skills, so feared during the attacks in 1815–16, were now recognised as a necessary and valuable contribution to the expansion into new country. Whatever anxiety remained among the British about travelling into the uncharted bush with an identified resistance leader—or, indeed, any nervousness Myles himself felt about travelling with men who put his name on a death list—was seemingly put aside.

Men like Myles (and some women) who acted as guides were invaluable to the success of expeditions in these first decades of British occupation. They possessed expertise in traditional knowledge and combined it with an understanding of British culture and language. Vital bush skills such as tracking, hunting and path-finding were as important as the ability to act as interpreters, intermediaries and diplomats through their understanding of neighbouring language or custom. Importantly, they could also negotiate with local guides along the way as a party progressed through less familiar country. Local Aboriginal knowledge was one of the most valuable resources that white explorers could acquire, for it provided an intimate understanding of the country through which they were passing.[27] Aboriginal guides accompanied almost every major expedition from Sydney before the 1820s, and continued to do so as the British pushed out from new settlement areas for much of the nineteenth century, yet few are known by name and fewer are recognised in the histories.

It was not long before Myles was called on by Howe. At Putty, where both Parr and Singleton had run into problems, Howe sent Myles and a second, unnamed Aboriginal man out to look for kangaroos and to search for a local guide. From Howe's own record, the second Aboriginal man does not appear to be the same as the one who had started out with them, for in his correspondence to Macquarie, Howe says that an Aboriginal man had left the party after two days, whereas it was day five when he sent Myles out. Whoever it was, the foray was not a success. The next day, they tried again. Howe wrote in his journal that he sent 'the two natives out for a native guide as we could proceed no farther in the direction I wanted to go'. In the evening, they returned accompanied by two young boys who would take them all to another guide who was waiting for them further along.

It appears from his journal, and the approach he took, that Howe had a more nuanced understanding of the way Aboriginal cultural practice and bushcraft operated than either Parr or Singleton. By sending Myles to find a local guide, he could overcome two issues: Myles not being familiar with the rough country they were entering, and obtaining the permission of the local people to travel through their land. Indeed, Myles may well have been instrumental in advising Howe to take this approach, understanding the need for a local for both guidance and right of passage. The guides proved to be instrumental in Howe's ultimate success. Within three days of joining the party, they had negotiated a path across difficult terrain through the mountains and, although not then realising it, had reached the floodplain of the Hunter River.

The day after the two boys joined the party, Howe and his men came into an Aboriginal camp of upwards of 60 people, men, women and children, many of whom had never seen white people or horses. Howe reported that the young ran from them and others climbed trees to escape. However, Myles, acting in his role as envoy, ensured that the party ate and exchanged food with the group. On the sketch of the route, Howe marked the camp with A-framed huts, although he gave no further descriptions of the dwellings. It is here that Howe most likely took up with the local guide, who he later identified as Murphy, before the party continued.[28]

Nine days out from the Hawkesbury, on 4 November 1819, Howe and his party, having been led by Murphy, looked out from a ridgeline over a heavy fog, which appeared to hang over a river. Howe noted:

> A very heavy fog ENE (which the Natives say is Coomery Roy & more farther a great way) appears very extensive, being seen as far as the eye can reach and has much the appearance of the bois-terous ocean, only the Fog is white and the Ocean appears green, over a Range of Rocks.[29]

Howe initially took 'Coomery Roy' to mean the fog itself, but later thought it referred to the country he was looking across, because on the same day his guides called a creek Coomery Roy Creek. He was in fact looking across the plains of the middle and upper Hunter, around Jerrys Plains and along the southern boundaries of the Kamilaroi nation, which extended over the Liverpool Plains and north-west to the Barwon and Namoi rivers near Walgett and Brewarrina. It is possible that Howe's guides were not describing the country as such but rather whose Country it was: what Howe heard as Coomery Roy being instead Kamilaroi.

The next day, after a morning of hard travel, Howe's party emerged from the mountains into a narrow valley that widened out until they reached the banks of a freshwater river. Howe had found his grazing lands. His enthusiasm and excitement over the discovery is obvious in his journal. The potential for grazing was clear; the country reminded him of that around Richmond, but with less timber. He estimated that just twenty trees stood on 50 acres (20 hectares) of land, with some areas having no trees at all. It was the finest grazing land for sheep he had encountered since leaving England.[30] The grass made a fine meadow, he wrote. His Hawkesbury experience also came to the fore. Coming from a river community susceptible to flooding, Howe noted the evidence of recent floods. Debris in the riverside bushes came up to breast height, but there was enough high ground around for stock to be safe. Evidence of the flood stretched close to two and a half kilometres back from the river in places.[31]

The group noted the sand and gravel beaches in the river bends and caught some perch. In the afternoon, before they could unload the horses and set up camp, the party was surprised by 'a strange native'. As Howe tried to get Myles or another of his men to approach and find out who it was, the man disappeared, and despite searching he could not be found. Myles and the other guides were alarmed, and Howe believed that they would have shot the man if they had had the chance. Half an hour later, five more Aboriginal men crossed the river around 800 metres away and came in close to observe the group, leaving as it began to get dark. This was too much for Myles and the other guides, and they threatened to leave Howe.[32] Although he convinced them to stay, a tight watch was kept overnight and Howe sensed this would be as far as he would go this time.

In the morning, Howe, who was by now feeling ill, convinced Myles and the others to go to the next reach on the river, whereupon they stopped, crossed the water and headed back towards their entry point into the valley. On the way back, Howe picked up a piece of coal from the riverbank near the modern town of Jerrys Plains, marking the first recorded extraction of coal in the upper Hunter.[33]

The return journey to Windsor was made in relatively quick time, with rations running low, Howe's health deteriorating and the packhorses struggling. George Loder left the returning party after two days, declaring his intention to return via Yengo, or Mount Yengo. Although on the way back towards the Hawkesbury, it was not the same route as Howe had taken, suggesting that Loder had already been through this area, possibly with Singleton or Parr in 1817. Singleton, for example, is thought to have skirted Mount Yengo on his first attempt.

After Loder left, the rest fell in once more with the Aboriginal group they had seen on the way out and to whom the local guide Murphy belonged. Howe recorded an unusual conversation with an elder named Whirle. The man and his son, noticing the change in the horses' condition, asked what was the matter. Howe explained that they were sick and the road had been rough. At this, Whirle asked Murphy which way he had taken the group. When he heard, he got very angry and said Murphy had taken them the wrong way, and that he and his son would lead them if they came back.

He could take them to a wide river that ran into the sea. Howe asked if this was the Coal River (Hunter River), but Whirle said no, it was further on, although when probed he did not know of Port Stephens. Howe, ever keen on grazing land, asked if there was much clear land near the river, to which Whirle replied 'too much! too much! too much! all about'.[34]

It is difficult to know what Whirle was referring to. Had he seen the logging being carried out by convict gangs around the Hunter River? Or was it a misunderstanding and he was merely saying how open the country was? Maybe as a man of the mountains he was expressing a preference for his Country over the flat and open floodplains that characterised the Hunter. More confusingly, why would Whirle be angry that Murphy took Howe the wrong way? There is no explanation in Howe's journal. Perhaps he was worried that Murphy had taken them too close to ceremonial or sacred sites, or maybe he would have approached Kamilaroi Country from a different direction to avoid unnecessary encounters. Considering the reaction of Myles and the others to the unknown warriors, the latter seems plausible.

As Howe's party left Whirle, they were joined by up to 60 warriors, who followed along and made camp with Howe that night. Groups of men came in through the night and, when gathered, performed a corroboree for Howe, who shared two kangaroos he had shot with them. This intimate encounter seems a fitting end to Howe and Myles' expedition. The following morning they continued on towards Windsor.

MYLES GOES BACK

Arriving at Windsor on 13 November 1819, Howe immediately wrote to Governor Macquarie to inform him of his expedition. He reported on his discoveries and told Macquarie that he had followed the river for approximately seven-and-a-half miles (twelve kilometres) through fine grazing land, regretting not being able to go further due to his health. No mention was made of the encounter with the Aboriginal men on the riverbank and his guides' refusal to proceed. Nor was there any mention of the difficulty of the path they had followed or its unsuitability for a road. He did, however, tell the governor of Whirle's offer to show them a quicker route should they return.[35]

On Macquarie's orders, Howe equipped Myles and a small party of Aboriginal men with rations and muskets to return north to where he had seen the fog and investigate the route suggested by the old man Whirle. Myles left on 9 December, leading what was possibly the first armed all-Aboriginal expedition in colonial Australia, and returned seventeen days later. The new path of Whirle was shorter and better, and the cleared ground more extensive than that which Howe's party had seen. Myles did not reach the river, however, having expended all the party's ammunition. What they had used the ammunition for—defence or food—was not recorded. Howe instructed Myles to attempt to convince Whirle and another man, Bandagran, who had first told Howe about the river, to 'come in' to a meeting with Macquarie at Parramatta. For his efforts Myles received a plate and musket, as promised by Macquarie for undertaking the journey.[36]

By following a pre-existing pathway known to Whirle and his people, Myles and his all-Aboriginal expedition had followed and recorded the first viable route connecting the Hawkesbury settlements with the Hunter Valley. The Putty Road follows this route very closely. For Myles, the reward of a musket and a plate was of note, but, maybe more importantly, he was rehabilitated in the eyes of Macquarie, having gone from wanted outlaw and hunted rebel to rewarded explorer in the space of three years. It would also appear that a level of trust had developed, and a personal

relationship between Myles and Howe enabled the successful collaboration. As both men were personally involved in the wars along
the Hawkesbury, their collaboration speaks of the ability of personal
reconciliation in a period of tension and mistrust.

HOWE AND MYLES' SECOND EXPEDITION: MARCH 1820

Howe wasted no time in organising another expedition based
on Myles' report. On 5 February 1820, he wrote an urgent letter
to Macquarie requesting a meeting to finalise the details of the
journey and establish a level of government support in terms of
equipment and supplies. His urgency was driven by the fact that
Macquarie had issued a proclamation that he was preparing dis-
patches for His Majesty's Government for the *Admiral Cockburn*,
which sailed on 1 March 1820, and that he would accept no further
applications except in an emergency.[37] If Howe was delayed too
long, he would be forced to wait or go in the colder months, something he feared due to his ill health.[38]

Macquarie agreed that Howe's request constituted an emergency and authorised provisions for Howe, ten men and two
Aboriginal guides. Among the list of supplies were twelve muskets,
with 24 rounds per man, suggesting that all members of the party,
including the guides, would be armed. On the final invoice for the
expedition, it was also noted that the party took 'three pounds of
tobacco for the natives', presumably for gifts or payments to any
Aboriginal people met on the way.[39]

The party left Windsor on 6 March 1820 with Myles as their
guide, and another Aboriginal man named Mullaboy, possibly
Myles' brother. He may have been the unnamed man on the
earlier expedition. The group had grown to sixteen, including
George Loder, Benjamin Singleton and convicts Charles Berry
and Nicholas Connelly who had previously accompanied Howe.[40]

With six packhorses, the expedition reached the river on 15 March 1820, coming out of the mountains at Bulga. Howe named the area St Patricks Plains in honour of the Irish saint whose feast day was 17 March. Following the Hunter downstream for six days, the expedition came upon the convict timber-getting parties at Wallis Plains. In a letter to Macquarie from Wallace [*sic*] Plains, Howe described the country he had passed through as being as 'fine a country as imagination can form . . . fit for cultivation and equally so for grazing'. The whole way through the mountains on the new route, they had only unloaded the packhorses once and he believed an easy road for cattle could be made from Windsor with little effort.[41]

The next morning, Howe and the group set off to return to Windsor. Taking a route across country back to their entry point, they noted several areas of extensive pasture they had missed on the way in, areas Howe considered as good as the lowlands of Richmond for food production. On reaching the edge of the mountains, Howe began marking the route by blazing the trees as they went, setting a clear path back to Putty and then on to the Hawkesbury settlements. His road was a mortal blow to the continuation of the penal station at Newcastle and would become the main path for the coming invasion of the pasture lands by the British and their herds.

For his trouble, Howe was promised a grant of 700 acres (283 hectares) at St Patricks Plains on the banks of the river he had 'discovered'.[42] As for Myles and Mullaboy, despite their pivotal role in making the expedition a success, leading Howe twice and going themselves once, they are not mentioned again by Howe and do not appear in the records after 1820 or in any of the written histories that follow. Myles likely returned to Windsor and rejoined his own people. In 1826, a man named Miles is mentioned in an article on a meeting of Aboriginal leaders at Richmond. He was then 'Chief of the Richmond tribe'. Seven years later, in 1833 and 1834, Miles—identified by his traditional name, Mioram—and another man,

Wolloboy or Jack, appear in a blanket list for Richmond, suggesting that both men stayed in the area after their time as guides.

It is not unusual in the context of colonial employment of Aboriginal guides that Myles, Mullaboy, Whirle and the other local guides would fall out of the narrative after a path had been marked by Howe. The role of a professional guide was a transitory one; the guide was only useful at the edge of the frontier, at the point where the British were pushing out beyond their own known boundaries. Once the way was known, the traditional Aboriginal knowledge was converted and claimed in a form recognisable to the British— paths that were marked and mapped.

While it is clear enough why the British would use a guide, it is less obvious why Aboriginal men and women would act in the role. Few guides have left any direct record of their motives, although the experience of Myles may give us some clues. By 1818 and 1819, it was no secret that British expansion into Country brought with it violence and dispossession. Myles had been, until recently, a wanted man. The very name given him by the British—Myles—suggests someone on the outer. It is possibly a derivative of the Sydney word *My-all*, meaning stranger or 'wild'.[43] For Myles, leading an expedition successfully would have given him some security on the potentially volatile frontier where he lived. For his own position in Aboriginal society, heading into another group's Country within an armed party may also have been a strong motivation. New knowledge of distant Country and new connections with other groups and leaders, such as Whirle, were in themselves important for status and position in the eyes of his own people as well as in those of the British.[44]

In addition to security and status, guides also had access to British goods and weapons. Clothes, tobacco and food were routinely handed out by explorers to Aboriginal guides and contacts. Others, as was the case for Myles, were rewarded with guns and muskets, which would have been highly prized.

The marking of the route by Howe hastened the end of the Newcastle penal station. To the large convict population still stationed at Newcastle and in the Hunter, the knowledge of an easy-to-follow, marked route running from Wallis Plains all the way back to the Hawkesbury was a powerful temptation for those inclined to chance a getaway.

As we have seen, the idea of moving the penal station had already been officially mooted by Macquarie in a letter to Earl Bathurst just over twelve months before. With a new, more isolated site for a penal station at present-day Port Macquarie, the rich and fertile lands along the three principal rivers in the Hunter were being considered as a site of settlement for the increasing population of free settlers. As Macquarie informed Bathurst, the area had the advantage of already being extensively clear of timber, making access to the land via the river easy and affording quick access to Sydney markets via Newcastle.[45] Although the penal station officially closed in 1821, it was not until 1823 that convicts were moved in numbers to Port Macquarie. In the meantime the first of the free settlers had begun to arrive.

Howe's route from the Hawkesbury established a link across the mountains from the first convict river settlement to the next— the Hawkesbury to the Hunter. Once known, his track became the main linkage and preferred overland route for the next half-century, over which thousands of men and women would travel. Of course it was not really Howe's route, any more than it was that of Parr or Singleton; it was an Aboriginal pathway, known for generations as a link between the two great rivers and the mountains in between.

CHAPTER FIVE

THE LAND RUSH

NEW ARRIVALS

Howe's arrival at Wallis Plains in March 1820 presented the Newcastle commandant, James Morisset, with new challenges. When he took command in December 1818, Morisset inherited a well-established convict station, with around 700 mostly male (but including approximately 50 female) convicts in Newcastle and in the timber camps upriver at Wallis Plains and Patersons Plains.[1] He had near total control over these men through a system of punishment and reward, surveillance and work. However, within two short years Morisset was being asked not just to supervise his convict workforce but increasingly to also police civil matters as settlers began to move in.

In July 1820, less than four months after Howe had returned to Windsor, four convicts from a cedar party at Patersons Plains disarmed their guards and absconded, following the path 'made by Mr Howe's horses'. Just as Morisset feared, the clear path was too much of a temptation to those convicts thinking of bolting.[2] Although the penal station and its timber camps were still in operation and still receiving convicts, Howe's overland route had seriously compromised the station's isolation.

Following Howe's success, Macquarie promised grants to him and others in his party. Although they were not immediately formalised, by September 1820 permission was granted to Howe to graze his flocks and herds on 700 acres (283 hectares) of land at St Patricks Plains. In November 1820, William Bell, son of Windsor magistrate Archibald Bell, claimed to have reached 'Comeroi' via 'Boottee' (Putty) by following Howe's earlier route. Bell spoke to his father of the undulating, open country covered in kangaroo grass and had probably moved his cattle there by early 1821.[3]

All the while convicts were still arriving in Newcastle. In December 1820, the five surviving members of what was known as the Cato Street Conspiracy were sent direct to Newcastle on their arrival at Sydney. James Wilson, Charles Cooper, John Harrison, Richard Bradburn and John Shaw Strange were all transported on the *Guildford* for high treason. The conspirators, all in trades threatened by the increasing industrialisation in Britain, had sought to kill the prime minister and his entire cabinet as a precursor to a general uprising in London. The men were betrayed before they could carry out their plot, with the five ringleaders executed and the rest transported.[4]

Shortly afterwards, the first free settler party arrived in Newcastle. In July 1821, the newly appointed chaplain for Newcastle, the Reverend George Augustus Middleton, came overland into the town. Accompanied by John de Marquet Blaxland (son of John Blaxland of Blue Mountains crossing fame), some convict servants and 174 head of cattle, Middleton had taken a different route to Howe, following the Macdonald River, as Benjamin Singleton had in 1817, before joining part of an Aboriginal trading path known as the Boree Track, which took them into the Wollombi Valley. From here they turned east across flat lands that skirted Mount Sugarloaf and led into Newcastle. The cattle, in particular, made a clear path through the bush, while Middleton marked the trees along the way. The track, known as the Parson's Road, soon became the new favourite route for escaping convicts.[5]

From Newcastle, Middleton sent his convict workers to land he had selected at Patersons Plains, where they started clearing the ground and felling trees. Blaxland wrote of the thick brush of cedar and rosewood along the riverbanks, the rich soil behind with abundant grass for cattle to graze on and the evidence of severe flooding all around.[6] Middleton was soon trading his cattle with the settlers already on the river—those convict farmers granted plots by Macquarie from 1812—although he himself spent most of his time in the parsonage at Newcastle, leaving the day-to-day running of the farm to his convicts.

Close behind Middleton, the three brothers George, William and Henry Bell arrived in September, probably retracing the route William had taken in November 1820. The arrival of the Bell brothers prompted Morisset to inquire whether anyone had been given permission to travel overland to Newcastle; none but the Reverend had been. As he feared more escapes, Morisset proposed that rewards be given to soldiers and bush constables for the return of runaways to encourage them to 'strive to greater exertions in the chase' and to help pay to replace clothing ruined in the pursuit. The governor agreed, but still men ran.[7] In December 1821, Morisset wrote, 'I am sorry to have to send you a long list of runaways, twelve of them went off in a body for the Parsons Road as it is now called'. By January 1822, the number on the loose had risen to 21, including Richard Bradburn, one of the Cato Street conspirators.[8]

It is possible that Morisset had some of these conversations directly with Governor Macquarie, who made his third and last visit to the penal station in November 1821 as part of his final tour of the colony.[9] Macquarie toured up the river to Wallis Plains, staying the night in the government cottage, a neat, commodious hut built by Wallis for the governor's visit in 1818, set above the freshwater Lachlan Lagoon and Wallis Creek. Macquarie undertook a brief tour of the district around Green Hills (now Morpeth), noting the store ship *St Michael* moored there, before returning to Wallis Plains, on the site of the present town of Maitland, where eleven families were settled on farms. As well as inspecting the farms and settlers, Macquarie and his wife Elizabeth, together with his entourage, were met at Wallis Plains by Bungaree, 'Chief of the Boan Native Tribe, with all his own family, and 30 more of his Tribe, waiting my arrival, having come on purpose to meet me'.[10] Bungaree and his group performed a corroboree for Macquarie in the evening. As we have seen, Bungaree had regular contact with the penal station in its early years, and although thirteen years had passed since Bungaree was last confirmed in the district—after his attack on Port Stephens Robert around 1808—it appears that he had maintained some connection to the area all along.[11]

Macquarie also confirmed one of the first land grants at Wallis Plains for a free settler. In late October 1821, as one of his final acts as governor, he ordered a grant of 1500 acres (607 hectares) be set aside at Green Hills for Lieutenant Edward Close of the 48th Regiment. Close had written to Macquarie requesting a grant on the high ground above the river near what is now Queens Wharf at Morpeth. Although land could not be granted to serving officers, Close had indicated that he would resign his commission to remain in New South Wales. In November, Close was appointed Engineer and Inspector of Public Works at Newcastle. His duties included superintending the convicts at Newcastle in the lumberyard, the mills, at the pier, in the mines, on the cedar parties and at the lime burners, all while his residence was in the officers' barracks at Wallis Plains.[12]

The appointment of Close no doubt lightened Morisset's workload, but his trouble controlling the penal station continued.

At Morisset's prompting, a notice was placed in *The Sydney Gazette* stating that travel overland to the Hunter was forbidden, but his frustration continued to build. Middleton's track provided a well-marked trail from Wallis Plains to Windsor, of which convicts took increasing advantage, including those who would otherwise have been 'quiet and contented'. The arrival of Governor Brisbane to replace Macquarie in 1821, and the proposal to move the penal station, led some convicts to believe that if they escaped to Sydney they would not be returned to Newcastle, further fuelling plots to run. Morisset did not have enough soldiers to prevent the absconding. Indeed, at least one convict had attacked a soldier in an escape attempt and was only stopped by the intervention of some Aboriginal men nearby.[13]

A NEW LAND POLICY

Increasingly, Morisset was required to deal not just with his convict workforce but also with the expectations of new, free settler arrivals. In the wake of his last visit to the area, on 24 November 1821 Governor Macquarie proclaimed in *The Sydney Gazette* that, having proceeded 70 or 80 miles (113–129 kilometres) upriver from Newcastle, he was of the opinion that due to the fertility of the soil and the access afforded by water travel, the country on the banks of the Hunter River merited attention for the development of pasturage and agriculture.[14] When Macquarie was succeeded as governor by Major General Sir Thomas Brisbane on 1 December 1821, a new approach to land settlement in New South Wales was also implemented, with an increasing emphasis on encouraging settlers with sufficient capital to develop agricultural and pastoral holdings on a large scale to migrate to the colony.

The new approach to allocation of land was based on the recommendations coming out of a report completed by John Thomas

Bigge and tabled before the British parliament between 1822 and 1823. Commissioner Bigge, under instructions from Earl Bathurst, Secretary of State for the Colonies in the British Government, had spent seventeen months in the colony, collecting evidence through interviews and documents for a three-volume report on the state of the colony, its agricultural potential and the effectiveness of transportation as a system of punishment. He spent time in Newcastle interviewing Morisset and others, as well as examining the laws, administration, reform of convicts, the state of the civil, judicial and ecclesiastical establishments and of agriculture and industry in the colony. During this process, Bigge interviewed most of the free settlers, officers and administrators, over 50 emancipists and hundreds of convicts.[15] Among his findings on the condition of New South Wales, Bigge's view of the treatment of convicts and the effectiveness of the colony as a place of punishment was that, under Macquarie, there had been a diminishing of the colony's intended role as a place of banishment and terror.[16] Macquarie's support of emancipists in particular, including his grants of land, was seen as an essential component of the undermining of the colony's reputation and the emerging view that it was a lenient place, especially in the main settlements.[17]

Bigge considered that the numbers of convicts in the towns of Sydney and Parramatta, in particular, exceeded the amount of work available for them and that they would be better employed by being assigned to free settlers in the pursuit of pastoral expansion. Grazing was his preferred option, over the more intensive crop farming in which many of the emancipist farmers were already engaged. For Bigge, grazing sheep and cattle had the potential to open up large tracts of land and provide exports of wool to English mills. He envisaged that the employment of convicts as shepherds under the supervision of free men would hasten the convicts' reform through hard work and their separation from the temptations of the towns. The size of estates would be determined by how many convicts a settler could afford to employ and how many cattle or sheep they could run. In his report, Bigge summed up the scheme thus:

> The principal object of these regulations is, to induce persons of respectability to engage personally in the rearing of sheep and cattle, on an extensive scale, in the interior of the country, to employ convicts in that occupation, and to provide as much control as possible for them, through the presence of their masters, or a free overseer.[18]

As well as encouraging grants to wealthy emigrants, Bigge sought to restrict access for emancipists and ticket-of-leave convicts. Those with tickets-of-leave would be forced to work as tenants or labourers for others rather than being able to have their own land. He thought this would prevent the complication of any ticket-holder resorting to the courts for rulings in land disputes, which had been allowed to occur in New South Wales despite being illegal under British law. Land grants of just ten acres (four hectares) would be offered to emancipists, compared to the 30 acres (twelve hectares) that was typical. Bigge considered that the larger acreage often resulted in land being left unoccupied, uncultivated or sold off soon after being granted. Land for emancipists should be set aside close to towns and settlements, especially for those with little experience or capital. In this way, they would be close to ready markets and, if they failed, could work as labourers in trades or otherwise in the towns themselves.[19]

Bigge considered the Hunter Valley a good place to put his ideas into practice. During his visit there, he received Morisset's report on the twelve farms at Patersons Plains and the eleven at Wallis Plains that were by then occupied. Bigge recognised the Hunter's propensity to flood, but agreed with Macquarie that the area be opened for free settlement due to its good soil and proximity to markets. While making no specific recommendations as to how the area should be settled, the implementation of his broader plan that grants be equated to capital would have a profound effect on the development of the region over the following decade.

With this new land policy in mind, in March 1822 Brisbane instructed Surveyor General John Oxley to begin surveying land around Newcastle and the Hunter River for partition into grants. Oxley in turn assigned assistant surveyor Henry Dangar to the task. In February, Morisset, aware of the plan, had already pledged whatever support he could provide to the survey and assured the governor that he would provide every assistance to newly arrived settlers in an endeavour to progress the governor's plan as swiftly as possible.[20] Dangar began his work on 14 March 1822, starting in Newcastle before moving inland.

Although Morisset pledged his support, his concern about the impact of free settlers on the convict station remained and once again he wrote to the colonial secretary, this time for an additional magistrate to help administer the district. Morisset suggested Edward Close, who had formerly served under him in the 48th Regiment. On 28 March 1822 Close was duly appointed by the governor, based at Green Hills. His land grant had been increased by Governor Brisbane to 2300 acres (931 hectares) in two portions, giving Close access to the river and to compensate for a section of swamp and marshland on the original portion.[21] Close was soon building a house on the high ground.

The role of magistrate was essential in the administration of law and order on the colonial frontier. For the more isolated settlements, as the Hunter River region was at the time, the magistrate was often the only representative of law and civil administration in the area, having to act as police, deal with convicts—including their assignment to settlers—and preside over local meetings, as well as dealing with local disputes between settlers. Prior to the mid-1820s, most magistrates were unpaid, had little or no formal legal background and were unsupervised by higher courts. Like Close, they were appointed as much for their standing in the community and their connections as they were for any legal training or experience.[22] One result of their isolation was a reliance on local interpretations of the law, especially as any formal guidance from authorities in Sydney could take weeks. For those with little or no legal experience, their interpretations could be loose on some aspects or applications of the law, especially when it came to dealing with convicts.[23]

As a new magistrate, Close was confronted by a certain level of ambiguity as to his role and his responsibilities. A range of options was available when it came to punishment of convicts, ranging from imprisonment or flogging to extra work, removal to a penal station such as Port Macquarie, or assignment to a road or gaol work party. As some measure of restraint, Governor Macquarie limited to 50 the number of lashes that a magistrate could order a convict to receive; however, this was often ignored in Newcastle by imposing multiple charges on convicts.[24] Close himself wondered about the limits, asking in December 1823 whether he had the authority to administer 100 lashes for a single crime, something he was already doing to absconding convicts before he sent them on to Port Macquarie.[25]

Unlike Morisset and his predecessors, as a magistrate Close not only had to deal with the convicts working in and around Newcastle but also had to preside over matters with newly arrived, wealthy emigrant settlers and their assigned convicts, and even settle land disputes as more people came to the Hunter. And just as the commandants at Newcastle had sometimes struggled with the isolation from Sydney when asking for directions, Close too was faced with long delays in official responses to queries. Although he was a short distance overland from Newcastle, the distance by river meant a good boat trip could take the best part of a day each way. Close was required to adjudicate as best he could. His increasing frustration led to his writing to the colonial secretary:

> The circumstances of this settlement have so completely altered within these few months that I am in many instances at a loss how to act particularly as I have received no official instructions how to proceed.[26]

HENRY DANGAR PLOTS THE LAND

By the time Bigge had completed and delivered his report, Henry Dangar was already undertaking a survey of the valley and marking out grants for the reception of settlers. Under instruction, Dangar divided the country into Townships (later renamed Parishes), each 36 square miles (93 square kilometres). Where appropriate, major rivers or streams were used as natural boundaries between each township; otherwise they were simply plotted out as squares across the landscape. Each was then further divided into sections of one square mile (2.6 square kilometres). As part of his work, he also took note of the soil and type of country as he went. He was instructed that, when setting out grants, no individual was to get more than one mile (1.6 kilometres) of river frontage, and he was also to survey and report on the convict farms that had been granted by Macquarie.[27]

It was hoped that Dangar's survey would bring some much-needed order to the fringes of settlement in the Hunter and prevent long-term disputes over land and boundaries. Morisset was already aware that some settlers were trying to take advantage of the uncertainty around land tenure by claiming extra acres. Even more concerning, he had heard rumours that emancipist farmers from Windsor had begun following Howe's path and were establishing themselves around Patricks Plains (the 'St' having been dropped from the name) beyond the area surveyed at the time. It was hoped that Dangar's survey maps would create a manageable grid across the inland that would allow Morisset and the colonial administration to exert their power in an ordered fashion. The mapping of the valley would push back the boundaries of what was unknown country, facilitating the possession of the land and allowing the process of a cadastral survey to work in tandem with a new system of land title, carving up the country of the Aboriginal inhabitants into a marketable commodity that could be sold, both literally and figuratively, to prospective new settlers in Britain.[28] The convict settlers around Wallis Plains were incidental to the scheme, while the Aboriginal people who owned and occupied the land from the ocean to the far mountains were hardly considered at all.

The urgency of Dangar's work was illustrated by the arrival of the first free settlers before he had even started. William Dun, James Philips Webber and John L. Platt all arrived between December 1821 and February 1822. Dun, arriving with his wife and two children in December, took up 1300 acres (526 hectares) on the Paterson River, which he called Duninald. Webber had permission to travel on the first ship to Newcastle bringing free settlers and received 2020 acres (817 hectares) at Patersons Plains, naming his grant Tocal. Platt, his wife and two children took up their estate at Ironbark Hill near Newcastle and began building in late February.

Dangar began his survey on the south bank of the Hunter River just outside the boundary of the penal station. Much of the land along the riverbank to the junction of the first branch, the Williams River, he noted as being swamp and marshland. The banks were thick with mangrove, which merged into dense brush and brambles. So heavy was the tangle that he noted in his field books that one small thicket was 'such that the Devil when he was a boy could not get through'.[29]

Besides the thick brush and forest, Dangar also quickly discovered that the topography of the valley also interrupted the artificial boundaries of his gridlines. Rivers, streams, creeks, swamps, ridgelines, hills and outcrops all got in the way. He advised the surveyor general that in parts he found it impossible to proceed with his survey without incalculable trouble.[30] By the time he had arrived in the upper valley, beyond the modern town of Scone, the landscape of the valley was such that his pattern was largely abandoned.

As Dangar moved upriver, he came to the farms of the emancipists that Macquarie had set aside from 1812 at Wallis and Patersons plains and realised it was not just the topography of the valley that could upset his plans. The emancipists and free settlers had already begun to extend their holdings, creeping along the river and into adjacent strips of fertile land in the belief that if they made improvements to it, the land would be added to their grants. Felled timber and cleared bush were evidence of their growing footprint. It was similar to a process that had taken place years before along the Hawkesbury, where small farmers and ex-convicts regarded the adjacent bush and wetlands as extensions of their own farms on which they could graze their stock or fell timber as needed. The attitude reflected the convicts' own belief that the colony was intended for them by virtue of it being they who had worked for it.[31] A sense of entitlement to the land had taken hold, encouraged by some governors such as Bligh and Macquarie; as the majority of the British population were convicts or emancipists, the idea became a source of tension and growing grievances in the Hunter as more free settlers began to arrive.

Dangar recorded the details and living conditions of twenty of the first settlers on the river at Wallis Plains and Patersons Plains. Most were living in cottages of wattle and plaster; three were in weatherboard houses and one in a log cabin. All twenty had pigsties and most had gardens or peach orchards. Some, such

as Benjamin Davis, who had been on his land since 1814, had
developed small farmsteads with a collection of buildings and outbuildings. Davis, who in 1816 had nearly lost his farm after being
suspected of harbouring runaway convicts, was living in a weatherboard and plaster cottage and had a log barn and peach orchard
valued by Dangar at £40. Mary Hunt, aka Molly Morgan, a Second
Fleet convict who had escaped back to England in 1794 only to be
retransported in 1804 and sent to Newcastle in 1816, owned a wattle
and plaster cottage with stockyards surrounded by a four-rail fence.
She also had a second hut with a skillion addition, a fenced garden
and peach orchard. Richard Binder, sentenced to Newcastle in 1813
and given a plot on the Paterson River in 1817, lived in a weatherboard and shingle house, with a cowshed, thatched log stable and
lumber house, thatched barn, pigsties and yards, cow yard with
five-rail fence, a hut for his convict workers, peach orchard and a
three-rail fenced paddock. His farm was 59 acres (24 hectares), the
largest among the former convict settlers.[32]

Nestled among the convict farmers was the 100-acre (40-hectare)
property of Surgeon William Evans, granted to him by Macquarie
in 1813. Until 1822, Evans had resided mainly in Newcastle, with the
farm managed by his convict workers. On retiring to the property
with his wife and children, Evans received an extra 1000 acres
(405 hectares), which he called Bellevue.[33] All the while, more free
settlers were arriving. By May 1822, John Brown had taken up his
2030-acre (822-hectare) estate, which he named Bolwarra, apparently after the word for flash of light as told him by an Aboriginal
guide who showed him the way.[34] Master mariner John Powell
occupied 60 acres (24 hectares) on the Paterson River with his wife
and two children, and by the end of 1822 had a wattle and plaster
house and 25 acres (10 hectares) of cleared land. The steady arrival
of free settlers saw growing consternation over the convict farmers
and their access to the land. John Bingle, a ship's captain who

brought free settlers to Newcastle, remembered in later life that the convicts and the support they received from the commandant in Newcastle were resented by the newcomers. His own feelings were clear when he wrote:

> They were called settlers, and unaccountable as it may appear, were not removed on the arrival of the free settlers, when the Hunter and its tributaries were thrown open . . . These convicts, so located, held these choice spots—the cream of the Hunter, without any authority whatever from the Government, but a dirty piece of paper under the commandant's hand, so in like manner those who were permitted to live out of gaol in the town, built themselves huts on it and were not removed by the Commandant to the cost of those free settlers.[35]

As they progressed, Dangar and his party of surveyors and convicts were often the first whites into an area. His reports became vital tools in land selection. His progress was hampered by the rugged topography, a want of horses for the team and a lack of shoes and trousers for the convicts. So dire was this situation that in August the men refused to proceed any further for want of shoes. The slow progress meant that land was being taken up quicker than he could survey it, leading to inevitable disputes over boundaries and access, which were not helped by some settlers failing to acquaint themselves with the sections he had surveyed for them.[36]

By the end of 1822, seventeen large estates amounting to over 24,500 acres (9915 hectares) had been granted between Newcastle and Patricks Plains, with a further 25,000 acres (10,117 hectares) granted before the end of 1823 to nineteen more emigrant arrivals.[37] When Dangar completed his work in November 1825, he had surveyed from Newcastle along both sides of the Hunter River as far up the valley as the mountains around Dartbrook and the 20,000-acre (8094-hectare) Segenhoe estate of Thomas Potter Macqueen, near the town of Scone. He had alienated land on both sides of Wollombi Brook, along the banks of the Williams and Paterson rivers and all the major creeks and tributaries of the valley. In total, over 380 individual parcels of land had been set aside, equalling more than 504,305 acres (204,085 hectares), for approximately 340 free settlers, with another 37 areas set aside for church and school estates. By the end of 1826, a further one million acres (405,000 hectares) had been alienated in the enormous pastoral grant made out to the Australian Agricultural Company on the edges of the Hunter Valley. This grant was made up of three parcels that ran from the northern shoreline of Port Stephens to the Manning River, from west of Willow Tree across the Liverpool Plains and along the Peel River near Tamworth.[38] These first settlers and their families represented the beginnings of a wave that would soon sweep into the Hunter from the east and south-west. The influx of settlers via land and sea led to an increase in the British population, both convict and free, from 1169 at the end of 1821 to 1673 by 1825, before almost doubling to 3260 by 1828.[39] By 1825, every piece of available land that fronted a watercourse was either occupied or promised to someone.

This rapid alienation of land into the private hands of settlers was being repeated in Tasmania and on the plains around Bathurst. In Tasmania, by 1831 almost 1.9 million acres (769,000 hectares) had been granted and, as in the Hunter, the vast majority of this had gone to free settlers rather than former convict families. At Bathurst, close to 92,000 acres (37,231 hectares) had been granted by 1825, and although this had risen to 295,000 acres (119,382 hectares) by 1828, it had long been outstripped by the Hunter Valley.[40] The settlers came with sheep and cattle, and were assigned a convict workforce to build and manage their vast estates.

LAND SQUABBLES AT PATRICKS PLAINS

By December 1822, Dangar had made it as far as Patricks Plains, where John Howe had entered the valley two years earlier. Here he found himself entangled in the beginnings of a land feud between explorer-settler John Howe and emigrant farmer James Mudie that would last almost a decade. Howe was in possession of 700 acres (283 hectares), the land Macquarie had promised him after his expeditions; Mudie had arrived in August 1822 to select a grant of 2000 acres (809 hectares). Mudie, having inspected and chosen a site with high and low land cut through by a creek, set his convicts to clearing, ploughing and planting. He had them begin erecting buildings and stockyards, with the intention of importing a water-powered grinding mill to harness the energy of the creek. After selecting the site, Mudie returned to Sydney, making his intentions clear to Surveyor General John Oxley and asking him to instruct Dangar to measure out the site before anyone else could claim it.[41]

Mudie believed that there was no one else within 30 miles (48 kilometres) of the land he had selected and assumed that as the land was unoccupied his right to it was assured. How he managed not to see what was by then a steady trickle of emancipist and free settlers coming into that part of the Hunter from Windsor is unknown, but he was disturbed by Oxley's response to his request. In a 'laughing manner', Oxley asked what Mudie had done to upset Mr Howe, who had already written to Oxley to complain of Mudie's behaviour and restate his stake on the land, with Macquarie's permission giving him first preference as discoverer.[42] Dangar was called on to adjudicate. He confirmed Mudie's claim but noted that, like others, Mudie had set out for his land before the selection had been marked on the charts.

Mudie was incensed not only by Howe but also by the fact that other settlers were also moving in from Windsor. In a letter to the colonial secretary, he fumed:

[H]ere I beg leave to observe that when I made inquiry of the
men in charge of the cattle to whom they belonged I received the
most impertinent answers, however I was able to learn that there
were a number of men (even now prisoners) who had cattle there
& that some of them had <u>no permission</u> whatsoever but that they
paid 10/– per head for their cattle grazing—and that the stock
yard which Mr Howe represents <u>as his,</u> was put up by a <u>number</u>
of individuals, who have not less than <u>1200</u> Head of Cattle about
1000 sheep some pigs & horses & while I have been obliged to
go round by Newcastle at a very heavy expense and fatigue those
people have been going over land from Windsor with carts and
even lately taken over a large timber carriage.[43]

Mudie's letter ran to over eight pages of complaint, with an
apology at the end for its length. In it he identified a number of
issues that would manifest themselves in the clash between wealthy,
free migrants being promised large grants in the Hunter and those
small-scale, colonial-born and emancipist farmers coming overland
from Windsor and the Hawkesbury. The area was being opened
on the cusp of a change in colonial policy when it came to land.
Macquarie and earlier governors had encouraged emancipist and
colonial-born farmers, based on the notion that the colony was a
place in which there was a right to land after sentence and that this
was part of the reform process. This approach was being challenged
by the post-Bigge reforms, which favoured large-scale pastoral-
ism driven by newly arrived settlers with capital. Both sides of the
argument felt equally aggrieved and would fight for what they saw
as their right to the land. Caught in the middle were the Aboriginal
people who were being dispossessed by the process.

Howe was not the only one on the land around Mudie. The
stockyard that Mudie noted in his letter was probably being
managed by Benjamin Singleton, who had also been promised

200 acres (81 hectares) at Patricks Plains. Singleton advertised in *The Sydney Gazette* in December 1821 that he would agist cattle for other Windsor farmers and would take charge of anyone's cattle at Patricks Plains for ten shillings per head per annum for a period of no less than three years.[44] The attraction of the extensive alluvial flats and reduced flood risk was as alluring to Singleton—who had been ruined twice by floods—and to the other Windsor farmers, compared to what they had endured along the Hawkesbury, as it was to the newly arrived free emigrants.

As Patricks Plains was beyond the easy surveillance of either Morisset or Close, disputes could escalate if left unchecked. It was also a place with direct connection to Windsor, meaning that people could slip in and out while avoiding the eyes of the authorities by bypassing Newcastle. In October 1822, Morisset had asked the colonial secretary who did, and who did not, have permission to travel there, after settler John Rotton had arrived in the district. Families were establishing themselves in the area, with crops of wheat growing and cattle grazing. For Morisset, still running a penal station, the newly formed tracks between Windsor, Patricks Plains and Wallis Plains were the main concern, as it was now 'utterly impossible to keep any Prisoner at this place who are sent here for punishment'.[45]

Morisset sent District Constable John Allen to Patricks Plains in December. He reported several families already there and so Morisset visited the place himself in February 1823. Morisset was happy to report no complaints made to him and everything having the appearance of as much regularity as could be expected for a distant settlement. He did take the precaution, however, of appointing Benjamin Singleton, who as we have seen was already there with his wife Mary and seven children, to serve as a district constable. A second constable to assist Singleton was also being considered.[46]

GETTING THERE AND AWAY

One of the complaints of Mudie and other emigrant farmers concerned the ease with which the smaller settlers could get to the area
from Windsor. The mode of travel to the Hunter was as much a class
issue as who had the right to the land itself. 'Legitimate settlers', as
Mudie described himself, had to first take a sea voyage, with all
the associated expense, inconvenience and potential danger, to get
from Sydney to Newcastle, and then had to make arrangements for
a trip upriver to the settlement at Greens Hills and Wallis Plains
before an overland journey to their grants. For Mudie and others
heading inland from Wallis Plains, the journey was longer because
many of them also had to arrange for local Aboriginal guides to
take them through the uncharted bush.[47] Howe and his ilk could
instead come straight across the mountains from Windsor, bringing
with them their stock, stores and supplies. The overland route was
not completely unregulated, and there were some restrictions. The
ease with which escaping convicts could move across these paths,
and the need to monitor the road, saw a system of travel passes
implemented for the journey from February 1823.[48] The pass was
specific to the road between Windsor and the Hunter, and applied
to all travellers, free, ticket-of-leave or emancipist.

The passes were issued in Sydney, with the particulars of the
travellers, their stock (including brand markings), where they were
travelling and for what purpose all recorded. For free settlers, the
pass also included the names of any convict servants they had with
them. Between May 1823 and September 1824, close to 2000 head
of cattle and over 600 sheep came across the road, along with
32 convicts and 33 settlers, some making multiple journeys, according to those passes that survive.[49] The passes were valid for between
seven and 21 days, depending on how far into the Hunter the group
was going and whether or not they were returning to Windsor.

Four days was the estimated time for someone to get across the ranges from Windsor.[50] Although free settlers could proceed to Newcastle from March 1824 without permission, passes for the road continued to be issued until at least September.

Although convicts and emancipists were conditioned to some form of official scrutiny when it came to their movements, the pass system caused resentment among the free emigrants. Robert Scott, who arrived in the Hunter with his younger brother Helenus in May 1823, wrote in his journal:

> There exists at present a dreadful drawback on all these advantages [at the Hunter River] but it can be removed at the pleasure of our rulers, I mean the system of Government pressure there: it is entirely a prison: and when one goes there it is like entering and subjecting oneself to the rules of Newcastle: the commandant (without saying anything of the Governor) has every power over you indeed of almost turning you out of your grant—several applications have been made to allow settlers to take cattle to their farms have been always refused. The Gov't are afraid of giving the convicts the facilities of escape . . . Major Morisset is a very proper person for such a Gov't but certainly not to have command and so unlimited a one, over free persons and men of character.[51]

STATUS, AUTHORITY AND POWER

James Mudie came to New South Wales as a retired military officer. He had served as a lieutenant in the Marines between 1799 and 1810. After he was bankrupted in a scheme to produce commemorative medals of the Napoleonic Wars, he used his connections to secure a letter of introduction from the Secretary of State for the Colonies for a land grant in New South Wales. For those wealthy free emigrant settlers, this was the usual way of establishing themselves, and most of the first waves of emigrants came equipped with such documents. Robert and Helenus Scott also had letters, although they were for their father, Helenus Senior, who had died on the ship on which they sailed to the colony. Although the brothers were aged twenty and eighteen respectively, they used the family connections to secure 2000 acres (809 hectares) each on the banks of the Hunter River at Patricks Plains, grants they combined to form their Glendon estate. Their neighbour, Dr James Mitchell, also came with letters of introduction, as did William Dun, who was armed with a letter from Henry Goulburn, under-secretary in the Colonial Office in London. In Mudie's letter of complaint, he reminded Oxley of conversations in the presence of Sir Thomas Mitchell regarding his land. All assumed that in this convict society their connections and presumed status would prevail in the frontier's social hierarchy.

For the most part it did, although not all were from quite as high in society as they liked to make out. Mudie himself had been discharged from the army, been declared bankrupt and identified himself as a major when he had risen no higher than lieutenant. For the emancipists, who were beginning to rise financially in the colony, these false pretences were particularly galling, especially when emigrant farmers would happily deal and trade with them but refused to allow them into the cloistered realms of their society. For the emigrants, there was little to lose in dealing in business with these former convicts, as their status as free settlers over convicts was seemingly assured: their reputations were only at risk in their dealings with other members of their own class.[52]

Military officers in particular used their connections to establish themselves, especially those veterans of the Napoleonic Wars. Edward Close was appointed magistrate at Wallis Plains by James Morisset, his former commanding officer in the 48th Regiment. Close's neighbours from the early 1820s, Thomas Valentine Blomfield and Francis Allman, were regimental comrades. Allman took up his land after having served as the final commandant of Newcastle between 1825 and 1826. Blomfield requested a grant of land close to Close, and the three men with their families were eventually settled within sight of each other. Blomfield noted that Close was two miles (three kilometres) away and Allman seven (11 kilometres) from his house but that he could 'see them with my glass almost as well as if I were there'.[53] This core of officers attracted other veterans and their families to settle in the Paterson, Morpeth and Maitland area in the years to come. Among them was Susan Ward, the widow of veteran William Gordon Ward who died prior to receiving a grant in 1820. Instead, Susan Ward was granted 600 acres (243 hectares) on the river at Paterson in March 1823 and was one of the few women granted land outright in the Hunter in the years prior to 1825. Former convict Mary Hunt, also known as Molly Morgan, received land under Macquarie's experimental scheme, while further up the valley near the present town of Muswellbrook sisters Elizabeth and Sarah Jenkins, free settlers, received adjoining grants of 500 acres (202 hectares) each on the banks of Muscle Brook, although there is no evidence that they ever actively farmed or used the land. William Ward's army comrade James Phillips, with his wife and six children, took up 2000 acres (809 hectares) at Bona Vista, adjacent to Susan Ward, in September 1822.[54]

Social connections and allegiances were just as important in the emancipist and colonial-born communities. As Mudie discovered, settlers like Howe could have some influence in the administration in Sydney. Oxley's 'laughing manner', as Mudie described it, hints at a level of acquaintance between Howe and Oxley, and an understanding of the mechanics of colonial society. As a long-term resident of the colony, chief constable at Windsor and an explorer, it is unsurprising that Howe was able to outmanoeuvre the newly arrived Mudie. Howe also had on-the-ground connections in the Hunter, as did others coming overland from Windsor. All six of the free men from Howe's second expedition in 1820 were on land at Patricks Plains by 1824, with one of the convicts farming there by 1828.[55]

LAW AND ORDER

Of Howe's party, the one who held the most influence locally was Singleton, who was appointed as the area's first district constable. The position brought him into conflict with some of the larger emigrant land owners, especially Mudie, whose disdain for Singleton led to clashes over the treatment of convict workers on Mudie's Castle Forbes estate and Singleton's authority over the emigrant settlers. His appointment nonetheless represented the spread of law and order outwards from the establishments at Newcastle and Wallis Plains. However, the increasing numbers of arrivals tested the limits of jurisdiction of the constables and Close as the sole magistrate. Each of the three settled districts—Wallis Plains, Patersons Plains and Patricks Plains—had one district constable and one bush constable, usually a reliable convict. The district constable supervised the district generally, dealing with disputes and issues between settlers, while the bush constable was responsible for pursuing absconding convicts and bushrangers, guarding prisoners and transferring them to the magistrate. As the only magistrate, Close was increasingly called upon to deal with issues arising between settlers, with little or no direction from Newcastle or Sydney.

For example, in September 1823, settler Joseph Pennington sent one of his convicts, John Hurst, downstream to Newcastle to be placed in the gaol on charges of insubordination and blasphemous language. Pennington had arrived in the Hunter from the Hawkesbury in October 1822 with his wife Ann and two daughters. He was joined by a party of eight convict servants, twenty head of cattle and two bullocks, which overlanded from the Hawkesbury in April 1823. Pennington eventually settled on 1500 acres (607 hectares) near the junction of the Hunter and Williams rivers, which he named Leigh Farm. When Hurst arrived in Newcastle, Morisset advised Pennington that, as commandant, he was not concerned with settlers' men and sent Hurst back upriver to Wallis Plains for Close, as the local magistrate, to deal with. But Close, with no direction on the limit of his authority, was unsure if he could remove Hurst as a bonded man and have another assigned to Pennington, if he could have him flogged or if he could send him on to Port Macquarie. In the end, he was returned to Pennington, only to abscond with four others in January 1825.[56]

As well as managing the settlers' convict servants, Close also found himself dealing with free emigrants over the conditions of their grants, especially in relation to the cedar and other timbers along the river. Cedar had been cut from the Hunter from the first years of the convict station at Newcastle but, by the early 1820s, the remaining stands of cedar were increasingly within the boundaries of private landholdings. Although licences were required for settlers to access the cedar, many ignored the orders due to its value, especially on the more remote and rugged properties where the last major stands were to be found. As early as October 1822, John Brown at Bolwarra, one of the first free settlers to take up his land, was caught illegally trading in cedar and hardwoods. Brown, with the help of four convicts from a timber gang working nearby, took 107 logs—30 cedar, 20 rosewood and 57 gums—before the timber gang guard noticed logs going upstream instead of down towards Newcastle.[57]

Lieutenant William Hicks at Melville, just upriver from Brown, confronted a timber gang in 1823 and threatened to shoot any who came onto his land. Hicks told Close that he considered everything within the boundary marked as his property to be his, except that timber required for naval purposes, which cedar was not.[58] Illegal felling of cedar trees continued across the lower Hunter throughout 1823 and 1824, with cases being regularly addressed by the colonial secretary in Sydney. Settler Alexander Shand, for example, was reported by his neighbour in February 1824 for illegally felling cedar on the neighbour's land and from the nearby government reserve.[59] The rules, which had been clear during the operation of the convict station at Newcastle, whereby all the timber belonged to the government, were now being blurred as more land fell into the hands of private owners.

Examples such as Pennington's convict and ongoing timber theft were soon overwhelming Close, with settlers increasingly sending convicts to him for removal to Newcastle, either because they were sick or for sentencing and punishment. With no passable road between Wallis Plains and Newcastle, convicts were sent by boat, which had to be requisitioned from settlers because of a lack of government vessels. To add to his frustrations, if six or more convicts were to be sent, they needed to go in two batches as Close did not have enough constables to guard them all. The remainder were detained in the small wooden lockup at Wallis Plains until he could spare the men. At times, the one-roomed hut was so full of prisoners that guards were forced to sleep outside.

Close struggled for direction. In December 1823, nearly two years after his appointment, he told Governor Brisbane that he sometimes had to resort to reading *The Sydney Gazette* for instructions regarding his authority and, as he had no clerk, he was also forced to write and respond to all correspondence himself. The confined population that existed when he started was now 'extended and troublesome', with the country overrun by free labourers, emancipist workers, sawyers and fencers, many of whom frequently disagreed with their employers over contracts or wages. Adjudicating these disputes, a task for which he was not being paid, was taking more time than he had and left him no time to manage his own estate or supervise his men.[60]

By the start of 1824, there were too many settlers in the Hunter around Patricks Plains for Close to properly manage. Finally, in April 1824, Robert Scott at Glendon was appointed as a second magistrate to serve the middle Hunter. He was joined the following year by John Reid at Luskintyre, approximately halfway between Scott and Close, and Peter McIntyre, agent to Thomas Potter Macqueen and manager of his estate at Segenhoe, inland from Patricks Plains. McIntyre had asked to become a magistrate, seeing the role as one of security not only against the roving bands of bushrangers and runaways, but also to help the smaller settlers keep their own convicts in 'subjection'.[61]

Not everyone who was approached accepted appointment as a magistrate. In 1827, Thomas Blomfield of Dagworth near Morpeth, a close friend of Edward Close and Francis Allman, was invited to become a magistrate. Although he acknowledged that the position would increase his respectability, he refused, telling his sister Louisa:

> Having seen the great trouble that magistrates are constantly exposed to, and from the ignorance of the laws of my country, I declined it. No doubt it adds to the respectability of a man in the eyes of the lower classes, but I should have been constantly exposed to an action at law through some confounded blunder or other.[62]

Although Peter McIntyre's view displayed his opinion of the place of convicts in the society, the growing numbers of constables and magistrates did provide a sense of order and protection for the isolated farmer. The increasing semblance of stability afforded to the small settlements by the extension of the law attracted people to the district to settle, which, in turn, attracted those who could profit from the provision of goods and services.

CHAPTER SIX

WORKING ON THE FRONTIER

Aboriginal people reacted and responded to the invasion of their valley in complex and varied ways. Violent confrontations in the mid- and late-1820s were the most dramatic and obvious response. The drama and tragedy of the frontier, which for many people was inescapable, has in part obscured other interactions occurring before, during and after that time: interactions that revolved around cooperation, alliance and work. The relationships of labour and living illustrate the sometimes blurred and fluid boundaries of the Hunter frontier. By looking at Aboriginal actions, exchanges and cultural practice, we can develop a greater understanding of Aboriginal experience and life in the Hunter Valley, rather than a viewpoint simply driven by the British lens of race and colonialism.[1]

Aboriginal people, both men and women, embraced a wide variety of roles in the colonial period across New South Wales. Henry Reynolds argues that labour was one of the most important exchanges between the two cultures, although, with the exception perhaps of the first guides, we must be aware that the exchange was rarely on equal terms.[2] Governors, missionaries and some settlers all believed in the civilising effects that work could have on Aboriginal people. Governor Macquarie hoped that their employment as labourers in agricultural work would make them increasingly useful as a labour force to the young colony, with Governor Gipps holding the same view in the 1840s.[3] Aboriginal people were forced to make profound cultural adjustments. To survive, many had to adopt new ways and learn a foreign language, all the while facing the almost overwhelming numbers of British settlers and their stock invading the country around them. Despite a reliance on Aboriginal skill, knowledge and bushcraft, many colonists increasingly considered Aboriginal people to be inferior and dangerous, fostering a growing inequality that meant Aboriginal people were excluded from the very economy they had helped establish.

SHOWING THE WAY

For many British settlers, employing an Aboriginal guide was their first encounter with Aboriginal people. As we have already seen, guides were essential in the exploration of overland routes between Windsor and the Hunter, with Howe, Singleton, Middleton and others all relying on men such as Myles and Mullaboy to find the way. They were also extensively employed by the commandants and officers of the Newcastle penal station to track and recover runaway convicts or lead hunting parties for sport, as they were in other parts of the colonial world, around Sydney, Bathurst and the Illawarra. Bungaree, Biraban and Burigon were all well-known for their skills and respected with a degree of friendship. Reverend Middleton was remembered as having a good relationship with local Aboriginal people once settled in Newcastle. John Bingle recalled going with Middleton and a group of over 100 Aboriginal people from Newcastle to Lake Macquarie around 1822, saying:

We enjoyed all the wild sports of Australian bush life in its primitive state as the Aborigines of the day (before they were contaminated with our vices) were accustomed to enjoy them. Shooting, fishing, kangarooing, and hunting—our game was ample for us all. They supplied us also, by diving, with the finest mud oysters, for which the waters of the Lake are noted, these we scalloped on our bush fires, and we spent five or six days of as much enjoyment as I ever had in any part of the world.[4]

Guides were equally important for the first wave of arriving settlers in the early 1820s. Most employed guides to find their way through as-yet uncharted bush to their promised grants along the river. Some settlers who would later be prominent in violence against Aboriginal people were reliant on them at the start. Despite the prevalence of guides, there are few sources that offer any Aboriginal perspective, leaving the reasoning and motivation of guides hidden from view. However, enough hints and clues survive in the letters, journals and writings of British settlers to allow us to partially recover the crucial role these individuals played.

The most complete, and certainly the most tantalising, account is that of a young guide known as Ben Davis, who assisted Robert Scott and his literate servant John Brown to navigate their way from the landing at Green Hills to their grant at Glendon in May 1823. As noted previously, Robert and his brother Helenus were young when they arrived in New South Wales, just twenty and eighteen respectively. They had accompanied their father, Dr Helenus Scott, who had served 30 years as a doctor in India but who died at Cape Town on the voyage out in 1821. Despite this family tragedy, the brothers managed to secure two adjacent grants of 2000 acres (809 hectares) each on the Hunter River at Patricks Plains, which they combined and named Glendon. The grant selection was left to Robert, as Helenus, still too young to manage his own affairs, had returned to England in May 1822, in the hope of gaining an appointment to the colonial service in India.[5] With Helenus gone, Robert and John Brown proceeded to Wallis Plains to select the grants. Brown kept a journal of the expedition, describing the employment of the guide, Ben Davis. Although guides were commonplace across the colonial frontier, Brown was interested enough to record their interactions on a day-to-day basis.

When Scott and Brown arrived at Wallis Plains, they hired a horse from a local English settler named Morgan and set off to claim their land. The best-known Morgan at Wallis Plains during this period was in fact Molly Morgan, enough so that some settlers referred to Wallis Plains as Molly Morgan's. Curiously, by 1823 Molly was married to Thomas Hunt. However, it is possible that Hunt himself was known as Morgan, taking advantage of his wife's growing influence and reputation. On the morning of the second day, as the party made their breakfast, a young Aboriginal man appeared from the bush and, recognising the horse, told them he was to be their guide. When questioned as to who he was, Brown recorded that he replied 'the White men call me Ben Davis, and he was going along with us, for Binghi Morgan sent him'.[6] Brown was very pleased to have Ben Davis join them, for they had attempted to secure the services of a guide at Wallis Plains to no avail.

The guide's English name most likely came from settler Ben Davis, one of Macquarie's farmers, who had been living on the river since 1814. Although Brown did not record a traditional name for his guide, he is probably a man named Munnoin who appeared under both names on a list of blankets distributed at Patersons Plains in 1834, near where the convict farmer Davis was settled.[7] The adoption of British names by Aboriginal people was common practice throughout the colonial period, particularly in the early years of contact, starting with Bennelong and Governor Phillip.[8] The acquisition or trading of a name was a significant custom in

Aboriginal society, a practice that was both a ritual of friendship and one of strategic positioning. A name assigned authority, with a British name offering evidence of patronage or, at least, of a connection that in turn afforded some level of trust, familiarity and even protection to the person, although this was diluted in later years as most known individuals were assigned an English name, which became increasingly derogatory and disparaging.[9]

Although John Brown's diary does not elaborate, it was likely that Scott had discussed a guide with Morgan. Morgan was likely acting as an agent for newly arrived colonists, with Aboriginal people equally taking advantage of his connections to gain employment as guides, and its associated access to British goods. Interestingly, it was not the first time that Scott had used a guide in his short time in New South Wales. Before settling on the Hunter, Scott and Brown had considered land over the Blue Mountains around Bathurst and had employed the services of a pair of guides whom he identified as Bungaree and a woman named Carawoolgal.[10] Whether it was the Bungaree so famous in Sydney has not been determined.

Morgan appears to have had a close collaboration or a working relationship with Ben Davis, and possibly other guides in the area. The connection reveals aspects of what American historian Richard White refers to as the 'middle ground': a period in a settlement history when Europeans and Indigenous people lived in a mutually comprehended and advantageous world immediately behind the frontier. It was still a potentially violent place, but also one in which both sides cooperated to a certain degree for their own mutual benefit. Crucially for White, who was looking at First Nations American history, it was a point when neither side could gain what they wanted through the use of force, therefore making it necessary to come to some arrangement to achieve particular objectives. Each side acted in its own interests, while having to convince the other side that any mutual action was fair and legitimate.[11]

A version of this was playing out in the first years of contact in the Hunter. Aboriginal guides were afforded a certain amount of protection by their British clients, while still keeping in contact with their Country. Their skills and knowledge helped the settlers move through the valley and avoid unnecessary confrontations along the way. The armed settlers, in turn, could act as a deterrent to any other groups that might otherwise stop Aboriginal people from different areas crossing their Country. This situation could only exist while both sides were on a relatively equal footing, and so lasted only briefly, but pockets of cooperation and coexistence remained a feature of the colonial Hunter.

Led by their guide, Brown continued to record the journey inland:

> We set off with Ben Davis as a guide and he seemed very much pleased, and kept talking all the way he went but we did not understand him but by what we could make out he was telling us about the country.[12]

Here Brown offers a tantalising glimpse of what Aboriginal guides like Ben Davis might have conveyed to the first wave of British settlers about their relationship to the Hunter Valley. This may not be a commentary on the physicality of the country but, instead, a deeper and more complex narrative about Country as understood by Ben Davis, the complex, interwoven physical, territorial and cultural understanding of the landscape through which they were passing. 'Country' is a multidimensional concept identifying people who live on, manage or are associated with it, the animals, plants, landscape, creeks, rivers and the lore attached to it. The country that Ben Davis was describing would have been defined by his multilayered understandings of the place.[13] While all this was new to Scott and Brown, for Ben Davis and other Aboriginal people the Hunter was a known place, inscribed with stories, knowledge, history and meaning learnt through generations.

Ben Davis was not only useful in showing them the way; he also acted as an interpreter and intermediary when other Aboriginal parties crossed their path. The morning after their arrival at the river near Patricks Plains, Scott and Ben Davis left to hunt kangaroo, leaving Brown to manage the camp and set dinner. Soon after, Brown noticed a group of Aboriginal men 'peeping from the trees', apparently as afraid of him as he confessed to being afraid of them. Despite his fears, Brown beckoned them in, showing a fish he had caught in the river the day before. The group of men came and sat down by the fire. By the time Scott and Ben Davis returned, Brown had learnt the name of the leader, Mytie of the 'Womby Tribe', and was busy digging yams with them among the trees. Ben Davis knew Mytie, proclaiming him a 'very good fellow', and the group stayed with Scott's party for three days, helping them fish in the river and having friendly contests such as spear throwing. Of this, Brown wrote:

> [W]e stuck a Buiscuit [*sic*] on the top of a stick and made them stand at a distance and throw their Spears at them and them that hit it had it, and in short time they would have got all the Buiscuits we had if we had not left off for it was no trouble to them to hit them for they could do it three times out of five at fourty [*sic*] yards [36.6 metres] distance with ease.[14]

The yam harvest and spear-throwing contest contrast starkly with Brown's acknowledgement of fear on both sides at their first meeting. It was likely that Ben Davis's assurances of the trustworthiness of both parties helped facilitate the friendly encounter, although the ease with which the biscuits were hit must have given Scott and Brown some pause for thought. The encounter also tells much about the mobility and connections across the Hunter between Aboriginal groups. Mytie said that he was from the Womby Tribe, the term used for Wollombi in the mountains to the south of Patricks Plains. Ben Davis, meanwhile, was from Patersons Plains to the east, and yet both met at Patricks Plains in the centre of the Hunter.

There is nothing more on Ben Davis or Mytie after these observations. After staking their claim, Scott and Brown returned to Wallis Plains and then to Sydney, where the grants were formalised. Robert Scott returned with his brother Helenus, who was back from England, in early 1823 and began clearing the estate. The two brothers lived for a short time in a bark and sapling shelter, modelled closely on an Aboriginal gunya, until work began on their house in 1824.

Locals and visitors alike continued to use guides throughout the 1820s, 1830s and as late as the 1840s, including in some areas close to the growing settlements. One such place was the land around Nelsons Plains, near the junction of the Hunter and Williams rivers. With its thick brush forest and swampy ground, it remained an area that the colonists treated with caution. Robert Scott was still finding his way in the bush here in October 1823, when he wrote in his journal:

M & I agreed to walk to Nelsons Plains across the country if we could have got a Native to show us the way . . . [however] it seems there is to be a grand Cobbra (grub) Feast somewhere in the neighbourhood and nothing in the world could induce them to be absent from such an entertainment . . . As we could not get a Native, Mitchell and I were afraid to trust ourselves in the forest, therefore we only walked to the same spot we disembarked last night.[15]

Scott's account gives us a glimpse not just of the ongoing need for guides on short excursions in some terrains, but also of some of the considerations Aboriginal people made in joining expeditions. In this case, the advantages of assisting Scott on what was a relatively small journey were not enough to outweigh the cultural drawcards of the cobbra feast and associated gathering.

Between 1822 and 1825, Dangar's ongoing survey made the valley increasingly familiar to the colonists and so reduced the need for guides in the settled areas. As well as his six convict workers, we know Dangar was accompanied by several Aboriginal people during the survey work, although neither his field books nor the detailed letters to the surveyor general regarding his progress make any mention of them.[16] One of these guides helped Dangar find a passage from the upper Hunter Valley to the Liverpool Plains in October 1824, the first recorded break-out from the Hunter into new grazing lands.[17] Later, in 1826, when Dangar assisted Robert Dawson of the Australian Agricultural Company to locate their land grant, Dawson commented on a hunting party of Aboriginal men near Maitland who were acquainted with Dangar due to his survey work and who chatted with him before continuing on their hunt.[18]

Dangar's surveys led to increased British penetration of the Hunter. In 1828, he published a guide for emigrants that included a map based on his survey work. It outlined the type of country in different parts of the valley, the large estates and landowners, and the types of agricultural or pastoral use to which areas were suited. Dangar hoped 'that the Map, with the Index . . . will enable persons of all descriptions to proceed to any part of the country there delineated, and there to describe with accuracy the position they wish to select'.[19]

While Dangar considered that his maps would make the valley knowable to all, ending the need for guides, those who wished to travel beyond the main estates and settled districts still relied upon guides well into the 1830s and 1840s. Although roads and tracks between settled areas and larger estates were increasingly well marked, known among the settlers and easily followed by visitors to the region, any deviation from these or explorations into the more remote parts of the valley remained for some a 'trackless wilderness'. Free settler James Atkinson wrote in 1826 that when travelling into unexplored districts, Aboriginal guides were usually procured. They helped carry equipment, including the fowling pieces (guns), and would erect bark shelters for themselves and the British party at night. Atkinson had more than once travelled long distances, including to the Hunter, with no other company than two Aboriginal guides 'whose fidelity I could rely on'.[20]

Roger Oldfield, the editor of the short-lived periodical *The South Asian Register*, wrote on a visit to the Hunter in 1828:

> In the course of our progress along the Hunter, we engaged a black fellow to be our guide, in which capacity the blacks are of a most essential service. A map and compass are useful: but the local maps, which are obtained directly or indirectly from the Colonial Surveyors, have very few natural boundaries laid down, for the guidance of a stranger; and the compass, is a very uncertain benefit, when standing on the margin of an extensive morass, or when fixed in the dilemma of a thicket.[21]

In 1833, William Breton reported that the Aboriginal people of the Hunter made excellent guides 'when well treated'. But, he added, if the party was on horseback care should be taken, because a horse could walk quicker than was convenient for a man, and if the guide was outpaced or if they felt hard-pressed they would take the first opportunity to 'give their employers the slip'.[22] Even at this later stage, Breton recognised that the guides still retained an element of power in the increasingly unequal relationship.

Lieutenant George Malcolm of the 50th Queens Own Regiment of Foot, visiting Robert Scott at Glendon in 1834, had a guide called

Ybai to lead him from Glendon to Charles Boydell's property on the Allyn River near present-day Gresford, a distance of approximately 32 kilometres. Today's Glendonbrook Road to East Gresford closely follows Malcolm's route. Malcolm employed two other guides to lead him from the Australian Agricultural Company estate at Port Stephens back to Newcastle, travelling through dense bush, across sand dunes and through swamps on the way.[23]

Even though the use of guides diminished locally, they continued to be engaged in expeditions beyond the boundaries of the Hunter Valley. What are now remembered as iconic colonial explorations, such as those undertaken by Sir Thomas Mitchell in 1839, the three expeditions of Ludwig Leichhardt between 1844 and 1848, and the disastrous journey of John Kennedy in 1848, all employed Hunter Valley men. Harry Brown, who accompanied Leichhardt on his first two ventures, and Jackey-Jackey, who accompanied Kennedy, were both from around Muswellbrook. Both men were lauded for their bravery, leadership and skill during expeditions to Far North Queensland and Central Australia. It is the tragic deaths of the British explorers that are remembered, however, rather than the Aboriginal men who accompanied them.[24]

The ongoing use of guides into the mid-1830s belies the idea that the settlers were instantly confident in their abilities to navigate through the landscape beyond the marked roads or tracks.

COMMON GROUND: EMPLOYMENT AND WORK

While convicts who were assigned to work as shepherds and herders, or those who absconded and became bushrangers, were acquiring knowledge of the remote country, many of the free settlers were only familiar with their own estates and, in many cases, this was limited to the immediate homestead area and surrounding paddocks. The mountains, steep valleys and surrounding bush remained as Aboriginal space. In contrast, the valley floor, the creeks and rivers were increasingly becoming common ground, the space where most interactions between Aboriginal people and settlers were taking place: a space that American cultural theorist Mary Pratt has referred to as a 'contact zone'.[25]

Pratt's contact zone was an area in which those peoples who had been geographically and historically separated came into contact with each other and established ongoing relations, both good and bad. In contrast to the British idea of a frontier, the concept of a contact zone acknowledges the Aboriginal movement back and forth across the limits of location and settlement boundaries that defined settler and official governance. Applying this lens to historical sources allows the interactive, improvisational aspects of colonial encounters to be seen not in terms of separateness but rather of co-presence and interaction.[26] This is not to suggest that it was free of violence and confrontation. In many cases, unlike a middle ground, the balance of power in the contact zone was beginning to shift, and those Aboriginal people within it were increasingly compelled to defend their culture, traditions and Country.[27] It was, however, a shared landscape, one in which increasingly interwoven histories began to emerge, especially as the number of Aboriginal people that were employed across the estates grew.[28]

Although the experience for Aboriginal people was very different to that of the British, with pressure on their Country from an invasion of settlers and their stock, violence, confrontation and racism, the two sides' histories were inevitably entangled. As both groups continued to live in the same space, crossing paths throughout the colonial period, they also shaped each other's lived experience of the place.

Missionaries such as the Reverend Lancelot Threlkeld believed that the employment of Aboriginal people would be a path to civilising them. Threlkeld had established a mission for the London

Missionary Society at Newcastle in 1825, before relocating to the shore of Lake Macquarie at Belmont. Threlkeld knew it by its Aboriginal name—*Bahtahbah*. In 1828, he moved again, continuing to run the mission for the colonial authorities on the opposite shore of the lake, near present-day Toronto—*Derahbambah*—until 1841.[29] While he employed Aboriginal people on his farm site, his legacy remains his accurate recording and translation of the Aboriginal language of Newcastle, Lake Macquarie and the Hunter people.

For those frontier settlers, estate owners and small emancipist farmers, the motivations to employ Aboriginal people were often quite varied. They turned to Aboriginal labour for convenience, to save cost or to exploit particular skills. This was particularly the case for emancipist farmers, who often worked smaller farms and with less money to employ extra workers. And it was these farmers in the Hunter, as it was elsewhere, that were the first to use Aboriginal workers on their land. In evidence presented to Commissioner Bigge in 1820, the then-commandant of Newcastle, Major James Morisset, reported that while Aboriginal people were very troublesome in stealing corn, they also assisted the settlers in harvesting it.[30] As much as being a response to the labour-intensive nature of the harvest, where more workers made lighter work, the employment of Aboriginal workers may also have been a method by which the isolated small settlers sacrificed some of their crop to the locals to stave off larger scale raids on it, as had been common along the Hawkesbury River in the 1790s.[31]

Aboriginal people continued to be employed at harvest time after the valley was opened to free settlers. Peter Cunningham wrote in 1826 that a farm on the way up the river to his own employed 50 Aboriginal workers to cut and carry the maize, for which they were paid a supply of boiled pumpkin for supper.[32] George Wyndham—who purchased the Annandale estate in 1828 from the insolvent David Maziere, renamed it Dalwood and planted

maize, wheat and orchards, before turning to wine grapes—
recorded employing Aboriginal workers from May 1830.[33] In his
diary, which also served as a workbook for the estate, he noted
that Aboriginal workers helped harvest the maize crop in June
1833, and there is some evidence of Aboriginal men helping with
planting grapevines on the property in the later 1830s.[34] Although
Wyndham actively employed Aboriginal workers, his maize was
still targeted by Aboriginal raids. His diary also records trouble
at the adjacent property, Harpers Bush, in February 1833, with
the mounted police and local men pursuing Aboriginal raiders.[35]
Charles Boydell, on his Camyr Allyn estate near Gresford,
employed Aboriginal workers to harvest tobacco in the 1830s.
One man, known as Jacky, taught Boydell the local language,
which he recorded in his diary.[36]

Alexander Harris wrote an account of his time working in
the Hunter and at Port Stephens in the 1820s and 1830s. Harris
advised newly arrived settlers to treat Aboriginal people kindly, not
only because they were of 'great service' on small farms as they
were skilled in 'stripping bark, showing new runs, tracking lost
bullocks and sheep, &c. &c.', but also because it was the 'secret of
restraining their tendency to furtive and vindictive depredations'.[37]
Harris observed that small farmers who could not afford to pay for
labourers, or had no assigned convicts, invariably maintained good
relations with local Aboriginal people for the sake of obtaining their
assistance in agricultural work. Echoing governors Macquarie and
Gipps, Harris observed

[if] there is anything to be done for the civilisation of the blacks
and to prevent their utter extermination, it will be found in the
encouragement of amicable relations which so easily establish
themselves between them and the small settler.[38]

Through his own employment on rural estates, Harris enjoyed contact with many Aboriginal people and small settlers—both of whom, he believed, were being forced from land that was theirs by right, through birth or work, by large landowners interested in nothing but profits and power. He believed that Aboriginal people could understand a convict settler having ten, twenty or even 50 acres (4–20 hectares), especially having witnessed the treatment that convicts received, but could not comprehend why anyone would want 20,000 acres (8094 hectares) or more 'with his countless flocks and herds, and white slaves—he has no sympathy whatever with him'.[39]

Employing Aboriginal workers on small settler farms was not only advantageous to those cash-poor settlers who could not afford labourers or convicts (whom they had to feed and clothe). It could also suit the traditional, seasonal cycles of Aboriginal people. The jobs on farms were often piecework or contract labour so people could come and go as the work required, allowing for traditional ceremonies and practices to be maintained, while the interaction with the colonial economy gave them access to goods for themselves or to trade with other Aboriginal groups. Much of the work also utilised the traditional skills of Aboriginal people, reassigned to suit the purpose of the small farmer.

Edward John Eyre, who went to the Hunter in May 1833 to establish a grazing farm, used Aboriginal workers especially around shearing time. Although he had been assigned six convicts, and he was working in conjunction with his neighbour and mentor William Bell and his men, shearing was very labour-intensive, particularly the work of washing the sheep prior to the fleece being removed. The sheep needed to be fully submerged for the dirt and grit to be loosened from the fleece; to achieve this, sheep were driven into and across the river, then turned and made to swim back where they were dunked before being penned together to await the shear.

A series of pens or races were constructed both on the riverbank and in the river itself to hold the sheep and to direct their movement through the stages of the washing. The pens were constructed using bark strips and slabs from box or stringybark trees growing on the property, and Eyre employed Aboriginal men to cut and prepare these strips for their construction. He had previously seen bark canoes on the river capable of holding between six and eight people, but noted that the method of preparing the bark for canoes was different from that used to make the pens and races, showing a change in practice to suit the British use of the traditional material. Eyre saw sheets of between six and twelve feet (1.8–3.6 metres) square cut for the sheep pens, flattened by heating them on the inside just as a cooper would heat his barrel staves. Eyre thought that the Aboriginal people were 'very skilful and expeditious'.[40]

Although Helenus Scott thought that Aboriginal people were unsuited to hard work due in large part to their 'wandering life' and their 'lack of strength', he too employed them extensively at Glendon for seasonal work, including gathering and husking the maize, weeding the land and occasionally hoeing and preparing the ground for planting. Like Eyre, Scott took advantage of their bark-cutting and -forming skills for roofing sheds and other buildings on the farm.[41]

One of the obstacles that presented itself was language. Scott used what could be described as a *lingua franca*, a form of hybridised English and Aboriginal language to communicate with his workers. In 1827, answering a query from his mother as to how he communicated with his Aboriginal workers, he told her he knew of only two or three settlers who could speak the language, and although some Aboriginals spoke good English, the general language was a corruption of both English and the Aboriginal language. As an example, he wrote:

[W]e say 'you bring it me badoo & me give it you ripo & mite, bell
me gammon' which means 'you bring me water (a bucket of) & I
will give you a water melon & a cob of corn, I will not deceive you'.
Badoo is water, ripo a ripe water melon (of which they are particularly fond), mite is the young maize before it is ripe and when
roasted or boiled is very good eating for whites or blacks, bel is no,
not, don't etc as in 'bel you go'; don't you go; he might answer in the
same Anglo-Black lingo 'How many you give it me bulla carbon
fellow? Bugeree you! Where sit down bucket?'; how many will you
give me? Two large ones? Very good. Where is the bucket?[42]

At his Lake Macquarie mission, Lancelot Threlkeld, who was
learning and translating the language, employed Aboriginal people
as part of his wider evangelical plan to civilise them, with the men
clearing the land and working the fields to supply the mission
throughout its operation. In 1827, he reported having nearly 60
Aboriginal men working to clear 25 acres (ten hectares) of ground
for cultivation, for which he paid them in flour and clothing. He also
noted that as new farms were established around his mission, they
too employed Aboriginal workers to help them clear their small
plots.[43] Whatever the benefits Threlkeld saw, Alexander Harris
considered his civilising work and that of others as quite useless,
saying it was 'intrinsically absurd in the nation which is robbing
another of its land and its means of subsistence soliciting that other
to adopt its religion'.[44]

On the one-million-acre (405,000-hectare) estate of the Australian Agricultural Company (A.A. Co.) north of Newcastle and
inland from Port Stephens, Aboriginal workers helped clear land,
chop wood and carry water. They also supplied fish to the British,
worked the sawpits alongside white workmates, manned the boats
to transport workers across the inlet and up the rivers and creeks
that fed into Port Stephens, and served as guides and scouts for the

company's commissioner, Robert Dawson. Indeed, Dawson had engaged an Aboriginal man at Newcastle to guide him and the other company agents to their Port Stephens grant when he had first arrived in 1826. The man himself informed Dawson that he was only visiting at Newcastle, having come across from Port Stephens just days earlier.[45] Aboriginal women were employed in domestic service in the huts of the company managers. Dawson recorded that, while he employed Aboriginal people in large numbers and he could get any work he desired done by them, they were not always the same people. Hundreds of Aboriginal men and women came and went from the company camps, working where and when they wanted for varying lengths of time before heading off again into the bush.[46]

In 1841, George Wyndham at Dalwood gave evidence to a New South Wales Legislative Council select committee on the employment of Aboriginal people on his estate. The committee was investigating the question of immigration as a means of combating the declining rural workforce as convict transportation came to an end, and sought opinions on whether Aboriginal employment might alleviate the labour shortage. Wyndham wrote that he occasionally employed Aboriginal people as shepherds, including one by the name of Roger who was lame in one foot due to a spear wound that prevented him earning his living from traditional means. Despite employing Roger, Wyndham wondered why, with food available to them through a few hours of hunting or fishing, Aboriginal people would agree to the drudgery of labouring for settlers at all. He noted that they were not labourers for the same reasons that gentlemen were not labourers, 'viz that he can live without labour. So also can they and as comfortably as they wish to live'. He remarked that they were not fools, and proffered, sarcastically, that the best way to induce them to work on farms might be to chop off their large toe, thus preventing them from climbing trees to secure possums.[47]

Wyndham's insights, although a little crude, offer a rare glimpse into the Aboriginal position in the Hunter twenty years after the opening to free settlers. His comparisons to the work ethic of gentlemen, while probably apt, may also have been too close to the bone. Not surprisingly, his replies were considered to be an insult to the committee and were withheld from the official publication of the responses.

The only other respondent from the region was Phillip Parker King, Commissioner for the Australian Agricultural Company between 1839 and 1849. Like Dawson before him, King acknowledged the usefulness of Aboriginal workers on the vast estates that made up the company holdings. He noted that Aboriginal people were particularly fond of being employed as stockmen but often went off without warning or consideration of the company's convenience. Their absence was often prolonged and when they returned, if re-employed, resumed as if nothing had happened. King had recently employed two Aboriginal shepherds to whom the company paid a wage of £8 per annum, rather than clothing and rations as was the norm. It was an experiment for the company to see if they stayed working longer. Twenty-two Aboriginal men were permanently employed, fifteen as shepherds, four as stockmen, one looking after the horses, one at the boat station and one as a constable. Others were employed as needed, including women in domestic service and men manning boats or acting as messengers.[48]

The evidence of both Wyndham and King confirmed the preference for piecework and for those jobs that kept a closer link to Country and tradition. Stock work and shepherding allowed some movement in Country, keeping connections to the land alive. These settlers, while expressing frustration at the habits of their workers, also appear to have accepted in some small way the comings and goings, although whether they had also developed an appreciation for the reasons is not clear.

Other Hunter estates also had Aboriginal workers well into the 1840s and even the 1850s. William Stevens, whose father worked as a free emigrant on the Glendon estate in 1841, recorded 'a lot of blackfellows' among the 150 workers gathering and pressing grapes in the Scott brothers' vineyard in 1841.[49] The letters of Helenus Scott himself also noted Aboriginal people working in and around Glendon: a young boy helped to bring horses to Glendon in 1848 and another assisted Helenus's brother-in-law Richard with packhorses in 1854. This man, known as Garry Owen, rode with Richard and collected honey from wild bees among the Glendon vineyards for the family.[50] Also in 1848, at Jerrys Plains, Aboriginal people were helping with the harvest of Richard Hobden's crop, the workers described as exhibiting 'an industry, perseverance, and skill in the execution of their task which cannot be surpassed by Celt or Saxon'.[51] As Hobden had taken up his 100-acre (40-hectare) grant in 1824, it is possible that he had employed Aboriginal workers from the start, 24 years earlier. At Raymond Terrace, Aboriginal men were employed as guides for hunting parties as late as 1848. In an early form of organised tourism, groups travelled by steamer from Sydney to Raymond Terrace, where guides would join them for the hunting. In one party, at least seven men were employed, two named as Jorrocks and Beeswing, and some armed with guns to assist. They also performed a corroboree for the party at the end of their safari.[52]

CHAPTER SEVEN

LIVING ON COUNTRY

ADAPTATION AND SURVIVAL

While Aboriginal people came and went from employment, they were also increasingly coming and going from the developing urban outposts and fledgling towns that were emerging in the later 1820s and 1830s. As work became available in these centres, more Aboriginal people were attracted to them. In 1825, Aboriginal men were working as boatmen at Newcastle, rowing whaleboats in and around the harbour for those taking up allotments in the new town.[1] In 1827, Threlkeld, from his Lake Macquarie mission, complained of the corrupting influence of Newcastle on his Aboriginal companions, who he said were drawn to the place to drink or work as prostitutes.[2] A correspondent for *The Australian* newspaper in the same year wrote that the Aboriginal inhabitants outnumbered the British in Newcastle, who totalled around 200, and that they were the willing servants of the lower classes, carrying wood and water for them for payment of tobacco or food.[3] Aboriginal people were a familiar presence in the town, with the correspondent noting: 'They go perfectly naked, and walk in and out of the houses before the eyes of the English females, without creating the smallest notice or concern. Such is habit.'[4]

In 1838, Threlkeld wrote that although their numbers had fallen and were now relatively low, Aboriginal people were performing so many tasks for the people of Newcastle that they were fully and constantly employed and could choose the jobs that suited their habits best. Threlkeld listed fishing, shooting, boating, carrying wood, collecting water and acting as guides as some of the task work undertaken by an embryonic population of urban Aboriginal people.[5] James Backhouse also saw Aboriginal people collecting water and cutting timber for the residents of Maitland in 1843.[6] Around the same time, a resident of Paterson, near Maitland, wrote of an Aboriginal man named Jamie who would regularly come and stay with the family for a week, working in the kitchen for the cook in exchange for food. Jamie was clothed and fed by the family, although when invited to sleep in the kitchen or one of the outbuildings, he would instead return to the bush, reappearing the following morning. The settler complained that the clothes would never last a week. Perhaps Jamie was exchanging them as a trade item or giving them as gifts, or he understood the significance of being clothed to the British but retained a more traditional appearance when returning to the bush and his people.[7] While towns offered potential for work, they also afforded some protection from the violence of the frontier and access to regular food, tobacco, alcohol and other luxuries. But the transition from bush life to town life was not immediate. It was a gradual shift, with many still living a traditional life and others adopting a sort of hybrid lifestyle, slipping back and forth from traditional to town life.[8]

In 1827, a correspondent for *The Australian* describing an excursion through the Hunter River district wrote of witnessing 'the army under King Bungaree . . . proceeding to the field with all the ferocity that dabs of pipe clay and smears of red oker [*sic*] could produce'. The men were armed with spears, boomerangs and waddies. Coming from Sydney, from where he presumably knew Bungaree, the correspondent was 'surprised to see them in such numbers, so strong and healthy'.[9] This brief account, while giving a glimpse of ongoing traditional life, perhaps more intriguingly places Bungaree back in the Hunter 26 years after first being recorded there as James Grant's interpreter in 1801.

Traditional ceremonies and gatherings were central to Aboriginal life in the Hunter. One Singleton resident, Henry O'Sullivan White, eldest son of surveyor George Boyle White and his wife Maria (nee Mudie), recalled a corroboree as a young man in the mid-1830s with over 400 in attendance, including men from the Hunter, Macleay and Manning rivers, on land next to their Greenwood estate near Singleton, with ceremonies continuing around Bulga, Singleton and Port Stephens into the later 1850s and 1860s. A ceremony at Bulga in 1852 reportedly attracted 500 participants from as far as Mudgee and Goulburn to a bora ground enclosed with carved trees—which were still evident into the 1920s.[10]

Some family groups camped regularly on the larger estates, which offered some of the advantages of the towns—such as a measure of protection—while maintaining a stronger link to their Country and traditions. One such group camped in the paddocks of Glendon in the 1830s. This camp was tolerated by the Scott brothers, with Robert Scott punishing convict servants who harassed and attacked them.[11] The Scotts even supplied muskets and guns to some Aboriginal men within these groups, despite this being illegal. A newspaper report in 1843 described a skirmish using guns and traditional weapons between Aboriginal warriors from Maitland, Sugarloaf, Wollombi and Glendon on one side and Port Stephens and Paterson River on the other in a field at the back of Maitland town. Six muskets were seen with the Glendon group, and two men were shot and killed on the other side. At the subsequent inquest, the Scotts were named as the suppliers of the guns, which they had made available for duck hunting.[12]

Camping on estates also gave access to new materials that could be adapted for traditional purposes. Archaeological sites excavated near Singleton during the 1940s revealed traditionally crafted blades and flakes made from green, blue and amber bottle glass, with a dump of the bottles used close by. Recovered on a site near the river, with other examples made from crockery, roof slate and even insulators, the collection provides evidence of a dynamic process of adaptation and traditional tool-making well into the second half of the nineteenth century.[13]

The movement of people back and forth between towns, estates and the bush, and the ongoing traditional practices of tool-making and ceremonies, point to a large and viable population of Aboriginal people in the district. The number of Aboriginal people in the Hunter after the invasion was rarely recorded and, when it was, it was a haphazard and fragmentary effort. Some idea can be gleaned from blanket distributions that took place from the mid-1820s, when the bureaucracy assessed potential populations. An informal census undertaken by magistrates and landowners in mid-1827 to determine the number of blankets required in an upcoming distribution reported approximately 1712 Aboriginal men, women and children living between Lake Macquarie and Newcastle and inland to Merton.

The largest concentrations were around Threlkeld's mission and in Newcastle, with 760 people. About 300 lived between Luskintyre, Patricks Plains, Wollombi and Dr James Bowman's Ravensworth estate, while a further 252 were recorded around Wallis Plains and Patersons Plains, 300 in the region close to Merton and a further 100 around the Merton estate itself.[14] The numbers were largely based on educated guesswork by the magistrates and did not include any groups around Segenhoe or Edinglassie, nor those around Port Stephens, who came and went from the valley, as no returns were supplied from there. It also ignored those who continued to live in traditional ways in the hills and isolated valleys of the Hunter. As Alexander McLeod at Patricks Plains explained in his return:

> [W]e have to state that no correct calculation of the numbers of Aborigines can be made, and that for many reasons, their wandering habits and constant intermixture one tribe with another: some frequenting the settlement and others keeping themselves entirely strangers—the statement of their numbers must therefore in great measure be a guess.[15]

To further complicate the count, estate owners such as William Ogilvie at Merton, Peter McIntyre at Segenhoe and Francis Little at Invermein all cautiously noted that the Aboriginal people they knew from their areas were also connected to groups at Mudgee and Bylong in the west, and others in the Liverpool Ranges. McIntyre, who had been subject to recent attacks, distinguished between those who were local and those who were 'wild', and noted the constant communication between both groups. Just over ten years later, in 1838, the numbers were similar, with a total of 1720 people counted at this time, although this included Port Stephens; less than half that number of blankets were ordered.[16]

The movement of people around the Hunter and their connections to adjacent regions such as Mudgee, Port Stephens and the Liverpool Plains reveal the great and continuing mobility of the people across the region. The colonists could only guess where they went between annual blanket distributions or after the harvest was completed, and they could only estimate the actual numbers of people who lived around them. Tracks and pathways crisscrossed the valley and led up and over the mountain barriers that confined the British, embedding the people into the wider knowledge of Country set down over hundreds of generations.

The apparent ability of Aboriginal people to appear and disappear around the estates and towns added to the unease felt by some colonists and laid bare the reality that the British had entered and were living within an Aboriginal world, a place already well-known and understood by the Aboriginal people who lived in it. Just as Aboriginal people came and went at will from the settlements, so too would travellers often come across Aboriginal people moving easily through the bush that they were struggling to negotiate. William Breton wrote that as his party of ten approached the Hunter near Wollombi in 1833,

> we fell in with several of the aborigines, and the further we rode the more we saw, until at length there were not less than sixty with us . . . It was entertaining to observe the different groupes [sic] wandering among the trees, for we were all more or less scattered, and the shouts of the wild denizens of the woods added to the effect.[17]

Eight years later, in 1841, young emigrant William Stevens wrote of 200 Aboriginal men and women passing by his family near West Maitland as they made their way inland to work at Glendon.[18] The experience of Breton and Stevens highlights that, despite falling numbers in the official blanket counts, the Hunter Valley in the 1830s, and even into the 1840s, was still very much Aboriginal Country.

NAMING COUNTRY

The obvious, although sometimes overlooked, indicator of the deep knowledge of Country and the long occupation of the valley was the many names given to every feature and aspect of the place. The process of Aboriginal naming was intense. The Hunter River itself had different names ascribed to it along its course. Near its mouth it was known as *Coquun*, while further inland it was called *Myan* and *Coonanbarra*.[19] The names acted like signposts in the landscape, understood through the stories and mythology that went with them, each place name being part of a larger narrative that was inseparable from the people with which it was associated.[20] The language of the people acted as the repository of knowledge about Country, inscribing a landscape of meaning across the Hunter. Anthropologists have referred to this integration of language and knowledge of Country as the speaking land, with a constellation of Aboriginal languages across Australia all contributing.[21]

Many of the estates took their names from Aboriginal language. John Brown (no relation to Robert Scott's servant), who arrived in Newcastle in February 1822, named his farm Bolwarra, reportedly as it had been used by his guide and was said to mean 'flash of light' (how accurate this was is conjecture, as Threlkeld recorded the word for lightning as *Pin-kun* or *Wot-tol*).[22] On the edge of the mountains north of Patricks Plains, surveyor George Boyle White and his wife Maria (second daughter of James Mudie) kept the local name of Mirannie for their first property. George Wyndham likewise kept the name Miangarinda for his second farm near the Goulburn River.[23] Susan Caswell and her husband William at Port Stephens called their property Tanilba, said to be an Aboriginal name for the area, which in turn was also adopted by her as the name for one of her own daughters born on the estate.[24] Houston Mitchell, brother of Sir Thomas Mitchell, took the name Walka for part of his estate directly across the river from Bolwarra near Maitland. As he explained:

The Aboriginal name for the hilly part of my grant is Walka and the lake is called Potay. This information I distinctly received from about 50 natives who were seated at their respective fires on the prettiest part of Walka.[25]

Houston recorded other names for his property from the Aboriginal groups camping around his estate, including *Coolumbundara*, which covered 515 acres (208 hectares) in the west of his property, and *Yawarang*, the name of the swamp, shared with him separately by two different Aboriginal men. Although these two names did not migrate into the British nomenclature, so taken was Houston with Walka that he not only named part of his estate (which survives in present-day Maitland) after it, but he also took Walka as a *nom de plume* for correspondence to the Sydney newspapers.[26]

Sir Thomas Mitchell, in his role as surveyor general, encouraged his surveyors and mapmakers to retain Aboriginal names where possible. The reasons why the British chose Aboriginal words and names for their estates were rarely explained in their letters and journals. Houston Mitchell's and John Brown's acknowledgement of the origin suggests that some adopted the names as the 'actual' or authentic name for their new home. It may have been a way to anchor themselves in a new place, or recognition of the deep roots that predated their own arrival. For others, it may have been an appropriation of the place, name and all, for themselves; a stamp of ownership over all the land and its identity.[27]

The early explorers and first arrivals also recorded place names. As noted earlier, John Howe wrote of the 'Coomery Roy' when he first entered the Hunter in 1819. Although wrongly attributed as a place name rather than the name of the people who lived there, the Kamilaroi, the name remains as a location in the Hunter. Bulga, the small village and district south of Singleton, took its name from the local word for mountains. As Helenus Scott explained to his mother in 1824 while describing his travels overland through the mountains from Sydney, while the British called the area where the road came into the valley Bulga, he believed that 'more properly "bulkra" is the native name for a mountain'.[28] Similarly, *Wallumbi* was recast as Wollombi. At Green Hills, later known as Morpeth, Edward Close recorded the names for the river, swamps and prominent landforms around the estate.[29] The name for Bishops Hill, where his residence was situated, was *Terrymilla*, the area of British settlement was *Illulong*, the river was *Coonanbarra*, and Wallis Creek was *Bomi*; the nearby swamps were *Daragen* (Morpeth Swamp) and *Bomabeg* (Back Morpeth Swamp). Of the place names recorded, *Tenambit* for the eastern point of a sharp bend in the river, called Narrowgut by the British, survives as a suburb of Maitland, while *Merrilong* (later morphed to Merrylong), identifies Day Hill, a park behind Close's surviving house in Morpeth.[30]

Surveyor Henry Dangar also recorded Aboriginal names on the map he drew in 1828 to accompany his emigrants' guide to the Hunter Valley. Across the entire region, Dangar noted approximately 40 Aboriginal names for prominent features such as hills, islands, harbour entrances, swamps and creeks. The majority were clustered around the harbours at Newcastle, Port Stephens and Lake Macquarie, where Threlkeld had established his mission. Around Newcastle, Aboriginal names were assigned to beaches, headlands and islands: *Tahlbihn* at the entrance to the river; *Burrabihngarn*, also near the entrance; *Corrumbah*, near present-day Stockton; and *Burraghihnbihng* for the large swamp on the western edge of the settlement. Except for the entrance to Lake Macquarie, which was identified as Reids Mistake, all the features named in this body of water and its surrounding shores (nine in total) were given their Aboriginal names, of which *Wonde Wonde* survives as Wangi Wangi and *Buhlbah* as Pulbah Island.

Inland, however, along the river where the farms were being surveyed, the Aboriginal names largely disappear from Dangar's map. Some of the farms appear to have Aboriginal names associated with them, such as *Yarraconill* and *Yarrabung* in the mid-valley, but these are surrounded by the likes of Melville, Rosebrook and Abergaveney. A few mountains and landscape features retained their Aboriginal identity, such as *Kolen kolen* Mountain and the *Bundanbing* Hills, or *Purandarra* Brook and *Munnimbah* Brook near Singleton (later changed to Jump Up Creek and Mudies Creek, respectively), but they are scattered. Of these, only Munnimbah is in general use today in the altered form of Minninbah, given to a grand house that overlooks the brook.

Despite the absence of Aboriginal names on the official maps, some settlers were aware of the cultural whitewash underway. The most vocal of these critics was the Reverend John Dunmore Lang, whose brother had a farm on the Hunter River. In his book *An Historical and Statistical Account of New South Wales both as a Penal Settlement and as a British Colony*, Lang noted the Aboriginal names of the principal rivers in the valley as the *Coquun* (Hunter River), the *Doorribang* (Williams River) and the *Yimmang* (Paterson River). The rivers were named after the governor and Colonel William Paterson of the New South Wales Corps:

> Preposterously enough! For all three rivers had had native names much more beautiful and highly significant, as all native names are, from time immemorial. Every remarkable point of land, every hill and valley in the territory, had its native name, given, as far as can be ascertained from particular instances, from some remarkable feature of the particular locality—insomuch that the natives can make appointments in their forests and valleys, with as much accuracy in regard to place, as an inhabitant of London in the streets of the metropolis.
>
> Surely then, when there are such unexceptionable and really interesting names affixed already to every remarkable locality in the country, it is preposterous in the extreme to consign these

ancient appellations to oblivion, in order to make way for the name of whatever insignificant appendage to the colonial government a colonial surveyor may think proper to immortalize.[31]

Although Lang stated that the Aboriginal names for the rivers were relatively well known in the district, he claimed that most of the settlers, when asked, could not give the traditional name for the river they lived on, having never had the curiosity to ask.[32] Breton had also noted the fact that the rivers' Aboriginal names had been replaced and, comparing them to the Aboriginal names for the rivers in County Argyle (around present-day Goulburn), wondered if their original titles may have been more euphonious.[33]

TRADING KNOWLEDGE

As well as the names and language, Aboriginal knowledge of their Country was also beyond the reach or curiosity of many of the settlers. An understanding of the seasons, the rivers and their flood patterns was essential for successful farming on the alluvial plains. Following devastating floods in 1857 and 1870, a parliamentary inquiry took evidence from some of the oldest British residents still living along the river between Maitland and Singleton in order to compare earlier known flood heights. John Eckford, a settler at Maitland since 1818; John Brown, at Singleton since 1823; John Kennedy Howe, son of John Howe who discovered the overland route to the Hunter in 1819; John Wyndham, son of George Wyndham of Dalwood; Alfred Glennie, brother to early settler James Glennie; and Alexander Munro, who arrived in Singleton in 1830, all gave evidence of their experience of the early floods.[34]

Some settlers were blinded by their mistrust of Aboriginal people. Munro told the commissioners that he did not think any settler would remember the floods of 1820. Although Aboriginal people had said the floods of 1857 were higher, he did not believe that the information given by them could be relied on in this regard.[35] Wyndham, however, gave evidence of the Aboriginal testimony to early residents and the warnings given by them. He remembered old Aboriginal residents saying that before the British arrived, floods had covered the hills outside Singleton, forcing them to climb the trees to avoid the water. Furthermore, the river terrace where Robert and Helenus Scott built Glendon had been inundated, with only a small section left dry. In the same flood at Maitland, all the kangaroos and emus that had escaped to the highest ground were trapped and subsequently swept away as the water continued to rise. Wyndham also recalled that John Lanarch and John Howe had both confirmed driftwood and debris in the trees on top of the two hills where the Aboriginal people had sought refuge and that Benjamin Singleton had seen driftwood and debris stuck in trees sixteen feet (five metres) above the ground.[36]

Deaf to the warnings, the earliest settlers all took land along the river. Helenus Scott explained to his sister Augusta that all the finest settlements were on the river and liable to be flooded, but they preferred the risk, as flooded land was so much richer than any other.[37] James Mudie's Castle Forbes estate was devastated by floods in 1825, with his house, farm buildings and crops all swept away. The damage was so great that Mudie requested a convict carpenter be sent by the government to help him rebuild. In the 1830s, William Breton noted the poor choice of site for the growing town of Maitland. While the government buildings, such as the gaol and courthouse, were out of flood reach, the houses of the residents were clustered along the banks of the river and a creek that entered it. Breton predicted that the next flood would wash them all away. However, for the residents, the convenience of the location, close to the wharves and loading stages for the trading ships that plied from there to Sydney and beyond, overcame any fears of inundation.[38]

Not everyone ignored the knowledge base around them. The convict Martin Cash, a herdsman for George Bowman at his farm on the Wybong River near Denman, supplemented his diet with fish such as perch and mullet. To catch mullet, he used a technique learnt from local Aboriginal groups, who he described as friendly, obliging and the only contacts he had on the isolated cattle runs. Instead of hooks, Cash used the bark of a local tree that he heated under the ashes of a fire, before placing it in a small net and plunging it into the water holes. The fish would soon after float to the surface and could be picked up with ease.[39] In other parts of the Hunter and on its fringes, settlers traded with Aboriginal people for fresh fish and other seafood. At Port Stephens, Susan Caswell, wife of Lieutenant William Caswell, traded tobacco with the local Aboriginal people for fresh fish and oysters from the bay to supplement the family diet.[40]

As well as the trade of Aboriginal knowledge, collecting was another common connection between Aboriginal people and settlers. Birds and animals had been collected from the Hunter Valley during the first years of British occupation, with Aboriginal people often employed in their pursuit and collection. In 1818, Governor Macquarie was presented with a chest made of Hunter Valley cedar and rosewood, and filled with birds, insects, shells, butterflies and marine specimens, with the fold-out panels painted with images of animals, birds and scenes around Newcastle, Lake Macquarie and other landscapes.[41]

In 1821, John de Marquet Blaxland, arriving with Reverend Middleton, used his Aboriginal guide to assist in collecting petrified wood.[42] Later, at Glendon, Robert Scott employed Aboriginal people in collecting emu eggs, regent birds, insects and other specimens for him. The Scott brothers had built two collecting boxes for insects but were struggling to find anything rare, although emu eggs could fetch between four and five shillings each around the Hunter.[43] At Dalwood, George Wyndham was also collecting specimens to send to his mother and family in England. In 1837, he sent some hawks, shells and marine sponges home, which, his mother remarked, would enrich the cabinet of natural history at Dinton, their English estate.[44]

In addition to the natural curiosities, Wyndham also sent home a collection of possum-skin cloaks. In 1835, and again in 1837, cloaks were sent first to his two sisters, then his mother Laetitia. While it is not clear from the correspondence how he came into possession of these cloaks, it is likely that they were acquired from local Aboriginal people. Possum-skin cloaks were worn in the upper reaches of the valley, in the mountains to the south and the north close to Wyndham's Dalwood estate.[45] For his sister Mary Ann, the cloaks were not simply curiosities from her colonial brother but an Imperial fashion statement. Returning from London, she wrote:

> I must now tell you that during our absence the Opossum Skin Cloaks and hawks arrived. The cloaks we were delighted with; they show so much native ingenuity. I shall certainly parade on the Terrace in mine. They are a great curiosity and we are much obliged to you for sending them.[46]

The relationships between Aboriginal workers, guides and traders and British settlers in the Hunter from the 1820s through to the 1840s were complex and changing. Reasons for working differed across the decades and across the employment. Guides had access to goods and sometimes weapons as payments, and increased prestige within their own community through a new knowledge. Aboriginal workers on the estates worked for different reasons: access to food or tobacco, protection, shelter or necessity. The work was not necessarily a matter of unequal exchange but, rather, just one aspect of a reciprocal relationship built up between local people who knew each other.[47] This reciprocity formed at the same time as violent clashes, reprisals and attacks were also increasing throughout the Hunter Valley.

Whatever the reasons, by drawing on their culture and economic traditions, Aboriginal people were able to negotiate a place for themselves in the rapidly changing world, a process that involved both accommodation and resistance.[48] However, as the population rose and the stakes over land and property grew, class and racial tensions began to manifest themselves in what for a time became a landscape of violence.

The Brokenback Ranges that flank the southern edge of the Hunter Valley. Aboriginal pathways criss-crossed these mountains for millennia. The British found their way through in 1819–1820. (Author's collection)

One of the most significant rock art sites in the Hunter Valley, Baiame Cave in Milbrodale is a powerful representation of the deep Aboriginal spirituality and connection to Country in the region. (Author's collection)

The *Lady Nelson*, in which Lieutenant James Grant undertook the first official survey of the Hunter River in June 1801. (State Library of New South Wales [SLNSW] ML 590)

Ferdinand Bauer's view across the settlement at Newcastle, 1804. This is the first view of the penal station and shows the rudimentary beginnings of the town. The house of the commandant Charles Menzies and the flagstaff are on the hill to the right. (SLNSW, SV1B/Newc/1800-1809/1)

Joseph Lycett's painting of Newcastle looking towards Prospect Hill, c. 1818. Comparison to Bauer's work from fourteen years earlier illustrates the spread of the penal station across the core of modern-day Newcastle. (Newcastle Art Gallery collection, Gift of Port Waratah Coal Services in 1991, NRAG Foundation)

The soldiers' barracks with Christ Church visible on the hill in the distance, c. 1820. This is one of a series of watercolour studies done by Edward Close during his time as Engineer and Inspector of Public Works at Newcastle. (National Library of Australia [NLA] PIC Draw 8631#R7273)

Portrait by Captain James Wallis of five unnamed Newcastle Aboriginal men and women, including one in a soldiers red coat, c. 1818. (SLNSW, SAFE/PXE 1072)

Portrait by James Wallis of five identified Newcastle Aboriginal men, including Burigon on the far left, Nerang Doll, Trimmer in full warrior dress, Walker and Nerang Wogee with the shield, c. 1818. (SLNSW, SAFE/PXE 1072)

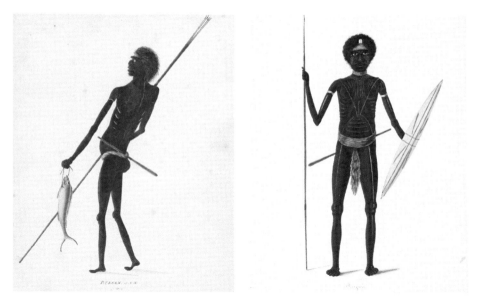

Two views of Burigon/Burgun by convict artist Richard Browne, c. 1819. Although rudely executed, Burigon is portrayed with the accoutrements of everyday life. In one he is shown with a four-pronged fishing spear or *mooting*; in the second he holds a single prong *camoy*, his body painted in red ochre. A waddy is stuck through his belt in both portraits. (NLA PIC Solander Box A64 #T2791 NK149/D [Left]; PIC R8947 LOC Box A65 [Right])

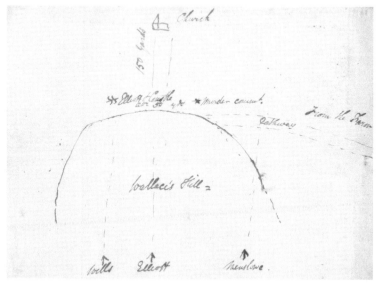

This small sketch map was presented as part of the prosecution case against John Kirby for the murder of Newcastle Aboriginal leader Burigon in 1820. (New South Wales State Archives [NSWSA] SZ792B Court of Criminal Jurisdiction Case Papers)

The Reverend Lancelot Threlkeld in 1816, just before he left London. Threlkeld was instrumental in informing Sydney on the atrocities playing out in the Hunter Valley in the mid-1820s. (SLNSW P1/1765)

James Mudie, owner of Castle Forbes estate and target of a convict uprising. (SLNSW ML1225)

Susannah Matilda Bedwell, c. 1850. Bedwell was the daughter of Susannah Matilda Ward, settler at Patersons Plains. Susannah Ward, a widow, was granted 600 acres of land on the river at Paterson in 1823, one of a handful of women to receive land in their own right in the Hunter Valley. (SLNSW ML 694)

Robert Scott (L) and Helenus Scott (R) in 1820. Robert and his brother Helenus, both shown here on the cusp of their journey to New South Wales, were to become two of the most influential and controversial of the Hunter Valley settlers in the 1820s. As magistrates and landowners, the brothers were at the centre of colonial politics and society, with their home base being the estate of Glendon, near present day Singleton. (SLNSW Min 354 & Min 355)

Glendon House, home of Robert and Helenus Scott, shown here in an 1837 painting by artist A.E.R., thought to be Amelia Rusden, sister of Helenus' wife Sarah Anne Rusden. (SLNSW SSV1B/SingD/1)

The camp of Colonel William Paterson on the banks of the Paterson River, painted by J.W. Lewin in 1801. This is the earliest known painting of the British in the Hunter Valley. It shows Paterson propped up on his elbow, his long-barrelled guns and the specimens collected. (SLNSW PXD 388)

A lone settler clearing and fencing his land near Morpeth, painted by Edward Close, c. 1824. A growing sense of entitlement and ownership over the land developed amongst the settlers as more farms were enclosed. (SLNSW PXA 1187)

Aborigines hunting water birds, by Joseph Lycett, c. 1818. This painting shows Aboriginal people flushing out and catching black swans in what is probably Hexham Swamp, just north-west of Newcastle. (NLA PIC MSR 12/1/4 #R5675)

An image of an exploring party, published in 1826 as part of James Atkinson's account of his time in New South Wales. It shows Atkinson's party with a professional Aboriginal guide, clothed and armed with a gun, and local guides assisting. Atkinson wrote of using guides during his time in the Hunter. (SLNSW SSV*/Expl/1)

A Joseph Lycett painting of a large party of Aboriginal warriors showering a British longboat with spears and rocks. Lycett was slightly wounded in a similar incident at Port Stephens in 1817. A speared hat floats in the waves, testimony to the accuracy of these weapons. (NLA PIC MSR 12/1/4 #R5688)

Corroboree at Newcastle, c. 1818, attributed to Joseph Lycett. This image is a montage showing a variety of different ceremonies that would have taken place over a period of time. In the distance the signal station near the growing town of Newcastle is visible. (SLNSW DG 228)

James Atkinson and his party building a bivouac, 1826. British explorers and settlers often took advantage of traditional Aboriginal skills and adapted them to suit their own purposes. (SLNSW ML 630.991/1A4)

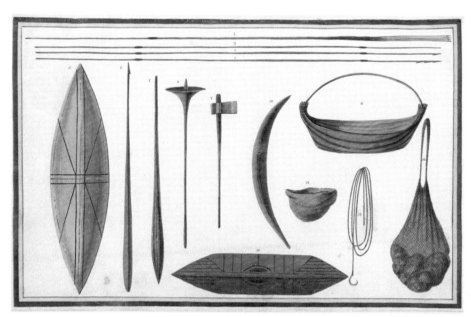

This selection of Aboriginal tools and weapons from Newcastle, drawn by convict artist T.R. (Richard) Browne for commandant Thomas Skottowe in 1813, includes a traditional axe with a British-made steel head, evidence of the adaption of new technologies by local people. (SLNSW SAFE PXA 555)

This simple settlers hut, known as the 'Germans Hut', was sketched by William Leigh near Gresford at Lewinsbrook, c. 1830. It demonstrates the timber and bark construction typical of first generation settlers. (SLNSW PXA 1988)

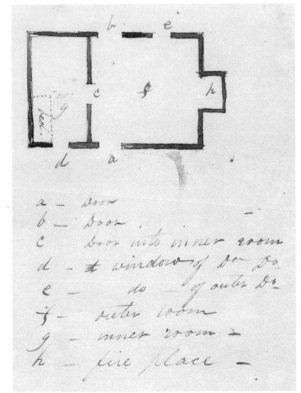

a — door
b — door.
c — door into inner room
d — a window of do do
e — do of outer Do
f — outer room
g — inner room
h — fire place

This plan shows the layout of Richard Alcorn's hut, in which a deadly melee took place between Aboriginal warriors and convict farmers in August 1826. The plan was presented as part of Robert Scott's report on the incident. A massacre of eighteen Aboriginal people followed just days later. (NSWSA CS 5/7951 26/5653)

Aust^n. Agric^l. Co^y. Coal Works: Newcastle.

The opening of the Australian Agricultural Company mines at Newcastle in the late 1820s transformed the former convict settlement and set the foundations for the modern coal trade in the Hunter. The steam ship *Sophia Jane* loads up at the company wharf, shown here in c. 1833. (SLNSW SSV1B/NEWC/1840-9/1)

Morpeth river port, c. 1845, by Edward Close. Morpeth enjoyed a thirty-year reign as the Hunter's main port for trade and migration, until the arrival of the railway in the 1850s. (NLA PIC Drawer 8631 #R7258)

George Townshend's Trevallyn house (formerly Charles Boydell's Cam-yr-allan). This is a fine example of the large mansions erected in the 1840s, which began to replace the first generation of settler homes. The older, single-storey Cam-yr-allan can be seen still standing alongside. (SLNSW SSV1B/Hun RD/3)

Burning Mountain near Wingen at the very top of the Hunter Valley. Known by Aboriginal people as far away as Newcastle as *Ko-pur-ra-ba*, it was an important site for the ochre used in ceremony across the Hunter Valley. (SLNSW PXA 3819)

The Kingdon Ponds in flood near Scone in 1856. Flash floods or gradual inundations were constant hazards for those who lived near or depended on the river. (SLNSW PXA 3819)

A portrait of Cumboo, also known as Billy Good-day, by William Nicholas in 1842. One of the few contemporary portraits of an Aboriginal person from the Singleton area, Cumboo appears on blanket lists at Patricks Plains from 1841 until 1856. (SLNSW DL Pd 59)

Cecilia Kelly, wife to convict Phillip Kelly, standing in 1906 (R) with Margaret, one of her daughters, outside the house Phillip built in Bathurst St, Singleton. (Author's collection)

CHAPTER EIGHT

RESISTANCE AND REPRISALS

In November 1825, *The Australian* newspaper reported the murder of a white settler in his hut in the district of Patricks Plains. His stockman had also disappeared and was presumed dead. The body, identified initially as John Greig, was found by two neighbours, Mr Allen and Mr Forsyth, who had come by to have breakfast with him. The deceased was described as a respectable and industrious man. Allen and Forsyth found him with his head beaten in, an open book of Robert Burns' poetry lying nearby.[1] Two other stockmen were reportedly found speared soon after, and a third narrowly escaped the same fate. Ten soldiers from the Newcastle garrison were dispatched to quell the violence and protect those isolated farms where settlers were reportedly living in a state of fear. While the report got the name of the victim wrong—it was in fact Robert Greig—the incident marked the start of a bloody, intense and destructive campaign of violence across the middle and upper Hunter, one in which the combatants often knew each other by sight or name and where friendships, allegiances and previous kindnesses could be the difference between life and death.

Settlers had been moving into, and farming in, the middle valley for four years when Greig and his stockman were killed. Initially, the establishment of farms and estates had little serious impact on Aboriginal people's movement across their Country. In the first months, and in some cases years, few of the estates had fences and many left the forest largely untouched. Aboriginal food sources were maintained to some degree. Kangaroo, possum, bandicoot and other small mammals were still abundant in the forests and across the open grasslands, and the rivers were plentiful with fish and shellfish, including freshwater mussels in the middle and upper reaches of the Hunter. Yams, a staple food, continued to grow in the alluvial soil along the river and its tributaries, with other plants such as *burrawang* (*Macrozamia spiralis*) and native cherry (*Exocarpos cupressiformis*) also readily available.[2]

However, the increasing numbers of livestock, growing areas of cultivation and farms along the rivers had begun to compromise access to and availability of traditional food sources by the mid-1820s. For example, in May 1823, the total number of free landholders and families was around 93 people on 33 farms with 179 convicts assigned. By 1825, there were approximately 1582 people, including over 950 convict men and women, 250 emancipists and around 320 free persons. By 1828, the total was closer to 3500. Stock numbers rose from around 610 sheep and cattle in 1821 to 13,500 in 1825 and 167,000 by 1828, including 120,000 sheep.[3] Colonial hunting of kangaroos and emus with dogs for sport disrupted this food source, scattering mobs from their feeding grounds. Flocks of sheep tended by shepherds, and herds of cattle let loose in the bush, gradually trampled native pastures. New settlers, now ensconced on their grants, worked to clear the land, erecting huts and planting orchards, while their convict servants built fences, systematically locking in land parcels. Their growing sense of entitlement and ownership appears to have worked to harden their views on an Aboriginal presence in their neighbourhood. Soon after many of these settlers had utilised the skills of Aboriginal guides and interpreters, they were putting in place measures, often threatening or violent, to exclude Aboriginal people from the very country that they had led them through.

SKIRMISHING ON THE EDGES

While much of the violence that was to come would occur in the middle and upper Hunter, a sense of threat and unease had existed from the first years of free settlement. In July 1822, Edward Close, magistrate at Green Hills, now Morpeth, recommended the deployment of three soldiers and a constable to the First Branch of the Hunter, now known as the Williams River. The same had already been approved for Wallis Plains and the Paterson River to 'protect those persons who may choose farms there against the Black Natives who are very savage at present'.[4] Close, a former soldier, considered that a show of force would change the behaviour of any Aboriginal groups that threatened the settler community.

Clashes were also being reported around Newcastle. In December 1824, John Platt, at his Ironbark Hill estate near Newcastle, complained to the colonial secretary about being harassed by Aboriginal raids on his property. Platt had arrived in February 1822 with his family and was the second-largest supplier of maize to the government stores by May 1825.[5] His house and mill sat atop rising ground overlooking the river. The land was cleared down to the water's edge and planted with wheat and maize. Platt's property was devastated by fire in December 1824, with his crop destroyed, a barn with the harvest inside burnt down, farm implements lost and some livestock killed. He did not state the cause of the fire in his letter, and it may have been accidental—or even the work of a disgruntled convict, as his farm had been robbed twice before by absconding convicts. He did make the point, however, that he had been targeted twice by Aboriginal raids on his crops, 'notwithstanding the severe example' he had made of several of them, and the implication was that the fire was the work of Aboriginal raiding parties once again. Fire was a well-documented tactic against maize crops and buildings around the Hawkesbury and the settlement at Prospect near Sydney, and Platt's uneasy relationship with local people could well have provoked such a raid as this.[6]

The maize crop of Robert and Helenus Scott at Glendon was also targeted. In May 1824, Helenus wrote to his mother about the ongoing trouble that they were experiencing. Bread had been taken from the convict huts and corn from the fields. Robert had caught one Aboriginal man and held him prisoner, making him work for the day before sending him off in the evening. The hope was that he would spread the word among his companions not to steal from the Glendon farm. As no more raids were reported by the brothers, the tactic may have worked.[7]

Other farmers took more drastic actions to protect their crops. John Powell, on the Paterson River, set spring-loaded guns in his crops with notices around his farm to warn people of their presence. Powell was a small farmer, on 60 acres (24 hectares) of land with his wife Charlotte, the daughter of the ex-convict Commissariat at Newcastle, John Tucker. As a small farmer, the loss of a crop could jeopardise Powell's ability to stay on his land, and the taking of crops has been suggested by some historians as a tactic used by Aboriginal people to force settlers off. They understood the economic importance and reliance on the harvest. By taking the crop, they could then undermine the settler while also giving themselves an easy food supply to sustain any resistance or supplement traditional foods that were under pressure due to grazing, land clearance and farming.[8] The posted warnings suggest that the guns were there to fire on Aboriginal raiders who would be less likely to be able to read or understand the notices. Either way, one gun succeeded in shooting convict Michael Fox from the nearby large estate of Captain George and Sarah Frankland at Paterson. Although Fox had been shown the public path through Powell's land the week before, he had entered the cornfield nonetheless and was shot in the thigh.[9]

Edward Close and Robert Scott, as the local magistrates, were tasked with investigating any reports of violence. Scott, as the closest magistrate, was increasingly called upon as the clashes became more frequent in the isolated middle and upper Hunter. In August 1824, he ordered district constable John Earl of Patricks Plains to apprehend an Aboriginal man known as Jerry, who had allegedly stolen one of George Blaxland's dogs from Perley, his farm near the junction of the Hunter and Goulburn rivers. Blaxland had a 'serious encounter' with Jerry, although he gave no further details. Jerry was also accused of assault and robbery of an unnamed boy, with a four-dollar reward posted for his capture (Spanish silver dollars were used as currency in New South Wales until 1849, and one Spanish dollar was the equivalent of 4s 4d).[10] Scott referred to Jerry as being part of the 'Patricks Plains tribe', a generic name for any Aboriginal people living around the district inland from what is now Singleton up to Fal Brook (Glennies Creek) and across towards the Goulburn River area. Although Scott was sure of Jerry's guilt, Earl was cautioned to bring the right person in as there were a number of men in the district known by the same name.[11]

RESISTANCE, PAYBACKS AND REPRISALS

The remainder of 1824 and much of 1825 were relatively quiet in the valley, as violence escalated in the western plains around Bathurst and Mudgee between Wiradjuri people and settlers. The ensuing fighting by troops of the 40th Regiment under the command of

Major James Morisset, former commandant at Newcastle, culminated in the declaration of martial law in August 1824 and the killing of at least sixteen Aboriginal people near Mudgee. A week after the killing, Morisset led an expedition of four parties to sweep north from Mudgee. One of these parties, led by George Ranken of Bathurst, entered the Hunter Valley through the Cassilis Gap, making campfires out of coal as they camped along the river.[12] For settlers in the upper valley, this proved that Aboriginal warrior bands could pass from the Bathurst region into the Hunter, and rumours began to spread throughout late 1825 that this was precisely what was happening. Attacks on isolated huts, including the taking of food and clothes from ex-convict farmer Joseph Onus, who lived at Bulga on the Wollombi Brook with his wife Ann and six children, and then raids around the Invermein district and new estate of Thomas Potter Macqueen at Segenhoe, appeared to confirm that the Wiradjuri had joined with Hunter Valley groups in raids.[13]

John McIntyre, the brother of Macqueen's overseer Peter McIntyre, pursued the raiding party into the hills surrounding the property. Here, the raiding party took up a strong position on high ground and forced McIntyre to retreat by rolling rocks and boulders down on him and his group. This was the same tactic used against Benjamin Singleton on his second attempt to find his way through the mountains in 1818, and had been a fighting technique witnessed around Sydney during Macquarie's campaigns at Appin and in the Hawkesbury in 1816.[14] The raids around Invermein were followed shortly after by a series of raids and robberies of lone travellers on the road above the large Ravensworth estate of Dr James Bowman and another attack on McIntyre's farm, where a dray was robbed despite the driver being armed with a blunderbuss.

The conflict began to escalate with Greig's death in late October 1825. Robert Greig was the cousin of settler James Greig, who had arrived in the Hunter in mid-1824. He came to New South

Wales in the brig *Amity*, in which he held a share before selling it to the colonial government on arrival. He had considered land in Van Diemen's Land, but settled on 50 acres (20 hectares)—later increased to 500 acres (202 hectares)—in the Hunter after inspecting the area. The death of his cousin Robert was widely reported in the colonial newspapers, with seemingly no reason for the brutal attack, although James himself had some idea. Writing to his brother in Scotland, he said that, although he could not tell the exact cause, since Robert had arrived in May he had been sober, enjoying hunting and fishing in the river that ran through the property. But James had been told by another friendly Aboriginal man that Robert had taken a man and beaten him, which had 'irritated the tribe he belonged to, and caused Robert Greig's untimely death'. He continued:

> I wrote to Mr John Greig Lythangie about ten months ago informing him of the unfortunate Robert Greig Lochgelly who was murdered by the Native Blacks in my absence, and likewise a convict servant who was left along with him on my Farm. Robert was reading Burns poems at the time he was killed in a second . . . Robert Greig is interred on my farm, I have put a Paling round his grave.[15]

James wrote a second letter to his friend Andrew Kettie, also in Scotland, the same day as that to his brother. Here he explained the situation further:

> Although the Black natives are by no means hostile, yet are always very revengeful when injured by any white person, the first that they meet with are sure to meet with their resentment. I am sorry to inform you that Mr Robert Greig of Lochgelly has fallen a victim to their resentment.[16]

Evidence of Greig's poor treatment of his Aboriginal neighbours was reinforced with later accounts of his behaviour. Robert Scott, in his magistrate's report written eight months later, noted that Greig's 'noted aversion to having the Natives about him, may have excited their hatred', while Reverend Threlkeld told the attorney-general, Saxe Bannister, that he had heard from his Aboriginal informants that Greig had struck an Aboriginal man and tried to drive them off the land.[17] Peter Cunningham, settler and explorer, writing a year later, added more detail. Cunningham claimed that the man who killed Greig was called Nullan-Nullan—probably a derivative of *nulla-nulla*, the word for club—who had approached in a friendly manner while Greig was reading Robert Burns, then sliding behind him, had struck him down.[18]

The combination of versions and evidence illustrates some of the complexities of the frontier in the Hunter Valley. Regarding James's version, although he was the settler, it was his cousin who was the target. James was away on business in Sydney at the time and, as Henry Reynolds has argued, raids on isolated properties, particularly those carried out as retribution or payback, were often preceded by periods of close surveillance.[19] Further, although Robert and the shepherd were killed, James's sheep were left alone, found later with his Scotch collie watching over them. Maybe the attack was postponed until James was away as, from his letters, James appeared to have an understanding of local law and was on friendly terms with at least some Aboriginal people—one having given him the details of Robert's behaviour that led to the attack.

Following the attack on Greig, the Aboriginal raiders withdrew into the mountains to the south, a move that the magistrates and Cunningham described as a retreat made in dread of British reaction. Two more shepherds were attacked, one being killed and the other badly lacerated near Mr Laycock's farm at Putty. The magistrate's report said that the group had joined forces with another group they referred to as the 'Wallumbi tribe', a group associated with the Wollombi and Wollombi Creek area. The potential for an escalation of the violence was not helped by a party of soldiers sent from Windsor to Putty to intercept the raiders. Instead, they encountered and killed several members of what was later discovered to be a friendly Aboriginal group.[20] Indiscriminate killings by settlers, soldiers and constables were a recurring feature of the violence and one that fuelled further troubles.

The attacks around Putty may have been quite separate to those playing out in the Hunter, events with roots reaching back to earlier encounters. In early January 1839, George Bowman (no relation to James Bowman of Ravensworth) wrote a brief account of his recollections of the violence in the Hunter Valley in 1825 at the request of Robert Scott, who had been called to testify before a Legislative Council committee on the 'Aborigines Question' in Sydney in October 1838. As George remembered it, the wounded shepherd was found on the road near Putty by his own overseer and men as they drove sheep from Windsor to the Hunter. The man was 'in a speechless state, his head crawling with vermin in the wounds received from the blacks'.[21] George Bowman told Scott what he 'supposed and believed to be true' from information related to him from other Aboriginal contacts—namely, that in 1816 the two men attacked had been instrumental in capturing some of the men on Governor Macquarie's list of ten Aboriginal leaders wanted for their involvement in attacks along the lower Hawkesbury River. Bowman remembered that the military had not attempted to take prisoners 'but shot all they fell in with and received great praise from the Government for doing so'. He recalled that two or three of the Aboriginal people among those named in the list had been brought up in settler families from their infancy but had become desperate murderers.[22] This list had included Myles, who had guided John Howe's party into the Hunter in 1819. If his recollection was correct, nine years had passed before the colonists involved in the killings on the Hawkesbury had been paid back.

The possibilities of Hunter, Mudgee and Wollombi groups acting together in the upper valley fuelled the fear of the settlers and prompted the deployment of troops from Newcastle into the area. Ten soldiers accompanied by two bush constables headed inland in June 1826 and were successful in capturing a number of Aboriginal men identified as having been involved. All managed to escape. While the soldiers were on patrol, the farm of George Forbes at Edinglassie was attacked, with sheep killed and a shepherd speared through the shoulder. The magistrate William Ogilvie, whose Merton estate was nearby, sent two constables to the property but no trace of the raiders could be found.[23] Ogilvie wrote to the then-commandant of Newcastle, Captain Francis Allman, that there were growing tensions in the area as isolated huts were the target of robberies and raids. Forbes' shepherd had been assaulted by a large group that had first come to the hut of the overseer and, on finding him alone, had proceeded to ransack it. The overseer was attacked by a warrior with a tomahawk but managed to force them outside and keep them at bay with firearms. He had then seen the shepherd approaching. He was driving a dray with the bullocks at a run with a pursuing party of warriors throwing spears, one of which struck the driver in the shoulder. When the overseer went to his aid, the first group raided the hut he had left unguarded.[24]

Ogilvie requested Allman dispatch a small party of mounted police as he feared it would be necessary to 'exercise some severity towards them'.[25] The mounted police had been formed after the violence around Bathurst—it was noted that mounted troops could more easily pursue fleeing Aboriginal bands than could foot soldiers. The new unit was a military force, manned by soldiers on regimental pay but with the cost of the horses and equipment borne by the colonial government.[26] Half the unit was sent to Bathurst in November 1825 to operate against bushrangers, while the other half, commanded by Lieutenant Nathaniel Lowe, was sent to Wallis Plains in February 1826.

The ability of the mounted police to respond quickly to reports of violence or attacks made them a particularly effective fighting unit on the open plains of the middle and upper Hunter. They were soon in action, capturing a man named Billy thought to be involved in the assault on Forbes' convict servant. Billy was taken back to Newcastle by Lowe and held in the lockup.

Before the mounted police arrived, Julia Pike, the wife of Ogilvie's neighbour Captain John Pike at Pickering, had contacted him in fear of the raiding parties. Ogilvie and his constables went to her to discover that large numbers of Aboriginal people had also plundered the huts of the convicts on that property. He followed the group into the mountains nearby, where they had taken the high ground and could defend themselves with ease. Ogilvie called to one by name and through negotiations came to an agreement that what was taken would be returned.

ESCALATING VIOLENCE

The deployment of the mounted police did not immediately stop the attacks. Although an officer and four mounted troopers were stationed in the upper Hunter to patrol and respond as necessary, soon after the attack on Forbes' Edinglassie farm the Ravensworth estate of James Bowman was targeted for the second time. This time two men were killed, a stockman stripped and left naked in the bush and a fellow watchman killed inside his hut. Two days later, another hut nearby, that of small ex-convict farmer James Chilcott on the banks of Fal Brook, only a few kilometres east of Bowman's, was attacked by what was presumed to be the same group. Chilcott managed to drive them off after physically wrestling with a man named Cato for a musket. Two men working on fences at Bowman's Ravensworth were ambushed by the retreating body of warriors, one wounded by seven spear thrusts.[27]

Threlkeld visited the wounded man from Bowman's some time later in the hospital at Newcastle. His conversation revealed a disturbing approach by the mounted police that would have ongoing consequences for the Aboriginal people of the upper Hunter. The worker told Threlkeld that he was chopping wood to build a fence when he was speared through the arm. On turning, he was wounded again but still managed to run before he was caught and knocked to the ground with a cudgel. The following day, the mounted police arrived at his hut with a suspect. He recognised the man as being part of the group, but not one of those who had thrown the spears. On hearing this, the soldiers took their prisoner outside, tied him to a tree and shot him, leaving him tied as a warning.[28] While the Sydney newspapers, particularly *The Australian*, and local magistrates screamed murder after every Aboriginal incident, it was now evident that the mounted police had employed summary executions in response.[29] Threlkeld had as yet heard only one example of what became a much wider campaign of terror carried out by the mounted police across the region.

More rumours were starting to swirl out of the upper Hunter, and Threlkeld got wind of Aboriginal people killed 'in peculiar circumstances' while in the custody of Lowe's mounted police. He wrote to Attorney-General Bannister in July 1826, and again in January 1827, with disturbing reports of more executions being carried out by the mounted police. Told to him by an eyewitness, Threlkeld described how another man—known variously as Jackey-Jackey, the Commandant or Jerry—thought to be involved in the attack on Bowman's men had been captured, identified and then brought down to the watch house at Wallis Plains under the direction of

Lieutenant Lowe. Here, on the night of 1 August 1826, Lowe and his mounted police took Jackey-Jackey to a place behind the watch house, tied him to a tree and executed him. He was shot four times, the first hitting him in the neck, the second in the face as he turned, the third missing and the fourth killing him from close range.[30] They were explosive allegations and something that the colonial authorities could no longer ignore. The killings continued, however, before any of this came to light.

The open nature of the country in the middle and upper valley was perfect for mounted operations. The troopers could respond rapidly from a central location and pursue escaping bands of warriors quickly. In sweeping through the valley, the mounted police had by August 1826 captured a number of men thought to be involved in the various incidents. The troops had been joined by some locals in the hunt, with John Lanarch (son-in-law to James Mudie of Castle Forbes) and James Glennie, a neighbour of Chilcott, both riding with them. Around 12 August, the party successfully captured a man close to Ravensworth and Glennie's property on Fal Brook. According to Lanarch, as told to an inquiry held later, as they suspected him of involvement at Bowman's, he was tied to the pommel of one of the horses and made to lead the group in pursuit of the larger party. Lanarch claimed that he volunteered, but this seems unlikely. In leading the group, the captive took pains to walk on the opposite side of any tree that the horses passed, thereby constantly catching and tangling the rope, delaying the party three or four times. The man appeared increasingly uneasy, which Lanarch took to be a sign of guilt. Eventually, the mounted troopers came into the clearing where Bowman's men had been attacked. Blood on the ground and on sheets of bark scattered around identified the place. Here the captive pointed in one direction and then another to show where the attackers had gone, claiming all the while not to have been involved. Then, according to Lanarch, he tried to escape and was shot down; his body was hung over a fence and left behind as a warning.[31]

Soon after, the troopers encountered a larger group and took at least seven men and some boys captive, although the numbers reported were vague. Four were captured near Glennie's hut, tied together and taken down Fal Brook to Chilcott's, where he identified them as the men involved in the recent attack at his hut. One was Cato. It had taken four troopers half an hour to secure Cato as he wrestled with them, and he was then beaten with the flat of a sword when he refused to cross the creek near Chilcott's. The prisoners were taken to nearby Captain Robert Lethbridge's farm but were not recognised there. Three of the party were merely boys and were released. As they were now close to his own hut, Glennie left the group here. Shortly after leaving, he heard a pistol shot. The troopers had killed Cato.[32]

With the remaining prisoners still tied, the mounted police started out back towards Wallis Plains. The troop was led by Sergeant Lewis Moore, with three privates, John Lee, James Fielding and George Castles. Somewhere along the way, three more of the prisoners were shot. Moore later testified to an inquiry that each had broken their ropes and fled, and the 'party did all they could to persuade them to return, but they continued their flight, under these circumstances the party were obliged to fire on them, where the three runaways were shot'.[33] The three privates gave similar testimony. George Castles added that, as they had other Aboriginal prisoners, the troops could not risk losing them by pursuing the escapees into the bush where their horses could not go, and so were forced to shoot them. The brutality displayed by the troopers was in part directed by the orders that Lowe had issued on their departure from Wallis Plains. The mounted police were to take into custody any Aboriginal men that they fell in with who were known to be involved in the attacks, and to secure them.

Lowe, having experience on the frontier around Bathurst, had instructed his men that in light of recent escapes, they were to fire on any who attempted to flee. If they did not fire, Lowe would be compelled to bring the troopers to trial for not doing their duty.[34]

As terrible as it all was, the actions of the troops were seen by the metropolitan newspapers in the context of the supposed outrages against settlers as the justifiable actions of those attempting to return with prisoners in difficult and confusing circumstances. But reports from Aboriginal people escaping to the sanctuary of Threlkeld's mission told even darker tales of executions and torture.

TAKING POSSESSION OF THEIR COUNTRY

Lowe's tactics appeared to have succeeded in subduing the attacks, and by mid-July 1826 Allman was reporting no acts of violence in the previous few weeks and that Lowe's 'exertions' gave reason to hope for no more.[35] But this was not to be. If anything, Lowe's tactics inflamed the situation and united large bodies of warriors across the upper Hunter. On 8 August, Threlkeld wrote to Saxe Bannister again, warning him that an Aboriginal man had come to the mission on Lake Macquarie with news that a large number of warriors were gathered in the mountains, threatening to descend into the valley and burn all the houses of the colonists. They demanded that Billy, captured after the attack on George Forbes' convict servant, be released from the Newcastle gaol as they worried that he would be shot like Jackey-Jackey.[36]

In the last week of August, it appeared that Threlkeld's fears were well-founded. At Merton, a property close to the junction of the Hunter and Goulburn rivers, a party of 200 warriors appeared, confronting Mary Ogilvie who was in the house with her children. Merton had been the focus of recent tensions. In mid-August, two boys, Tolou and Mirroul, had been arrested for killing cattle and, despite Mary's insistence that they worked for the family and were not involved, had been taken down to Newcastle.[37] Then, the day before the warriors appeared, two mounted police had enticed some local men onto the farm on the pretence of acting as guides in the search for bushrangers. Instead, they seized one, again named Jerry, who they suspected of being involved in the killing of a stockman at Forbes' property.[38] Mary intervened, convincing the soldiers that Jerry was not involved, and he was released. Fearing the anger of the local Aboriginal groups, the mounted police decamped in the night, leaving Mary and the property undefended.

As William Ogilvie was away in Sydney on business, Mary came outside to speak with the 200 painted and armed warriors. They were led by Jerry, wrapped in a possum-skin cloak and armed with a *nulla-nulla* stuck in strips of fur around his waist. In a display of the intimacies of the colonial frontier, Mary's younger son and daughter, who were playing outside, did not bother to run as the warriors approached, as they knew Jerry as a friend and he shook their hands as he walked towards the house.

Mary, also confident of their safety, approached the group with her eldest son William, who had learnt the local language, to ask why they had come armed to the farm. Jerry, angry at his own treatment, was suspicious as to why Tolou and Mirroul had been taken when Mary had enough influence over the soldiers to ensure his own release. William explained that his mother had tried to get the release of the two boys, but the soldiers had taken them in the night, and without his father around there was nothing they could do. Jerry, agreeing that he had never been treated unjustly by the family, turned to the assembled warriors and declared that the Ogilvies had done no wrong, and the group left.[39] Before departing, however, they brandished their weapons and told Mary to tell the soldiers never to come meddling with 'Master Ogilvie's blacks'.[40] When William Ogilvie senior returned, he in turn travelled to

Newcastle and secured the release of the two boys, informing Allman that he did not fear any further hostility despite there still being large groups of warriors in the vicinity of Merton.

The story of Mary Ogilvie's stand-off with Jerry and his warriors was quickly reported in the newspapers. *The Australian* praised Mrs Ogilvie's 'great degree of resolution', while Peter Cunningham, writing in 1827, remarked that it was

> A fine instance of intrepidity, and of the influence of female power over the minds even of rude savages . . . when Mrs Ogilvie, rushing fearlessly in among the brandished clubs and poised spears, by the firmness and persuasiveness of her manner, awed and soothed them into sentiments of mercy.[41]

Considering the clashes being reported across the upper Hunter from late 1825, and the growing anger and frustrations of the Aboriginals and settlers caught up in the experience, Mary Ogilvie's actions could well be considered fearless. However, her experience also demonstrates the intimate nature of the frontier. The knowledge of language, the personal friendship with Jerry, the intervention on his behalf and the trust between the two groups all combined to defuse a potentially deadly confrontation.

Just a few days later, on 28 August 1826, fifteen Aboriginal men gathered at the hut of Richard Alcorn, overseer for Captain Robert Lethbridge on the Bridgman estate at Fal Brook. The small hut stood just over 800 metres along Fal Brook from Chilcott's hut, scene of the earlier confrontation. It was typical of the back-country workers' huts of the period, with two rooms: one large outer room with a fireplace, and a smaller, inner room with a bed. There was a single exterior doorway and three windows, two in the living area and one in the bedroom. The doorway had no door and the windows no glass or shutters.[42]

Around midday, John Woodbury, a convict servant to Thomas Cullen at Pitt Town, arrived at Alcorn's hut to find the fifteen Aboriginal men already there. Woodbury was minding Cullen's cattle, which he had brought across the mountain road for agistment. Inside the hut was Alcorn's wife Charlotte, her young son Richard Jr, and baby Sarah Jane. She was worried at the number of Aboriginal men around and, while Woodbury sent Richard Jr off to fetch some other men working nearby, Charlotte offered kangaroo to the warriors for food. As the kangaroo roasted on a fire built for the purpose, Richard Jr, who had been followed by one of the warriors, returned with two convicts to the hut. There was no sign of violence or threat at this stage.

At approximately four in the afternoon, Richard Alcorn arrived. Alcorn recognised three among the group as having been suspected of the attack on his neighbour James Chilcott and, with Woodbury, decided to ask the group to leave. Three of the group were inside the hut with the family; when told to go, they called out to the remainder around the fire, who rose and advanced towards the hut. Richard Jr, seeing them coming, cried out in alarm, and Alcorn, Woodbury and the others rushed to the main room, where their weapons were, while the warriors surrounded the house. Charlotte and the children huddled under the bed for protection.

With no doors or window panes, the hut was particularly vulnerable. Before Woodbury could discharge his musket, he was struck by a spear in the hand, forcing him to drop the weapon and drag out the spear. Henry Cottle, one of the two convict workers, was struck in the left breast by a spear and fell dead. As Woodbury recovered his musket, the second convict, Morty Kernan, was also struck while firing from the bedroom doorway. Spears were now flying in through the windows and open doorways, as Woodbury and Alcorn fired their muskets back out. But with the shot for the muskets in the outer room, exposed to spears, both men were forced to fire powder only, hoping to fool their attackers into thinking that they faced loaded weapons. With spears exhausted, the warriors pressed forward with clubs and stones, gaining entry to the hut and killing the wounded Kernan with a blow to the head.[43]

In desperation, Alcorn had tied a bayonet to a long pole and used this as an improvised pike to thrust out at the warriors in the outer room, while Woodbury took a large wooden box to block the window. The box was soon smashed in, the bayonet broken and Alcorn knocked senseless. At this, the attack began to break up. A shepherd, alerted by the shooting, was observed by the attackers going to fetch the mounted troops who were stationed at Glennie's property nearby. The adjoining workers' huts were raided for bedding and blankets, and the warriors retreated into the bush. The mounted troops pursued the group but did not find them.[44] Robert Scott, the nearest magistrate, arrived the next day, filled with 'shuddering horror', to examine the scene. He found the bodies as they lay in the hut, surrounded by broken spears, stones and debris. His interview with Woodbury revealed the details of the encounter, made all the more dramatic by a sketch of the hut with each incident marked on the plan. Woodbury identified four of the men involved—Ball, Murray, Togy (who had been at Chilcott's) and another man named Brandy. One of the boys captured and released at Glennie's was also involved.[45]

MASSACRE

Woodbury and Alcorn claimed that the attack was unprovoked; however, the ferocity of the attack and its eruption soon after Alcorn arrived suggest instead retaliation for some unknown offence. Although it was quickly established that these men were not the same as those who had appeared at Merton, the timing caused Scott and others to worry about coordination among the groups, and a request for the mounted police to be deployed in force was made to Sydney. In the meantime, Scott, with five of the mounted police stationed at Glennie's farm, four settlers and four Aboriginal trackers, went after the group.

Three days later, and approximately twenty miles (32 kilometres) from Alcorn's hut, the mounted group came upon an Aboriginal camp. From here, the accounts of what happened next vary. In his general report, compiled in October 1826, Scott wrote that the party 'came up with the murderers on the morning of the third day where a skirmish took place and one European was speared through the face, and it is supposed that two of the murderers were killed and some more wounded: as reported by a Black woman who was taken prisoner'. Captain Foley of the mounted police, who arrived at Glennie's farm with twenty troopers as Scott was returning, reported to his superiors in Sydney that Scott had found the group with the aid of the trackers, and two of those involved in the attack on Alcorn's were killed and several wounded.[46]

Some weeks later, *The Australian* newspaper gave a more detailed and disturbing account of the event. According to their informant, the mounted party came upon the camp in the evening, alerted to its position by the light of campfires. One European and one Aboriginal tracker, each armed with a musket, crept forward to reconnoitre their position but were seen and, as a cry went up from the startled Aboriginal group, the two scouts opened fire before moving behind trees to reload. A spear struck the tracker in the face, passing through his cheek and out the other, through a hollow 'occasioned by the loss of a tooth'. Hearing the firing, the rest of the party rushed in to join the melee; 'A hot conflict followed, the natives maintaining their ground, and making the most dexterous use of their spears. At last they were obliged to yield, betake themselves to flight, leaving behind them about eighteen of their comrades who were numbered with the dead . . . The attacking party sustained no loss of life.'[47] One man and one woman were taken prisoner.

The killing of eighteen Aboriginal people in a prepared assault on a campsite by Scott and his party amounted to a massacre, and yet little was said on the matter beyond the report in *The Australian*. The incident, although remembered by Aboriginal people in the Hunter, was lost in White Australia's colonial memory among the increasingly violent reports from Tasmania in the later 1820s and the shocking accounts from Myall Creek in 1838.

Although having just arrived in the upper valley, Foley was forced to withdraw his mounted police due to difficulties with provisioning them, leaving just seven men spread between Bowman's, Glennie's and Chilcott's farms, as well as a smaller detachment under the direction of Sergeant Moore, who had already shown his worth in dealing with Aboriginal prisoners. Foley gave him instructions to 'use every means to secure the surviving members of the tribe known to have been involved in the affray'. He then rode to Ogilvie's, leaving five men there, another five at Macqueen's Segenhoe estate and two more at Captain Pike's Pickering farm. Nineteen mounted men in total were stationed across the farms that had been subject to some sort of raid or attack.[48] Foley was confident in the knowledge that the mounted police in the district would prevent further attacks. There was one further incident at Ravensworth in early September, with five fencers saved from ambush by the barking of their dogs. After this, the violence did appear to ease off as 1826 drew to a close.

CHAPTER NINE

A LANDSCAPE
OF VIOLENCE

Governor Darling was shocked by the reports coming out of the Hunter Valley in late 1826. The brutality was too much to ignore and so, in October, he ordered an inquiry into the rumoured execution of the prisoner, Jackey-Jackey.

Although Darling had been given directions from the Colonial Office to oppose any Aboriginal incursions by force if necessary, the actions of Lowe and the mounted police in the Hunter went beyond what was considered acceptable.[1] Darling wrote to Earl Bathurst in London that while there could be no doubts as to the 'criminality of the natives', it was no justification for 'the massacre of prisoners in cold blood as a measure of justifiable policy'.[2] Darling hoped that the reports would be unfounded; he found instead that the rumours were true. Instead of quelling the violence, the actions of the mounted police had sparked the worst of it in the valley.

The first inquiry yielded few details and was inconclusive, due in large part to Lieutenant Lowe being unavailable. Darling ordered Captain Allman in Newcastle to convene a second investigation, conducted by local magistrates Robert Scott and Edward Close, sitting at Scott's Glendon homestead. Lowe and his troops gave their version of the events around the capture and killing of the prisoners, in a series of depositions. A report detailing all the known events in chronological order was also prepared by magistrates Scott and Alexander McLeod, starting with Greig's death in 1825 and ending with the attack on the five fencers at Bowman's Ravensworth estate.

However, the report did not cover all the details that were emerging. Inconsistencies in the first magistrates' report, followed by further obfuscations in the second inquiry and the urging of Threlkeld's letters to the attorney-general, resulted in Darling ordering a third investigation. After a false start, acting Attorney-General W.H. Moore travelled to Newcastle and Wallis Plains in January 1827 before reporting to the Executive Council in Sydney.[3] By then it was hardly a secret that terror was a weapon employed by the British against the Aboriginal population. A report in *The Australian* by a 'wandering' anonymous correspondent in the Hunter in February 1827 explained some of the methods used by settlers:

We saw the skull of a black fellow who had been shot dead with a pistol ball, in the act of making his escape from a party of police. The respectable settler in whose house it is preserved, suffers it to remain carelessly on a table or shelf opposite his door, and the blacks who look on it with a superstitious dread, will hardly come near the house much less enter it; the skull acting as a powerful talisman to keep them off at all hours.[4]

The depositions from Allman's inquiry had hinted at some of the other goings-on, and Moore, with little information himself, sought Threlkeld's opinion on the events that had taken place. Threlkeld described to Moore three incidents that he had heard of from his own Aboriginal informants. The first was the reported execution of Jackey-Jackey. Threlkeld had sent his servant to interview a witness to the event, discovering that the body had been buried behind the privy of the government house, before being disinterred and moved to avoid detection.[5]

Threlkeld's second example came from a sergeant involved in the capture of three Aboriginal men. While sheltering from the rain on the verandah of Threlkeld's Newcastle house, the sergeant, with two Aboriginal captives, told him that a third had been shot near the river while escaping. A servant of Mr Cobb—either George or his brother James at Anambah, near Lochinvar—had told Cobb, who in turn told Threlkeld, that the soldiers had wanted to shoot the Aboriginal man at the farm and throw him in the river, but the servant had begged them not to as they drank from that water.[6]

The third report related to an alleged hanging. At Bowman's Ravensworth estate, a man was taken during the pursuit of those involved in the spearing of Bowman's stockman. This man was brought in to Bowman's hut, where a rope was secured around his neck. He was then marched a mile (1.6 kilometres) into the surrounding bush, forced to climb a nearby tree and tie the rope to a branch. The troopers then proceeded to fire their muskets at him, wounding him twice before he fell and was left hanging in the tree. Threlkeld said that the person who supplied the rope had told his informant of the incident.[7] This was not the first report of Aboriginal people being hung from trees in the district. In July 1826, Threlkeld had been told by Biraban, his interpreter and intermediary, that a man caught stealing corn had been shot and hung from a tree with the corncob stuck in his mouth as a warning to others.[8]

The rumours and stories coming out of the Hunter Valley finally prompted official action in Sydney. Threlkeld's correspondence with Attorney-General Saxe Bannister provided too many details to ignore. On 4 September 1826, he wrote that he feared a war, that the settlers were all in arms and more soldiers were being deployed after the attack on Alcorn and the massacre. Threlkeld's brother-in-law had reported coming across 200 warriors on the road to the Hawkesbury who, while not harming him, threatened vengeance against Dr Bowman. Helenus Scott wrote to his sister in the same month about the disturbances and the fighting upriver, saying the 'natives' had acted very treacherously but had now been severely punished and appeared rather frightened. He went on:

> If the governor had acted as he was advised by persons on this river and as he ought to have done, the blacks would have been quiet in a short time without so many whites and blacks having been killed.[9]

Helenus confirmed that the trackers that went with Robert were indeed from Glendon. He speculated that Governor Darling's indecision was in part because he was afraid of being ridiculed in London if he declared war on the Aboriginal people, as had happened to Governor Brisbane before him. The use of the trackers illustrates some of the complexities playing out in the violence, where personal allegiances and connections shifted across both sides of the conflict. Fears across the frontier prompted eleven settlers, on estates from Lochinvar in the lower valley to Segenhoe on the front line of the frontier, to write to the governor on 4 September 1826, asking for troops to protect their property from 'the revenge and depredation of these infuriated and savage people'. It is possible that the use of the word 'revenge' gave part of the game away, suggesting that the petitioners were acknowledging an initial wrongdoing on their part, or a wider injustice by settlers across the valley. Bowman at Ravensworth signed, as did Peter McIntyre at Segenhoe, both estates having been subject to multiple attacks. William Ogilvie at Merton also signed it, despite his better relations with the local Aboriginal people.[10] Robert Scott and his brother Helenus, although directly involved in the action, were confident enough in their security that they did not sign the petition either.

The impression that the violence was driven by the settlers and their employees in the first instance was already in the minds of the colonial authorities. Threlkeld reported raids on Aboriginal camps and the abduction of women through 1825 and 1826. In December 1825, he told of an overseer for a road gang in Newcastle attempting to abduct a girl ten years of age, and beating her father when he tried to stop him. Threlkeld went further in a letter to Saxe Bannister concerning the reasons for the attack on Greig:

> I have not yet had one tangible instance of assault, although I am convinced of many, and have heard the shrieks of Girls, about 8 or 9 years of age, taken by force by the vile men of Newcastle . . . There are now two Government stockmen, that are every night annoying the Blacks by taking their little Girls . . . My wonder is that more Whites are not speared than there are considering the gross provocation given.[11]

Governor Darling also believed the underlying cause of the troubles to have been abuse by stockmen or 'irregularities' carried out by convict servants. While he thought that Aboriginal outrages should be punished, he did not accept that they had been entirely unprovoked.[12] Later, in 1833, William Breton confirmed that stock-keepers around Port Stephens raided camps, kidnapped the women and shot others for fun.[13] White men—including convicts and ex-convicts, as well as some owner–settlers—across the Hunter and through the A.A. Co estate were regularly reported as having raided camps and taken women away. If Aboriginal men resisted, violence often ensued.[14] The evidence appeared overwhelming.

The settlers' petition was dismissed outright by Darling. It had arisen due to Darling having recalled Lowe and his men to conduct the second inquiry into the reported executions under Lowe's command. Darling suggested that if the petitioners were so worried about their estates then they should spend more time on them rather than in Sydney, where he understood the majority resided permanently and where they were all during the outrages. He counselled that settlers should set an example to their servants and prevent the 'irregularities' that, he suspected, were in many cases the cause of the conflicts. Ominously, he also declared that if the settlers united to take vigorous measures for their own defence, they would be more effective than a military force in protecting themselves, but assured them that they would receive every necessary support for any exertions in their defence that they might make.[15] In this vein, he also rejected Saxe Bannister's call for the imposition of martial law, based on the success of the same in Bathurst, commenting that the threat was minor as the warrior groups were in the minority when compared to the settlers.

THE TRIAL OF LIEUTENANT LOWE

At the same time as encouraging the settlers to defend themselves, Darling had Lieutenant Lowe brought to trial for the wilful murder of Jackey-Jackey. Word of the pending trial drove a wedge between the authorities in Sydney and the magistrates and settlers in the Hunter. The acting attorney-general, W.H. Moore, having replaced Saxe Bannister in October, reported that the investigation had been hampered by the magistrates, especially Edward Close. A former military officer, Close was not one to welcome government interference in what he saw as local matters. But the securing of a crucial witness in Thomas Farnham, a constable at Newcastle, meant that the trial could proceed. It also gave Darling the evidence he needed to dismiss Close as a magistrate in March 1827. Captain Allman resigned soon after.[16]

Lowe's trial was unique. It was the first in the colony's history where a military officer was tried for the death of an Aboriginal person. It put the question of Aboriginal rights and sovereignty under British law to the court and highlighted the disparity between the way the law was viewed in Sydney and the actualities on the frontiers of the settlement. Although under the command of a central authority, the mounted police operated largely unsupervised, often with civilian auxiliaries, in what settlers viewed as a defence of their lives and property. While violent attacks perpetrated by convicts on Aboriginal people had occasionally been investigated and punishments handed down by magistrates, the actions of settlers, often framed in the language of self-defence, had rarely been officially questioned. Thus, the trial of Lowe was viewed by many Hunter Valley residents as a threat to their own security.[17]

The case went before the Supreme Court in Sydney in May 1827, with Lowe defended by Dr Robert Wardell and William Charles Wentworth. Through his newspaper *The Australian*, Wentworth had already made clear his views on the need for settlers to defend themselves against Aboriginal attack. The case opened with a challenge on the jurisdiction of the court to even prosecute Lowe for murder, arguing that Aboriginal people were not British subjects and no treaty had been made with the King on their behalf. Further, even if considered subjects, it was impossible to bring Aboriginal people to trial, as defendants required a jury of seven military or naval officers, which to be fair would mean a jury half of British subjects and half of Aboriginal people. As Aboriginal people could not serve on a jury, nor be punished under British law, the only recourse was summary punishment for any wrongdoing, which, Wardell and Wentworth argued, was exactly what Lowe had carried out. He could not, therefore, be tried for murder. The argument was rejected.

The prosecution relied on eyewitness statements from three individuals: Thomas Farnham, the constable from Newcastle who had been stationed at McIntyre's Segenhoe estate and who had escorted Jackey-Jackey to Wallis Plains; William Salisbury, an ex-convict at Wallis Plains; and William Constantine, employed as a messenger at Wallis Plains. Each gave damning accounts, identifying Lowe and Sergeant Moore as the principal participants in the execution. Constantine testified that he had helped bury the body, had seen it disinterred and moved, and then been urged by another to keep his mouth shut once it was known that an inquiry was to proceed.[18]

With the prosecution case laid out, the defence team turned to discrediting each of the witnesses in turn. The three principal witnesses were all serving or former convicts, with character witnesses stating that each was idle, untrustworthy and their statements not to be trusted. Constantine and Farnham's involvement in the capture and burial of Jackey-Jackey was also used against them. Some witnesses changed their story from earlier versions, and Farnham's own deposition appeared to contradict his original statements taken during the inquiry. It took the jury of seven military men just five minutes to find Lowe not guilty. Free, Lowe soon after joined his regiment in Tasmania, before leaving the colonies for England in 1830.[19]

The trial, described by Lowe's supporters as a solemn judicial farce, highlighted the disjuncture between the lawmakers in Sydney and those on the periphery of the settled areas. The trial had not been welcomed by the settlers in the Hunter, who expected to be protected whatever the cost, or by the local magistrates, who represented the law on the frontier. Close, Scott and others, whose loyalties were to their local community first and the colonial government second, saw the whole business as an investigation into their own behaviour as well as that of the mounted police. Many in Sydney suspected that it was the behaviour of the Hunter River magistrates that had stifled the first two inquiries, by preventing witnesses from coming forward and causing others to change their statements during the trial period. Although Close was dismissed from his post, Robert Scott remained, thus ensuring that his involvement in the massacre of eighteen Aboriginal men and women after the raid on Alcorn's hut would never be investigated.

AND THE FIGHT GOES ON

By the time of Lowe's trial, the violence had reignited across the Hunter. As with the events of 1825 and 1826, the targets did not appear to be random or indiscriminate but, rather, represented reverberations of the events of the past years as part of the ongoing resistance of Aboriginal people.

In late 1826, John Elliot, a blacksmith at Segenhoe, was riding home to the estate through the bush at night. As he was approaching the farm, an Aboriginal man he was friendly with appeared from the darkness to warn him of an ambush ahead. Elliot had seen the glow of a fire, which his informant told him had been set by a party of warriors to burn the body of the approaching rider, whom they believed to be John McIntyre, brother of Peter the overseer at Segenhoe. Elliot's friend had tried to convince the ambushing warriors that it was Elliot who approached and, when they did not believe him, he had slipped away to warn him. John McIntyre, the intended target, had been involved in a series of events at the start of the long wave of violence. He had chased a party out of the maize crop at Segenhoe; in reprisal, one of his drays was plundered on the road. More recently, Jackey-Jackey had been detained at Segenhoe before being taken down to Wallis Plains. The complex nature of relationships on the frontier is further illustrated by the fact that it was Elliot's wife Martha who was on friendly terms with local Aboriginal people, making it entirely possible that it was her influence and friendship that had saved her husband.[20]

Soon after, in November 1826, the twenty-month-old daughter of John Hunt, a district constable at Patricks Plains, and his wife

Catherine was abducted from their hut.[21] The suspect was an Aboriginal man known to the settlers as Bit-O-Bread, and to his own people as Birrybirry.[22] Four months later, in March 1827, Birrybirry and King Jerry were identified among a large group of Aboriginal men that surrounded the hut of George Claris, a convict assigned to John Howe on his Redbournberry estate at Patricks Plains. Claris believed that the men would have attacked but for the arrival of two other men who were travelling up to work for James Greig. Birrybirry was after vengeance for being wrongfully accused of the kidnapping, and King Jerry declared that he would assemble 1000 men and kill any white man that they encountered if Birrybirry was hurt. They were not afraid of the soldiers, they said, and gave a demonstration of how they would attack.[23]

Three days later at Fal Brook, Samuel Owen, an overseer for James Bowman, was returning to Ravensworth from Wollombi Brook. He encountered a party of fifteen Aboriginal men, who immediately surrounded him, blocking his way. One he recognised as Jackass, who 'had done so much mischief about Dr Bowmans'. Jackass may have been either a man called Yerriman, 34 years of age, who was later counted among those living around Merton, or, more likely, Girrogan, 25 years old, from the Patricks Plains area, close to where Owen encountered the group. Whichever it was, he asked if Owen was the 'big constable' and, when he answered yes, drew his waddy and flourished it. Owen kept him at bay with his musket. The remaining men stood in a circle with their spears, but did not interfere. It was a one-on-one contest: a version of the traditional Aboriginal ritual contests where a lawbreaker would face their accuser's spears and clubs in payback.[24] As each lunged and parried, Cobborn Mary, the wife of the accused kidnapper Bit-O-Bread, intervened. She spoke to the Aboriginal men in their language as she circled Owen, hitting the ground with a pointed stick. After some time, the men backed down and left, leaving Owen

with Cobborn Mary. She told him to avoid going into the bush, as
the men were determined to kill him.[25] Why Owen was challenged
is unknown, but Mary's intervention in the contest suggests some
authority over the situation. The same day, James Glennie and
Benjamin Singleton both reported that cattle on their properties
had been speared.[26]

Tensions remained high throughout the first half of 1827. In
May, as the trial of Lowe was playing out in Sydney, Robert Scott
wrote to the colonial secretary to express his 'apprehension that
the Aborigines in the district of St Patricks Plains were showing
symptoms of a hostile feeling towards the Europeans'.[27] The testimony of his own Aboriginal informants had convinced him that
Bit-O-Bread was responsible for the kidnap of Hunt's daughter, but
Scott was constrained in his actions. As Aboriginal evidence would
not be admissible in a court, 'it would be worse than useless' arresting Bit-O-Bread, despite having no doubt about his guilt.[28] He was
convinced that any move to capture Bit-O-Bread would result in
bloodshed, as the neighbouring Aboriginal groups had already
threatened to descend on the settlers if he was taken in.

The same applied to any attempt to arrest those identified
as being involved in the attacks on Bowman, which included
Jackass, who was accused of having speared Bowman's fencer,
and those who attacked Alcorn's hut. As these groups now only
appeared near settlements in number, it would require considerable force to overcome them and 'it is pretty evident that they
cannot be taken without bloodshed in the first instance, and open
war and retaliation afterwards'. He summed up his dilemma thus:
'On the one hand there appears to be an absolute necessity to
bring these wrong doers to justice and to regain the child, and on
the other almost a certainty of further violence ensuing should it
be attempted.'[29] Why he would be concerned about catching those
he suspected of involvement in the attack on Alcorn's hut when he

himself had led the party that reportedly massacred them all he never explained.

THE INTIMACY OF VIOLENCE

After nearly eighteen months of attacks and skirmishing, the Hunter frontier, while remaining tense, began to quieten down. The settlers and authorities viewed the period as a series of coordinated attacks, one leading inexorably onto the next as bands of Aboriginal raiders moved through the middle and upper Hunter. They feared and talked openly of war, and it increasingly resembled one as foot soldiers and mounted police were deployed. However, a closer examination of each event shows another pattern, one of targeted raids and attacks on specific people and places. While raids on crops and livestock may have been opportunistic, every incident where spears were thrown appears to have been in retaliation for something. A few estates appeared to be particular targets. Ravensworth and James Bowman, in particular, were the subject of regular violence, with at least four separate incidents. The deployment of the mounted police marked a moment of intensification that swirled around Bowman's estate.

In contrast, the experiences of Mary Ogilvie and John Elliot showed that a foundation of friendship, a calm demeanour and some understanding of language and culture could help avoid conflict. These encounters also illustrated an important aspect of the frontier, one that confounded the invaders. The attacks appeared to be random, spread out across the landscape. The frontier existed not as a definable boundary, behind which one was relatively safe, but, instead, was more a collection of individual frontiers, one for each farm or settler. The unknown could be as close as the fence line across a paddock, beyond which uncleared bush camouflaged any approaching raid. Reynolds has likened it to the guerrilla tactics employed by Spanish rebels against the French in the Peninsular War in Spain and Portugal, a practice with which some of the officers and men in the mounted police would have been familiar.[30] It was a style that suited Aboriginal resistance and was played out in a familiar landscape.

To further upset the invaders, there was a level of intimacy that gave an unsettling aspect to the violence. Both sides often knew each other by name, lived in close proximity and were, at times, on friendly terms. This added to the invaders' perception of the treachery of the Aboriginal people around them. Governor Darling also made the point, as reported by the troops at the front line, that the 'murders have invariably been perpetrated by the natives domesticated on the establishments of the settlers'. It was claimed by a correspondent to *The Australian* that Bit-O-Bread had lived around the hut of the Hunt family for some time prior to abducting their daughter, while John Woodbury at Fal Brook knew four of his assailants.[31] The unpredictability fostered a sense of constant vigilance among settlers, particularly those isolated from the main settlements around Wallis Plains and Patricks Plains. This, in turn, generated a level of fear and disorder that was difficult to control.[32]

But fear also spread throughout the Aboriginal community. An Aboriginal group that was camped on the Scotts' estate at Glendon during the height of the troubles was disturbed by one of the men accusing another of being involved in the killing of settlers upcountry. At the utterance of the accusation, the accused leapt up and fled into the bush. The man was well known to the Scotts, who considered him a friend. Robert Scott was sceptical of the charge and, upon investigating, found that the man was not within 50 miles (80 kilometres) of the attack at the time but, rather, had recently beaten the accuser in a contest over a woman.[33] Fear of settler vengeance was being manipulated by some to sway traditional lawmaking and to attempt to bring punishment by leveraging British suspicions of involvement in deadly attacks.

In 1833, William Breton, while travelling through the Hunter, bluntly summed up the result of the years of violence:

> We have taken possession of their country, and are determined to keep it; if therefore they destroy the settlers, or their property, they must expect the law of retaliation will be put in force, and that reprisals will be committed upon themselves.[34]

Fighting had not necessarily involved every settler or every Aboriginal group, but many were caught up in it. The violence and the fear fuelled a cycle of retribution and counterattack that rippled through the country for years to come.

MYALL CREEK AND ITS AFTERMATH

While the killing in the Hunter Valley appeared to slow, on the valley's boundaries it continued apace. The move by squatters over the mountains and into the Liverpool Plains in 1827 opened a new front in the conflict. With many of these men being Hunter Valley residents, the terrible outrages that were to come are inexorably linked to the events of the 1820s.

On 9 July 1838, Edward Denny Day, the police magistrate at Invermein (Scone), received a letter from William Hobbs, overseer at Henry Dangar's Gwydir River estate.[35] The one-page note was the first report of the shocking massacre of 30 men, women and children that became known as the Myall Creek massacre. Of the many atrocities committed on the frontier, few others resonate so strongly today.[36]

Day and his mounted police went to the estate, arresting eleven stockmen, a mix of convicts and former convicts, who were returned to Sydney to await trial. The eleven eventually stood trial twice, acquitted at the first trial but with seven found guilty at the second.

As the first trial drew near, towards the end of November 1838, Robert Scott chaired a meeting of settlers at Patricks Plains, during which a memorial to Governor Gipps was drawn up. In this the settlers, who claimed to regret the clashes with Aboriginal people, called on the governor to intervene to prevent further bloodshed, lest they be compelled to take action themselves. Known as the Black Association, this group, led by Scott and including Dangar, ran a ferocious campaign against the trial and raised £300 for the defence. Gipps took their memorial as a veiled threat of their intent to act outside the law and an admission of their having done so in the past.[37] It is likely that this strengthened the resolution of the prosecution team to pursue the case to its conclusion.

Robert Scott made no secret of his position. After visiting Governor Gipps to deliver the petition, he then walked to the gaol to talk with the accused. Here, he was overheard telling them that they had little to fear as he had devised a plan to discredit the only witness through a claim of insanity. The month before visiting the governor and the prisoners, Scott had given evidence to the Legislative Council committee on the 'Aborigines Question', testifying that his sixteen years' experience with them had convinced him that the only principle Aboriginal people understood, especially in clashes with Europeans, was force.[38]

His arrogant venom, displayed at the committee and in the governor's office, was topped by his appearance at the trial, where he sat close by the defence barristers that he had helped secure and finance. It was too much for Gipps and, with the conclusion of the trial and the execution of seven of the defendants, Scott was informed that his name would not appear on the list of magistrates for the coming year. Like Close eleven years earlier, he was dismissed.

CHAPTER TEN

CONVICT REVOLT AND RUINED REPUTATIONS

On the morning of 21 December 1833, a melancholy procession made its way through the bush towards James Mudie's Castle Forbes estate. Sitting on top of two coffins in the back of a one-horse cart were two shackled convicts, Anthony Hitchcock and John Poole, two of six men charged over a convict uprising at Mudie's estate in November. Hitchcock and Poole were to be hanged on a scaffold erected at the side of the road for their participation in the uprising at the farm six weeks earlier. At the same time, John Perry, James Riley and James Ryan, just seventeen years old, were mounting the gallows in Sydney. Only one of the six men, David Jones, escaped with his life, being transported to Norfolk Island for life instead.

Hitchcock and Poole had travelled under guard from Sydney by steamer, then by cart from the Green Hills wharf to Castle Forbes, the place of their execution. With no blacksmith available to strike off their shackles and no minister of religion to read them their last rites, the fatigued prisoners offered no comment from the scaffold and the convict crowd watched in silence as the sentence was carried out. In Sydney, with the Reverend John Joseph Therry attending, Perry, Riley and Ryan went to their deaths in front of one of the largest crowds at an execution in recent memory. Their deaths represented the end point of what has become known as the Castle Forbes revolt. A relatively minor event in itself, it came to represent the climax of a decade of tension between emigrants, emancipists and convicts in the Hunter Valley.

THE REVOLT AT CASTLE FORBES

Early on 5 November 1833, three of Mudie's convict servants were being transferred under escort and in irons to Maitland to join an iron gang. Just two-and-a-half kilometres along the road, the three men, Hitchcock, Jones and Stephen Parrot, and their unarmed escort were stopped by five armed men: Ryan, Perry, Riley, Poole and James Henderson. Hitchcock, Jones, Parrot and Ryan had robbed and assaulted some other convicts in an isolated hut on Mudie's estate a week earlier. Ryan and the others had bolted from Castle Forbes before their arrest; Henderson had run from an iron gang a few days earlier. The group released the prisoners before chaining the escort, Constable Cook, and Parrot, who refused to join them, to a tree then fleeing.[1]

Around midday, the gang appeared at Castle Forbes. Armed with muskets, fowling pieces and double-barrelled guns, they rushed into the main yard, rounding up the convicts and workers, and locking them in the wood store. Mudie's daughter Emily, wife of settler John Lanarch, attempted to escape with her female servant by clambering out the window of her kitchen but was also caught and pushed into the wood store with the rest. They were warned that anyone who attempted to escape would be shot. Emily was told by Riley that they intended to find her husband and bring his head back to stuff in the chimney for his harsh treatment and excessive use of the lash. Mudie, who was in Sydney at the time, was also on their hit list.

After ransacking the house, stealing food, clothes, silver forks and spoons, guns, ammunition and three horses, the gang corralled the remaining convict workers into the wool store and headed towards the nearby river, where Lanarch was washing sheep in preparation for shearing. The next few minutes sealed their fate, and transformed them from absconders into bushrangers with a price on their head.

As Lanarch worked, the gang approached unseen, spreading out to prevent any escape. Lanarch heard someone demand 'come out of the water every bloody one of you or we'll blow your brains out'. Turning, he saw three men with guns aimed at him advancing along the riverbank. Hitchcock fired. Lanarch turned quickly and scrambled for the opposite shore. As the others began to fire at the fleeing Lanarch, Hitchcock and Poole screamed out that he would take no more men to court and they would take care that he never flogged another man. He was a villain and a tyrant they yelled, as both Poole and Henderson discharged their weapons. At the top of the bank, Lanarch stumbled. Thinking that they had hit him, the gang offered no pursuit as he escaped across open ground towards his neighbour Henry Dangar's farm.[2] Safe from his pursuers, Lanarch did not think to send anyone to check on his wife and family.

Assuming Lanarch done for, the gang fled on horseback to Henderson's hide-out in Lambs Valley, tucked away in rugged country approximately 30 kilometres distant. The news of the raid spread alarm in the district, with settlers arming themselves and fortifying their estates. The mounted police, although stretched thin across the valley, began patrols on the Windsor Road, expecting the fugitives to make a dash for the Hawkesbury. A £10 reward was offered for the capture of each of the seven men.[3]

Three days later, the gang struck again. They robbed the farm of William Bowen at Black Creek, close to the town of Branxton, taking a horse, saddle and bridles. A week after the first incident, on 12 November, two more properties were raided. Although the intention had been to attack Castle Forbes again in the hope that Mudie would be there, it was on high alert and strongly defended. Instead, the fugitives raided the adjacent property of Rusholme, where George Spark was overseer. Here, the anger and resentment of their various mistreatments at the hands of their masters manifested itself in a brutal assault on Spark. David Jones, accused by John Lanarch of losing sheep and being absent from the farm, had been sent to the Singleton magistrates' bench by Spark in October, receiving a total of 75 lashes for the two charges. Spark was quickly overpowered by the gang, tied to a post in his kitchen and allegedly flogged 300 times across the lower back and loins, with the lash whipping around to the soft skin of his belly. As the strokes rained down, his attackers called out the names of all the convicts who had been sentenced to be flogged by the local magistrates the day before, giving rise to the suspicion that they were in touch with local sympathisers.[4]

Taking saddles, guns, clothes, flour and other personal items, the gang moved on to the farm of Henry Dutton, where they stole another horse, guns, ammunition, more clothes, food, frying pans and supplies. Frying pans and food suggested that the men intended to stay in the area, so while some mounted police maintained a watch on the Windsor Road and others stayed at Castle Forbes, two others joined local magistrate Robert Scott to hunt them out. Scott had assembled a large party, including John Lanarch and twenty others—two settlers and eighteen convicts—as well as two Aboriginal trackers to begin the search, and it was not long before they had the information they needed. When word of the raid on Dutton's came through, they quickly rode to the farm. Heavy rain through the night had left the ground soft and the tracks of the gang clear in the mud. The trail was easily followed and led the pursuers to the remote Lambs Valley.

As the party approached, a scout was seen running from the ridgeline and soon the smoke from a campfire was spotted. Fearing they would escape, Scott ordered his men to charge forward and the bushrangers' camp was quickly overrun. In the ensuing melee, Henderson was shot and the rest quickly rounded up by the mounted pursuers. Henderson died from his wounds a few days later, and the rest were held in the Maitland lockup until they were transferred to Sydney for trial in the Supreme Court.

The news of their capture quickly spread. Robert Scott was rewarded with a piece of silver plate costing £106 raised by subscription from 65 of his grateful free-settler neighbours. His compatriots shared the £70 reward.[5]

While Scott and the others were rewarded, the reverberations from the short-lived revolt rippled across the valley. In late November, a runaway convict called Herbert Owen attacked an Aboriginal camp on Scott's Glendon property. Owen was a friend of James Riley and had been part of the raid on Spark's farm. Assuming that the Aboriginal men were the same trackers Scott had used, Owen attacked the group with an axe. He struck one man known as Joe Priest across the back and arms, and another known as Jimmy in the face, breaking his jaw, knocking out several teeth and leaving his face gashed open.

TRIAL AND INQUIRY

The trial of the six captured men was a sensation. The prisoners were all charged with capital offences, with the death penalty the very likely outcome. In these circumstances, few convicts had the benefit of being represented in the court, as any legal representation needed to be paid for and few convicts could afford to do so. In this case, however, an anonymous benefactor put forward the money and Roger Therry was appointed for the defence.[6] The case for the defence was not strong, and Therry chose to argue that the treatment of the men at the hands of Mudie and Lanarch had been so severe and beyond the boundaries of what was considered normal that the death penalty should not be considered.

In describing the trial, Therry observed 'the whole scene caused a shudder that thrilled, not only through the Court, but through the heart of the Colony'.[7] The newspapers lapped it up, reporting in detail on the proceedings, especially the statements to the court of the various defendants. Sydney readers were eager to hear the lurid details of life on a distant estate, and letters and opinions in support of both sides were published in a *de facto* public debate over the convict system in general and Governor Bourke's apparent policy of humane treatment in particular. Bourke had been fighting with estate owners in the Hunter and elsewhere since introducing his *Summary Jurisdiction Act* in 1832; this had established a new Court of Petty Sessions and set new parameters around the role of local magistrates and their powers to punish. Magistrates in country areas were outraged at what they saw as a limitation of their powers, with those in the Hunter Valley raising a petition in opposition. Sent in August 1833, just months before the revolt, the petition, signed by 130 landowners, claimed that the new laws undermined the authority of the magistrates and had led to a rise in crime and insubordination across the district. It was the same outrage as that expressed when Lieutenant Lowe had been withdrawn and then tried in 1827, with many of the same names attached. The Hunter Valley establishment felt that the colonial administration in Sydney was again interfering in matters of which they had little understanding and that were best left to local authorities.[8]

For those who believed that the revolt was a direct result of the leniency under the new laws, the trial appeared to confirm their fears. Mudie and Lanarch, especially, stoked the argument with their testimony of the indulgences and privileges that had been extended to some of the defendants, especially to Poole. For those who considered the system barbaric, there was enough in the evidence of the accused to satisfy as well. In their defence, Hitchcock and Poole both made impassioned pleas to the court, claiming their behaviour was that of men with no further options due to harsh treatment and cruel punishments at Castle Forbes. They accepted their fate but implored the court to initiate an inquiry into the excessive floggings, bad rations and withholding of tickets-of-leave and other indulgences. Hitchcock began to list those estates where convicts were poorly treated and tried to show his lash-scarred back but was stopped by the court from doing so.[9] To Mudie and Lanarch's horror, despite five prisoners being sentenced to death and one to exile, Governor Bourke took note of their plea and ordered an inquiry into treatment of convicts at Castle Forbes and the performance of the bench of magistrates at Patricks Plains.

The inquiry ran for one week in late December, with witnesses called to answer the questions of the solicitor-general (later appointed attorney-general), John Plunkett, and the principal superintendent of convicts, Frederick Hely. They heard from both Mudie and Lanarch, six of their convicts, and neighbouring settlers, farmers, overseers, constables and convicts on surrounding estates. The claims made by Hitchcock and Poole over rations, treatment and work practices were all investigated. Lanarch and Mudie's conduct was found to be no more or less severe than many others, nor their treatment of convicts unduly harsh or oppressive. The inquiry did, however, expose some unusual methods and revealed a collapse in estate management and dysfunction in handling the complaints made by the convicts stationed there.[10]

Trouble had been brewing at Castle Forbes for some time. With 64 convicts working on the estate, careful management of work and culture was needed; with Mudie often away, this was left to his son-in-law, Lanarch. The robbery and assault of fellow convicts by Hitchcock, Ryan, Parrot and Jones was evidence of a breakdown of work practices on the estate.[11] Mudie and Lanarch, with adjacent estates, had effectively combined their workforce and used the men in a variety of roles across the farms.

Although many of the convicts had trade skills, most were rarely utilised, leaving the men working at farm labour as required. For some convicts, including the conspirator John Poole, this fostered a feeling of resentment that their skills were wasted on the farm. Poole was a skilled joiner by trade and had been employed to work with engineer Hugh Thompson to erect a windmill on the estate. He was allowed to make plough blades on the side, which Mudie sold to neighbours, and was given extra rations and extra money, some of which he gave to Mudie to buy a music book and flute. Despite this treatment, Poole had a volatile temper and held grudges; although he appeared to have a working relationship with Mudie, with Lanarch it was toxic. He thought that he should have been in Sydney, where his trade could earn him more, and he had threatened to take to the bush if punished. Hitchcock too was a skilled tradesman and earnt extra money by making straw hats and baskets.[12]

Offering rewards, such as extra rations or other privileges, for extra work was not unusual. Mudie's neighbours, including Henry Dangar, James MacDougall, John Earl and Patrick Campbell, often rewarded their convicts in this way. Mudie also allowed the convicts to keep gardens to supplement their rations, with some also owning dogs for hunting and protection when working in the bush. Again, this was a regular feature on many of the neighbouring properties. These small indulgences were as much strategic as practical. Allowing the men a small measure of autonomy was designed to encourage good behaviour, a level of trust and a measure of

respect. This system was deemed most effective with a large workforce employed across many isolated parts of the estate, with no
possibility of keeping everyone under guard or surveillance. For
some convicts, the isolation of the far-flung paddock was liberat-
ing. Martin Cash, assigned to George Bowman at Wybong Run
near present-day Denman, wrote of working as a shepherd on the
isolated runs that 'though a measure cut off from society at the time,
our calm and undisturbed mode of life [was] free from the daily
annoyances and petty tyranny which at that time men of my class
were generally subjected to and which has ever been the bane of
my existence'.[13]

Daily annoyances and petty tyranny went to the heart of what
many convicts considered the main problems with the assignment
system under which they laboured. Even when they accepted their
sentence, convicts still expected to be treated fairly. Alexander
Harris, who wrote of his time working in the Hunter in the 1820s
and 1830s, noted that among working men there was a 'strong and
ineradicable and very correct sense of what is fair' and if masters
did not act in fairness, workers would 'assuredly endeavour to right
themselves'.[14] Brutal treatment could quickly lead to a breakdown
in order on an estate.

Lanarch appears to have employed a level of brutality that went
beyond the tolerance of his workers. As Mudie was so often absent,
it was Lanarch who ran the day-to-day operations, with a number
of witnesses at the inquiry hinting at his use of the lash and other
summary punishments to manage the workforce. The convict James
Brown, on loan to Castle Forbes from George Boyle White's estate,
reported that Lanarch revelled in being known as a tyrant, declaring that he would flog anyone who spoke against him. As if to prove
this, James Harvey, the only convict to speak up at the time, was
sent to the bench and received 50 lashes for insolence the following
morning.[15] In contrast, James Dodds, a free settler who had been in

the colony twelve years and with fifteen convicts assigned to him, testified that he rarely had any trouble and attributed it to 'myself being constantly with them, and I give them no cause to complain'.[16]

Dodds displayed a level of fairness that translated into a certain security as well. If the men complained of bad meat rations, he issued fresh meat; if offences on the farm were small, he refrained from sending them to the magistrates. He trusted his workers and was rewarded by having never been robbed. Likewise, George Wyndham, although not called to the inquiry, had escaped the rampaging gangs after one of his convict servants posted a note on his front fence saying Wyndham was a good master and was not to be robbed or hurt.[17] John Elliot, who—as described in the previous chapter—had been saved from an Aboriginal ambush near Segenhoe in 1826, also claimed to have been spared by bushrangers through his friendships and connections. Again it was the kindness of John's wife, Martha, that protected him. She had a reputation for tending the convicts on the estate, especially those who had been flogged, and had been taught a secret whistling code that served as a passport in the bush. At least once John had been bailed up near Segenhoe, only to be allowed to pass unmolested at the whistle of the Irish rebel song 'The White Boys of the Wicklow Mountains'.[18]

BUSHRANGING

The Castle Forbes men were not the first bushranging gang to roam in the Hunter. Since the convict station and the first farms in 1812, runaways had stayed in the area surviving on theft and raids. Even in the years after the convict station closed, the vast majority of those classified as bushrangers were, in fact, runaway convicts, most caught within days or weeks of their escape. The authorities in Sydney put much of the blame on absentee masters, which also emerged as a factor in the Castle Forbes revolt. Prior to the Castle Forbes incident, the worst year had been 1825, with numerous robberies and raids on isolated properties. While some estate owners assured the authorities that they could look after themselves when it came to desperadoes, there were others who called for more magistrates and constables to be appointed. These would protect the small settlers and have the added bonus of discouraging convicts from joining any gangs, keeping them in 'due subjection'.[19]

Of the early gangs, the depredations of that known as Jacob's Irish Brigade or Jacob's Mob were the most brutal. Between July and October 1825, the mob, made up of three men from Vicars Jacob's estate near Lambs Valley, as well as at least five others from other estates, including Mudie's, rampaged through the district. Much of their activity was through the middle and lower valley, ranging from Branxton to Maitland, and they hid out in the surrounding mountains as far north as Dungog and south into the Broken Back Range. Over four months, the gang robbed their master's farm and nine of his neighbours, abducted the wives of two settlers and torched the house of James Reid, who had sent one of them before the magistrates.[20] To add insult to injury, in August Robert Scott had captured the gang with help from some of his convict servants, other settlers and Aboriginal trackers, and had transferred them to the lockup in Maitland. Despite the men being in handcuffs, they had managed to overpower their guards, take their weapons and make their escape, continuing their depredations. Scott wanted the soldiers charged with neglect of duty.[21]

As Jacob's Mob ranged through the area, a hefty reward was posted for their capture. Francis Allman, the last commandant at Newcastle, sent a detachment of the Royal East Kent Regiment, better known as the Buffs, to join Scott in the hunt. The gang, now numbering five, were finally cornered in a hut near Hexham in October 1825. Leader Patrick Riley was shot and another member, Aaron Price, surrendered. Patrick Clinch (or Clynch), Lawrence

Cleary and Michael Cassidy all managed to escape but were caught by Scott and his group soon after. The four survivors stood trial and were sentenced to death.

In a twist, one of Jacob's neighbours, Alexander McLeod, who had also pursued the bushrangers, took the unusual step of writing to Attorney-General Saxe Bannister immediately after the trial, reporting on the treatment that the men had received at Jacob's farm. McLeod informed Bannister that Jacob had recently left the colony, he was rarely at his estate prior to this and the men were forced through desperation and hunger to take to the bush. He stated that 'this among many other instances of the same kind is one of the great evils arising from granting lands to non-residents'.[22] What influence McLeod's letter had is not known, but all four men were spared at the gallows and their sentences commuted to transportation to Moreton Bay and Norfolk Island.[23]

Jacob's Mob embodied many of the fears of the settlers on the Hunter. Magistrate Edward Close claimed that they were being assisted by emancipist farmers around the Williams and Paterson rivers, some of whom were transporting the bushrangers along the rivers in boats to avoid detection. He also thought that they had bribed Aboriginal groups and were paying for assistance and information. These claims reflect a deeper fear that the convict settlers had allegiances to their own class and could organise themselves against their former masters. A growing geographic knowledge and a social network of sympathisers made the bushrangers increasingly difficult to counter. Worse still, bushrangers and Aboriginal groups were possibly working together, at a time when skirmishes with Aboriginal groups were on the rise.

As we have seen, some convict runaways in the years of the penal station did work in collaboration with Aboriginal men to rob and assault their victims, and it would happen again. In 1831, George Clarke, otherwise known as George the Barber, a runaway assigned to Benjamin Singleton, was captured by mounted police on the Liverpool Plains. Clarke was said to have lived among the Kamilaroi people, disguised himself by blackening his face and skin and had the traditional scarified markings of a warrior. With a gang of bushrangers, Clarke roamed the Liverpool Plains and into the top end of the Hunter Valley. A settler said of him in 1832 that

> the only runaway who has succeeded in hiding himself from the police is a man of the name of Barber—who lives with the black natives beyond the range of civilised society—This man has by some artificial means made his skin resemble that of the blacks and has adopted all their habits of life, and very surely shews himself amongst his old comrades.[24]

LABOUR, POWER AND PUNISHMENT

As the Castle Forbes inquest continued, it was Lanarch, rather than Mudie, who became the focus. The convicts interviewed complained of his threats and bad treatment, and Lanarch himself admitted to striking more than one of the convicts involved in the revolt. He had whipped Michael Duffy and another with a riding crop. In his own words, 'I admit that I have corrected the boy Duffy and also Stack, with a strap of leather, and another time with a riding switch, and with a stick. I never punished them more severely than a younger brother and when I have done so, it was in aggravated cases.'[25] He had also beaten the young Patrick Ryan after Ryan had lashed out at him with a stick. Both men had also been sent to the magistrates afterwards, receiving a further 75 and 150 lashes, respectively. James Riley and John Perry, both involved in the revolt, were punished more than any other convicts at Castle Forbes in 1833. Riley had been sent to the bench six times and received 275 lashes, and Perry five times for a total of 200 lashes.[26]

Convicts were intimidated by the relationship between Lanarch, other estate owners and the local magistrates, rarely complaining for fear of being sent to the bench for punishment. It was the same issue that Governors Darling and Bourke had wrestled with during the Aboriginal resistance in the late 1820s. Convicts complained that Lanarch would concoct a charge to have a man flogged and that any word of complaint was taken as insolence or neglect of duty. Convicts believed that there was little use in taking any complaint to the bench anyway, as the magistrates were all friendly with each other and a fair hearing was unlikely.[27]

Small settlers also noticed. Edward John Eyre considered the magistrates fair in their treatment, but noted that their similar interests, occupations and backgrounds meant that they often held the same views when it came to convict discipline. On attending court to witness the proceedings against a neighbour's convict, Eyre noted that not one convict called before the magistrate escaped being flogged.[28] The punishment books that remain for the Singleton bench between 1833 and 1839 show that floggings were ordered 1146 times in that period, in nearly 60 per cent of all cases, while only 235, or twelve per cent, were acquitted or discharged. The rest were sent to the lockup, Newcastle gaol or an iron gang. The figures were much the same for other benches. At Muswellbrook, out of a total of 156 cases between October 1834 and March 1835, 91 of those charged were flogged (again, almost 60 per cent) with another 24 having their ticket-of-leave cancelled or suspended. Only thirteen per cent were acquitted or discharged.[29]

Although the law forbade a magistrate from presiding in cases involving their own servants, in the Hunter Valley the sitting magistrates supported their fellow gentlemen. At the Muswellbrook bench in 1832, 58 per cent of all convicts charged with breaches of discipline came from the farms of the two most active magistrates, William Ogilvie and John Pike.[30] This trend can also be seen at the Patricks Plains bench between 1833 and 1839. The highest recorded referral rate to the bench came from Robert and Helenus Scott (222), followed by Dr James Bowman (181) and the combined efforts of James Mudie and John Lanarch (201).[31]

Other questionable practices were also exposed. It appeared that the Singleton bench of magistrates was circumventing the *Summary Jurisdiction Act* by doubling up punishments, charging convicts for multiple offences on the same day and sentencing them to cumulative floggings. Cases abounded of extra punishments and multiple floggings. Lanarch and others were also involved in labour-swapping, moving convicts between estates, in some cases as payment for debts. James Brown, a convict originally assigned to George Boyle White, Mudie's other son-in-law, claimed to have been lent back and forth in exchange for goods and services. He had worked at White's farm, Mudie's, and on those of settlers John Howe and Henry Dangar. Maria White had also threatened him that if he complained he would be sent back to Mudie's and she would see him flogged there.[32]

CLASS AND SOCIETY

Perhaps the most interesting outcome of the inquiry was its re-ignition of the long-running antagonism between Mudie and his emancipist and colonial-born neighbours. One of the sore points in the district was work on Sundays. It was generally accepted that Sunday was a rest day, with church services or work that could not be done at other times the only activity. It was part of the moral code of conduct between masters and convicts. Mudie admitted to making some convicts work on Sundays, but they were compensated for it with extra rations, a day off during the week or extra pay. Lanarch also told the inquiry that men worked on Sundays, but usually during periods such as the harvest, shearing or when bullock drivers returned from the steamer at Maitland. It was a case of business as usual.

However, some of their neighbours contradicted them. James Chilcott, an emancipist farmer who employed only seven men, said no work was done on Sunday and he only ever saw Mudie's drays on the roads. James White, Bowman's overseer at Ravensworth, said men only worked at feeding animals as required. Nathaniel Powell, who was Robert Lethbridge's overseer, concurred. John Earl, William Brooks, James MacDougall and his brother Andrew also agreed. While it appears a small matter, it raised suspicion that other practices at Castle Forbes that were outside accepted patterns had also been going on for a lengthy period.

Ten years earlier, in 1823, as the settlement around Patricks Plains was in its infancy, district constable Benjamin Singleton had alerted Edward Close to Mudie working his men on Sundays. Five Sundays in a row, Singleton had witnessed Mudie's carts on the district roads. He claimed it was undermining his authority as a constable and making the muster of convicts difficult. Close was disappointed that Mudie was showing such contempt for the regulations and reported him to Sydney.[33]

The complaints ignited Mudie's deep-seated resentment of emancipist and colonial-born farmers, whom he considered a separate and lower class. This applied especially to Singleton. For Mudie, the purpose of the colony was to prolong the punishment of transported felons and have them labour for the landowner. Convicts were unworthy of trust, and this, in turn, extended to ex-convicts and their families. They could not expect the same rights or freedoms as wealthy emigrant settlers because of the infamy attached to them. To make his point clear, Mudie coined the term 'felonry' to describe convicts and emancipists as a way to distinguish them from his own class.[34]

The so-called convict stain was a real and powerful social barrier in Mudie's world. The problem with this attitude, however, was that the day-to-day running of an estate meant that one had to get along with convicts or emancipists, as they were the ones who did the bulk of the work. Mudie's own overseer was a former convict, Patrick Crehan. Indeed, as Patricks Plains and other settled areas began to coalesce into villages, most of the essential services were run by former convicts: mills, warehouses, river transport, inns, hotels, policing and just about everything else.

The bush constabulary was particularly heavy with former convicts or colonial-born men from convict families. Many, particularly those first- and second-generation colonial-born men, were the product of convict families. Their parents had worked for their freedom, and they considered the country of their birth as rightfully theirs. Wealthy emigrants who took up large estates made it increasingly difficult for some to gain a foothold.

When Mudie had returned to live on his grant in January 1823, he had found Singleton with his wife and family already on the land. Mudie had already clashed with John Howe over the land, but allowed Singleton to stay temporarily while his own grant was sorted. Mudie's grant had good access to the river and a creek, with rich alluvial soil and, importantly for the district, an area of higher ground out of flood reach. Singleton, who had already been flooded twice at the Hawkesbury and had a claim in for extra land, said Mudie was robbing him of the land he deserved. Mudie responded that in this part of the valley, he was the only one who could be called a 'gentleman settler' and that he had nothing to do with Singleton or any of his party in the way of social contact, pointing out to the magistrate Edward Close that 'Singleton is on a perfect footing of equality with his convict servants, mine or any he comes in contact with, in a word Ben Singleton (as they call him) is a fine fellow'.[35]

Mudie was not the only one who resented Singleton. John Earl, who took up land next to Singleton's on a sweeping bend in the Hunter at Patricks Plains, took exception to Singleton being a constable and considered him to be 'ill-disposed to all free settlers'. Singleton was, of course, a free settler himself, his only crime being that he was the son of a convict. There was little love lost between the two men. When questioned by Earl over the number of cattle he was keeping, Singleton told him that he and his companions would keep as many cattle as they liked and run them where they wished as 'the Government had no right to give so much land to free settlers and so little to those that are borne [*sic*] in the country'.[36] Singleton was subsequently dismissed as a constable and replaced by Earl, who, in turn, was dismissed after being accused in his role as local pound keeper of stealing sheep from the flocks at Mudie's Castle Forbes.

Mudie's sneering contempt for Singleton, and Singleton's own declaration of property rights, encapsulate the class tensions and land disputes that dominated colonial politics in the Hunter Valley. It showed a social divide between free settlers and emancipists that was so rigid at times as to represent a type of class system. Helenus Scott considered all small settlers as lazy drunkards, especially those settled on the alluvial river flats where soil was so rich that they hardly needed to work to grow their crops. His brother Robert had written home soon after arriving in Sydney in 1822, declaring that

a broad line is to be drawn between a convict and a free settler. Men of the lowest and vilest character suddenly raised to opulence know no bounds to their arrogance and self-conceit, and thus it is here. Their manners disgusting and their vanity insufferable.[37]

Houston Mitchell, Sir Thomas Mitchell's brother, also complained about his emancipist neighbours. Although his main property was at Walka, in April 1830 Mitchell took up land at Wallis Plains fronting Wallis Creek, a site known as *Yarawang* by the Aboriginal people who lived in the area.[38] Here, he regularly clashed with his neighbour, John Smith. Mitchell was surrounded by Smith's fences on three sides, with the fourth side of his property fronting Wallis Creek. The only dry access was via Smith's farm. From April to November 1830, the two neighbours squabbled and fought.

Smith was one of Macquarie's convict farmers, having come onto his land in 1818 after being a prisoner at Newcastle for twelve months before his appointment as chief constable at the penal station. By the time Mitchell arrived, Smith had gained his freedom, married and started a family. He had built a large house and inn on a lease at Newcastle, was trading wheat and flour from the government mill—which he ran—had boats sailing the trade route to Sydney and employed a number of convicts to work his farms. His Hazelwood estate at Wallis Plains was over 775 acres (314 hectares), on which he built another house and a series of cottages for his workers.[39]

Smith refused to survey the boundaries of his farm surrounding Mitchell or to allow an access road to be built. He also stopped Mitchell's convict workers from crossing his land to get to their work. Mitchell was forced into the humiliating position of having to negotiate with his emancipist neighbour for the right to access his own farm. As the brother of the surveyor general and a free settler, this was an intolerable position. Mitchell described Smith first as a complete pest, and later as a 'most incorrigible vagabond'.[40] His opinions were confirmed in his own mind upon finally discovering Smith's convict past: transported the first time in 1809 as James Sidebottom, escaped New South Wales in 1812 and returned to England, caught and retransported in 1814 before being sent to Newcastle in 1817. Houston wrote to his brother:

So much is the return of John, alias Gentleman, Smith coloured,
if he ever were in want again I am sure he would hang, he is one
of those characters so completely preposterously disgusting offing

[*sic*] several miserable airs of some men who go by the same appellation as himself.[41]

The saga ended with a public road finally being built to give access to Houston's land. Smith outlasted Mitchell in the area, dying in 1870 a wealthy property owner with land in Maitland and Newcastle.

The antagonism between Smith and Mitchell illustrated the different positions of the emigrants and the emancipists when it came to land and who belonged on it. Although locally influential, Smith would still have been at a disadvantage in his dealings with the likes of Mitchell. The one advantage he did have was his land and the control over access through it; an advantage that he used effectively to frustrate his new neighbour.

The convicts' awareness of their position in the economy was of particular concern to some. In 1835, convict William Rigby was confronted by his overseer over his apparent absence from work. Rigby told the overseer, Robert Patterson, that he did not give a damn about him and that he was better than him 'or any other freeman that came to the country'. Rigby continued, 'What would he [Patterson] or any freeman do if it was not for the prisoners?' When told to hold his tongue, Rigby replied that Patterson 'might bring him to hell' if he liked. He did—Rigby got 50 lashes for his insolence.[42]

Despite their numerical superiority, emancipists and the colonial-born children of convicts were never considered on an equal footing, at least not by their free emigrant neighbours. In the 1828 census, approximately 34 per cent of the valley population were identified as emancipists or native born, 52 per cent under sentence as convicts and just 13 per cent free emigrants, including some such as Sarah Hill, Frances King and Ann Morley, all free women with their husbands assigned to them.[43] Yet, despite their numbers, of the 119 farms granted before 1828 that were 500 acres (202 hectares) or more, only fourteen were owned by colonial-born or emancipist farmers.[44]

Although a certain amount of business contact was tolerated, mainly through necessity, social contact was still unacceptable to many. A settler in 1842 noted:

> I do not mean to say that, among the class called emancipists, consisting of persons who have been convicts, there may not be found men and women who have become thoroughly reformed and fit to adorn society. This, however, is the exception not the rule. A large majority of the class in question are quite unfit for any company but that of a low pot-house.[45]

Despite the apparent antagonism, the day-to-day reality was that emancipists were sought after as employees for their industry, integrity and standing in the community. An anonymous diarist wrote in 1832 that

> the emancipist is the most active and industrious, and consequently the most thriving class—from the discipline they have undergone whilst serving their sentence they acquire new habits and become inured to the climate—When their sentence expires or they obtain the indulgence of a ticket of leave they find they have everything to gain—they know that by honesty they will gain character and by industry wealth and in a short time they find character will do as much as capital.[46]

Many were re-employed by their former masters once they gained their freedom. George Wyndham at Dalwood re-employed some of his former convicts all the way into the 1850s, finding them better to deal with than free servants who 'had such airs it was better

without them'. One former convict, a 'great old character' named
Eugene, would scare the children with Irish folk tales and stories
of banshees.[47] Susan Caswell was also happy with her convict
servants, who she found steady and willing to work. Caswell also
had a convict cabinet-maker 'who makes excellent furniture. He
made me an elegant wardrobe and work table and is going on with
furniture for a good house.'[48] Convicts were also cheaper. James
Greig commented in 1826 that free people's wages were so high
that no farmer could afford to employ them for any length of time.
Thomas Blomfield at Wallis Plains thought servants or mechanics
(tradespeople) arriving free were a bad addition to a farm. They
came from England, where work was scarce but workers plenty, to
the Hunter, where it was the reverse. Many who came on a bond
left their employer as soon after their arrival as possible, knowing
that they could earn 'twenty times as much' selling their labour
elsewhere.[49]

Edward John Eyre, working in the upper Hunter, noticed that
nearly all the workers were former convicts and marvelled at
their well-behaved and industrious conduct. He thought it 'quite
extraordinary how well the men behaved considering their large
numerical majority compared with their employers and the manner
in which the latter are scattered about the country and separated
from each other'.[50] The threat of convicts organising themselves in
some form of rebellion was a key reason for the public execution of
Hitchcock and Poole at Castle Forbes. The foundation of the penal
station itself, way back in 1804, was, of course, triggered by the
convict uprising at Castle Hill the same year. However, there is little
evidence that the convicts in the Hunter considered the possibility
of any action as an organised class. As Hamilton Collins Semphill
wrote in 1833 while manager of Thomas Potter Macqueen's
Segenhoe estate, despite having the largest workforce of convicts in
the valley, as far as convict insubordination in his district went 'such

a thing does not exist, and has not existed nor do I have the slightest idea where it did exist or where it does'—runaways and bushrangers being the exception.[51]

In many cases, law and order was managed by former convicts in the roles of bush constables, lockup keepers and scourgers. Of the 66 overseers working in the Hunter in 1828, 48 were serving convicts, ticket-of-leave men or emancipists. This work could be potentially very dangerous, not just because of the need to chase and confront armed offenders, but because for many convicts it was seen as transgressing whatever class camaraderie might have existed among them. In February 1835, Thomas Dunn, a constable, previously assigned to John Rotton at Patricks Plains, and Michael Duffy, a scourger, both with tickets-of-leave, were attacked at a store by nine men. Dunn was knocked to the ground and kicked about the head until Duffy fought off the attackers.[52]

While there may have been some form of bond between convicts and emancipists employed in various roles, there was a clear distinction between those who gave orders and those who were expected to take them. Dunn had received his ticket-of-leave for his assistance in capturing a bushranger, an act considered by many convicts as one of betrayal. As he had been assigned to John Rotton at Patricks Plains, his background would have been no secret. As for Duffy, as a convict scourger he was considered close to the bottom of the pile, just one up from the hangman. As instruments of the law, both men needed to be careful, and when in this case they were caught outside their zones of authority, they were held to account by their attackers.

It was not just other convicts those employed in the law needed to worry about. Thomas Dunn was working as a constable for John Bingle of Puen Buen on Dartbrook, one of the local magistrates. Bingle sent Dunn to Segenhoe to apprehend John O'Donnell, also a constable, who had been dismissed for neglect of duty.

On presenting the warrant, O'Donnell snatched it away, refusing to go. Once O'Donnell was secured and on the road back, Dunn was stopped by Hamilton Collins Semphill, a settler, overseer at Segenhoe and magistrate, who not only refused to allow Dunn to continue with O'Donnell but, angered at Dunn's insistence, warned him 'to mind the consequences, for he would write immediately to the Government'.[53] The dispute had little to do with Dunn but, rather, was part of an ongoing tussle between local magistrates for power and influence. It was one in which the life of a ticket-of-leave constable such as Dunn, or O'Donnell, could be seriously impacted.

COLONIAL CLASS, CONNECTIONS AND REPUTATION

Class consciousness was as apparent among the emigrant settlers as it was between them and the emancipists. Many of the emigrants had known each other or their families in England, some even travelling to New South Wales on a recommendation. George Wyndham's mother wrote to him from England in 1829 to tell him they had located his house on Mr Dangar's map and to ask if a family friend, surveyor Felton Mathews, could seek George's advice and introductions when he arrived in the colony.[54] Mathews stayed with Wyndham and with James Mudie while working in the Hunter in 1830. Helenus Scott described Wyndham, whom he had known at Cambridge, in a letter to his mother as a gentleman with a fine wife and child and who now (in 1828) lived just ten miles (16 kilometres) downriver. In contrast, he advised his mother that they could not take on a 'gentleman' convict whom she knew and who was being transported as he would be useless to them and bring much trouble.[55] Mary Singleton wrote to her brother Joseph Sharling in Calcutta in 1833, advising him to prevent their brother Lawrence coming to the Hunter given the lack of available work.[56]

Many settlers took advantage of their connections when they first arrived. Thomas Blomfield had requested land near his army comrades Edward Close and Francis Allman at Morpeth; others stayed at various properties as they found their feet. A regular circuit for first-time visitors developed across the estates, with Alexander McLeod at Luskintyre, George Wyndham at Dalwood, James Mudie at Castle Forbes, the Scott brothers at Glendon, James Bowman at Ravensworth, George Forbes at Edinglassie and William Ogilvie at Merton all regularly hosting guests and visitors.[57]

Susan Caswell received an invitation in July 1830 from Mudie to stay with him while her husband, Lieutenant William Caswell, readied their new house at Tanilba, near Port Stephens. She and her two children stayed for two months. With Mudie and his daughters also in the house, it must have been quite cosy, as Castle Forbes was described by another visitor at the time as being humble, considering Mudie had lived there for eight years.[58]

Social connections were maintained through visiting, and were especially important for those isolated farms and estates. Edward John Eyre, at his farm close to Jerrys Plains at Leamington, recalled the 'innocent amusement' of visiting neighbours as an antidote to boredom. Mostly he visited on Sundays, as there was no church service close by. Dinner was often a feature of the day, but not all visits went smoothly. Eyre accompanied a visitor to a neighbour's farm one afternoon, only to find himself embroiled in an awkward stand-off between the lady of the house and his companion over the time for dinner. As it was the custom for most to eat early, they had arrived at two o'clock. However, with the eldest brother out working, they were told dinner would be at seven o'clock. Eyre's companion, put out by the inconvenience and calling it a great nonsense to wait for just one person, called the family to a vote, which he understandably lost. Only after they were embarrassingly forced to withdraw did Eyre discover that his companion was not well-liked by the family and any dinner invitation had been unlikely from the outset.[59]

Visiting served the purpose of more than just a convenient meal. With many more men in the valley than women, social calls were a way to begin a courtship. In 1835, Houston Mitchell excitedly wrote his brother that he was in want of a wife and had a high esteem for Jessie, eldest daughter of Mr Winder of Luskintyre. She was seventeen, pretty and properly educated, remarkably good-tempered and unaffected even though she was 'currency' (that is, Australian-born).[60]

Mary Singleton, like other wives on the frontier, could find life lonely and isolating. Although her family included seven children, she wrote to her younger brother Joseph in Calcutta in February 1824 in great excitement that, having recently obtained his address, she could now write to him after twelve years of not hearing from him. It gave her 'great pleasure to hear you are both alive and well' and would give their mother and father, also alive, equal pleasure to know of his situation. The only other letter to survive from her comes nine years later; aged 34 and now with ten children, she has grown accustomed to her situation, signing off to her brother 'I am settled'.[61]

No matter one's social connections, one's own reputation could be quickly sullied if disputes with neighbours escalated. Robert Scott realised this early. In 1825, he wrote to his mother:

> I wish you could see us my dear mother, I am sure it would make you happy—I believe we are very well liked and I am glad to see I have gained a good deal of praise in my duty as a magistrate . . . it is the only means I have in my power of making myself known.[62]

For those thought to be gaining advantage over their free, emigrant neighbours, reputations could be permanently damaged. Henry Dangar, assistant surveyor and the man charged with marking out grants, ran afoul of Peter McIntyre, agent for Thomas Potter Macqueen at Segenhoe, over land parcels claimed by both men. As a result of a series of complicated land surveys for multiple emigrants and Dangar's own personal interest in riverside land, McIntyre accused Dangar of selecting the best land for himself. His claim that Dangar refused to survey land for McIntyre and his employer, Macqueen, led to Dangar's eventual dismissal from government service in 1827, a point that was brought up in the Myall Creek trials eleven years later.[63] Ironically, in his attempt to defend himself, Dangar travelled to England and on the way drew up a survey map of the Hunter accompanied by an index and guide for emigrants that became one of the main publications encouraging more settlers to come to New South Wales. It was on this same map that Wyndham's parents had located Dalwood, and it was this map that won Dangar the position of surveyor to the vast Australian Agricultural Company, whose land flanked the northern edges of the Hunter.

Back at Wallis Plains, Houston Mitchell was also struggling with reputational damage, this time with his brother. Although Houston had occupied the estate at Walka and the other properties around Wallis Plains, it was his brother, Thomas, who owned them. Houston believed that the arrangement was he would pay the purchase price plus interest when the farm was viable. On this understanding, he had declared himself the owner of the land to anyone who was interested. Whereas Walka was dominated by low-lying swamp and marshland, his eight acres (three hectares) at Wallis Plains were alluvial and the crops sustained the entire enterprise. In 1833, after three years working the farm and as Houston began to drain more swamp to extend his holding, Thomas stopped him doing so, informing him that the land was not his and never would be. Worse, he put Walka on the market as his own, depriving his brother of his main residence and exposing the fact that he had never owned it. Horrified by his brother's actions and with his reputation tarnished in the community, Houston told Thomas 'you make me a liar a downright horrid liar, of all other characters the worst on earth'.[64]

As for James Mudie, despite the inquiry into his conduct finding there was nothing particularly untoward in his treatment of convicts and casting more blame for the situation onto his son-in-law John Lanarch, the very fact that there had been any questions raised inflicted enormous reputational damage. For two years, he led a local campaign against Governor Bourke and his administration, whom he blamed privately and in published pamphlets for both his situation and the apparent deterioration of convict discipline across the Hunter. Many of his neighbours supported him. Finally, Bourke, having had enough, refused to renew his commission as a magistrate and, like Edward Close and Robert Scott before him, Mudie's time was up. In January 1836, he announced that he was selling Castle Forbes and soon after returned to England. He published his personal account of the events of his last few years, including his views on Governor Bourke and those associated with him, most notably Chief Justice Francis Forbes and Judge John Kinchela. Titled *The Felonry of New South Wales*, it was seen by many back in the colony as a gross, libellous and self-serving publication and cemented public opinion against him. The final ignominy came in 1840 when, on an ill-advised return to Sydney, Mudie was confronted in George Street by the son of Kinchela, who struck and knocked him to the ground with a horsewhip. The £50 fine imposed on Kinchela was quickly paid via public subscription.[65]

CHAPTER ELEVEN

THE CONVICT VALLEY

The Hunter Valley was a rural, agricultural landscape for much of its colonial life, dominated by farms and estates with large populations of convict workers. Grand houses had begun to appear on some, surrounded by workers' huts and workshops, giving the appearance of small villages, while others remained as modest working properties unadorned by ostentatious developments. The only true urban settlement before the mid-1820s was Newcastle.

Throughout the years of the penal station, each of the nine commandants who presided over the settlement had also added piece by piece to an emerging town.[1] However, before the appointment of James Wallis in 1816, Newcastle remained a rudimentary outpost with a firm focus on the industrial employment of the convict workforce in the mines, the lime kilns, the saltworks and the timber gangs rather than the urban development of the station.

A rapid influx of convicts into New South Wales between 1815 and 1820 (with 14,000 being transported from England) corresponded to an increase in the convict population at Newcastle from 287 in 1818 to 1051 by 1821. On top of this were around another

115 people working in the civil and military detachments, including the commandant, storekeepers, superintendents, soldiers, officers, bush constables and their wives and families.[2]

By 1821, Newcastle had the appearance of a town, though it still functioned as a penal station. John Bingle, a shipowner who first visited in 1821, remarked on the tidy, whitewashed huts and government buildings set against the backdrop of the sparkling harbour and splendid ocean views but, having never before visited a convict station, was equally struck by the arbitrary power, severe discipline and punishment, which 'to a stranger's eye . . . seemed very un-English':

> Walking out with the Commandant [Morisset] to see the beauties
> of the harbour, the splendid ocean view, and above all the magnifi-
> cent and unrivalled prospect from the church close, and to give me
> an idea of the awe in which he was held, I found no convict passed
> us walking; all drew up, head uncovered, long before we reached
> them, and every coal cart drew up and stopped.[3]

Morisset was the final commandant of the penal station. When he was replaced in 1823 by Captain Henry Gillman, 3rd Regiment of Foot, the decision to remove the convicts to Port Macquarie had been made and the process was underway. Gillman arrived in December 1823, and by January 1824 there were only 200 convicts still at the station. Of these, 46 were in the town gang, 35 worked in the mines, sixteen were watching the herds, sixteen more sailed the government boats, seven worked in the police department, with the remainder spread through the town at various jobs. His orders were to get the number down to 100 and to find out how many convicts those settlers on the land needed, including the convict farmers and the first free arrivals. Gillman was also to inform the settlers that the government herd was to be relocated to Castle Hill, and that the 957 cedar logs on the beach near the lumberyard and eight of the 22 government boats would be sold by public tender.[4]

In what was possibly an early attempt to distance the emerging settlement from its brutal past, Governor Brisbane renamed Newcastle Kings Town in late 1822, honouring Governor King who had established it in 1804 and reviving its early, informal title.[5] Newcastle became the name of the parish, although most who lived in or visited the town, and all the colonial newspapers, continued to use Newcastle as the town name. Indeed, Kings Town gained no traction outside officialdom and was dropped in 1829, with Newcastle reinstated.

With the transformation from convict outpost to township, surveyor Henry Dangar was instructed to lay out a new town plan. Dangar's grid ran seven streets west, from Pacific Street to Brown Street, and three streets south, from Hunter Street to Church Street, with a large market square and reserved land along the waterfront. Allotments were allocated under lease to settlers who were taking up land in the valley, with each expected to build on their town plot within a set time or forfeit it. The intention of planning a new town over the top of the old convict station was all well and good, but Dangar ran into early difficulties on the ground when he discovered that some of those convicts and ex-convicts who had built huts, opened small shops and settled in were now in the way of his survey lines. As the plan required the demolition of some of these dwellings, 'considerable discontent prevailed'.[6] From the start of this new town, it had at its core a population of urban convicts, so recently confined to the place, now determined to maintain their right to land that they considered their own.

Although Dangar was laying the foundation of what would eventually emerge as the main city in the region, initially this plan fell flat. With the convict station gone and new settlers taking land further inland, the purpose of the town went from administrative headquarters to stopping point for ships and settlers going upriver. Although 47 allotments were taken up in the first year, the population dwindled to approximately 200 people. Work on civic projects such as the breakwater stalled, then stopped, and even the church, once the pride of the town, was deemed unsafe as its steeple threatened to collapse. The coalmines, still in government hands, were blamed for much of the trouble. Their inefficient methods, using convict labour to mine, hand-winches to extract and push-carts to haul the coal, kept their output to a minimum. In 1827, four years into its life as a free town, Newcastle was described by one visitor as going to ruin and in a state of decay, although with a few stores and warehouses and two 'tolerable inns' there was at least a hint of an entrepreneurial future.[7]

WALLIS PLAINS REINVENTED

While Newcastle struggled to establish itself on the coast, upriver the logical place for a new town was Wallis Plains. Governor Macquarie visited the outpost in 1818, naming the timber camp after the commandant at Newcastle, Captain James Wallis, and Wallis had the convicts there build a government cottage and barracks for Macquarie and his party to stay in. Set on a rise overlooking a deep-flowing creek, which Macquarie christened Wallis Creek, the hut and barracks offered expansive views over the convict farms along the river nearby and provided a good vantage point to spot absconding convicts or unauthorised travellers.

From here, soldiers could also look down on the growing settlement at Wallis Plains. As the furthest point navigable on the river for boats coming up from Sydney or Newcastle, it was here that a small commercial town took hold. By 1824, the nucleus of a village was forming. A wharf, a store for grain and some cattle yards had been built by James Mudie on the riverbank in late 1823, and by

July 1824 there were enough people coming and going for a regular boat service from Newcastle to be established. Named *Perseverance*, it ran twice a week—from Newcastle on Tuesdays, returning on Fridays from Wallis Plains.[8]

In October 1825, merchants William Powditch and Frederick Boucher opened a general store on the river at Wallis Plains run by their agent John Stronach. Powditch, who arrived free in 1821, first established himself as a trader in Sydney before taking an allotment from Dangar's plan in Newcastle. At Newcastle, 'having himself experienced the great want of a store or general warehouse', he built and opened one near the town wharf in June 1825 before following the opportunities upriver to Wallis Plains. The traders also ran a boat service, *The Comet*, between Newcastle and Wallis Plains to transport goods and produce for their customers and eventually established the first bank in the district, the Bank of Newcastle, in 1828.[9]

In 1828, their agent Stronach was working as a baker at Wallis Plains, with three horses and 53 head of cattle but no allocated land. His livelihood was based not on the produce from any farm or estate but, rather, on the provision of goods to those other settlers around the district; as such, he represents the first wave of true town-dwellers in the Hunter outside Newcastle. By late 1828, a brewery was nearing completion, as was a new inn, and a collection of stone houses was beginning to replace earlier slab and weatherboard dwellings.[10] The inn was George Yeoman's, the colonial-born son of a settler on the Hawkesbury. Yeoman had married Benjamin Singleton's eldest daughter, Elizabeth, before moving from Patricks Plains to Wallis Plains to build the Angel Inn. By 1829, the small village, clustered around the junction of the Hunter River and Wallis Creek, consisted of around 40 houses, most close to the river and subject to flooding.[11]

At the same time, another settlement was evolving around Edward Close's Illulaung estate at Green Hills. Close had been at Green Hills since 1821, with his wife Sophia Susannah Palmer, daughter of the former Commissary in Sydney, John Palmer. On the river below Close's house was a wharf, the highest point a boat could safely reach when the river was in flood. Moored nearby was the former convict transport *St Michael*, converted to a store ship for the district in 1826. Although less than five kilometres by land to Wallis Plains, the tortuous meandering of the river meant that it was over 24 kilometres by water, making Green Hills an attractive option for a new town. For the moment, however, the lack of roads was a problem. A bridle path suitable for a horse or for walking linked Newcastle and Wallis Plains but skirted Green Hills, which was hemmed in by swamps and marshland. The river became the major highway. For example, with no formed road or bridges between Newcastle and Wallis Plains, those wanting to take carts inland had to transport them by river first. At Powditch and Boucher's wharf at Wallis Plains, the riverbank was easier to negotiate, and so the road ran from there towards Patricks Plains, giving Wallis Plains the early advantage in attracting settlers. In February 1827, Molly Morgan's pledge to donate £100 towards building a school for children at Wallis Plains further cemented the settlement's early dominance.[12]

Molly's donation took two years to come to fruition, with tenders called in March 1829. A small brick schoolhouse was constructed near the government cottage on the rise overlooking the growing settlement below. This was the first school established in the Hunter Valley outside of Newcastle. Fourteen students enrolled in its first year under the tutelage of John and Susan Simpson. The school also held church services until the first church was built some ten years later. Another small but significant sign of progress was the establishment of a regular mail service between Newcastle and Wallis Plains the same year, with delivery to Patricks Plains coming soon after.[13]

As a community grew, the location and name of the official government town of Maitland was already being planned. In May 1828, Assistant Surveyor George Boyle White had been directed to make preliminary surveys for the town at Wallis Plains. The town was set to be built out of flood reach on the slope around the government cottage and barracks. It also took in part of the farm of John Smith, one of Macquarie's convict farmers and scourge of Houston Mitchell. On his farm, the roads from Green Hills and Wollombi intersected with the road from Newcastle at what is now East Maitland. A bridge over Wallis Creek on Smith's farm, built in 1827, allowed the road to pass onwards to Wallis Plains.[14] Always the entrepreneur, Smith built a series of cottages, a windmill, stores and hotels along the road and surrounding streets as the town was developed. By 1830, there were about 40 houses strung along the roadways, enough for Houston Mitchell to tell his brother, Surveyor General Sir Thomas Mitchell: 'I am quite contented to remain here for ever—my ideas are now concentrated on how I will remain if possible without a wish to go from Hunters River.'[15]

Meanwhile at Green Hills, by now linked by road to the new Maitland town, a wharf capable of serving ships coming from Sydney was joined by stores and warehouses to take the trade coming upriver and produce from the farms inland. In November 1831, the new steamship *Sophia Jane* made her maiden voyage from Sydney to Green Hills via Newcastle. Although her schedule was irregular, she was joined in February 1832 by the paddle-steamer *William the Fourth*, built at Clarence Town on the Hunter River for Joseph Grose, who had opened a store at Maitland in 1831. The two steam packets ran regular mail runs and passenger services using the *St Michael* as a wharf. The success and speed of the new vessels also served to divert traffic away from the mountain roads from Windsor, which were now largely used for driving stock to the valley or by those who could not afford a steamboat passage.[16]

In 1832, land sales began around Molly Morgan's at Wallis Plains. This effectively set up a three-way competition between Maitland as the government town (developing at what is now East Maitland), the private town around Close's land at Green Hills and the riverfront close to Powditch's wharf.

The rivalry was expressed no better than in real estate advertisements as town allotments went for sale. In 1834, with a sale of nine allotments at Green Hills on high ground, the sale notice promised:

The present site of the township of Maitland is 3 miles [5 kilometres] beyond the navigable part of the river, and otherwise disadvantageously situated, consequently, from superiority of position there can be no doubt this [Green Hills] will ultimately become the chief town on the Hunter.[17]

Advertised as Green Hills, the town that followed was officially named Morpeth in 1834, with Green Hills fading from the maps, plans and memories.

UPRIVER AT PATRICKS PLAINS

As the rivers had determined where the emigrant farmers took their land, so too did they determine, for the most part, where the towns would begin to form. For while water was a necessity for the success of any town, having to cross that water was often the seed for its development. The road from Wallis Plains to Patricks Plains had been taking settlers overland since 1822. At Patricks Plains, the road crossed the river at a ford on Benjamin Singleton's estate, passable except when the river was running high. By 1826, a small roadside inn, known as the Plough Inn, had been built by Singleton to accommodate travellers overnight. His brother Joseph took over its management in 1827. Although at this time there was no formal settlement, a traveller noted the possibilities:

Patricks Plains by reason of the extent and fertility of the land, is capable of supporting a very thick population, and some day or other must be a place of great consequence. At present there is neither magistrate, school nor medical man—the nearest doctor being forty miles [64 kilometres] away.[18]

Singleton's inn was a popular spot, made all the more so by the fact that Singleton also ran a punt across the river when it was high. The township was more embryonic than real, although with around 200 people in the district there was enough of a population to warrant a racecourse and an annual race day from July 1826. Of the four races run at the first meeting, Benjamin Singleton won the first, his business partner Otto Baldwin the second, his future son-in-law George Yeoman the third and his daughter won the last.[19]

A second inn did not appear at the crossing until 1833, when John Browne opened the Governor Bourke Inn directly opposite Singleton's, now being run by John Johnston as the Good Woman.[20] Even with two inns, there was hardly a town to speak of. A lockup, courthouse and post office made up the remainder of the building stock.

And so it was for the remaining town sites across the valley, where the appearance of an inn or a government outpost heralded the first stirrings of urban life. In 1832, the mounted police moved their headquarters from Maitland to Jerrys Plains to be closer to where they were needed. Upriver, a watch house was opened at Merton, with the court sitting at Ogilvie's house of the same name. John Bingle had a watch house and lockup built at Fal Brook (now Glennies Creek), with convict constable Thomas Dunn in charge. Nearby, Richard Alcorn, survivor of an attack by Aboriginal raiders in 1826, had opened the Greyhound Inn. A post office opened at Paterson the same year, with an inn at Black Creek, near the present town of Branxton, also operating by this time. Although progress was slow, each of these developments attracted something else to the area. Inns, mills, stores and stockyards became focal points along the roads that were slowly being surveyed up the valley. As with other colonial communities, the interdependence of buyer and seller, producer and consumer, encouraged further economic activity, which in turn provided an alternative to farming for new arrivals or ex-convicts with no land.[21]

ISOLATION

These emergent settlements were hampered for the most part by their isolation. Those beyond Patricks Plains were constrained by bad or, in some places, non-existent roads. The first roads had formed as a series of cart tracks made by those settlers heading inland to their grants, or later connecting the farms and estates to each other. Other than the road across the mountains from the Hawkesbury, roads were not a priority in the early years, as the open nature of the country above Wallis Plains meant that carts or riders could traverse the grassy plains between widely spaced trees with little difficulty. Where roads were made, Henry Dangar described the method thus:

> The first settler, or party of settlers, proceeding with their men,
> teams, and baggage into any new and distant country, having,
> as is usual before made a journey to such, and having obtained
> every information the Crown surveyors of the district can give,
> he or they, on entering upon the journey, keep two or three men
> following the carts, and with axes mark the trees, by fractures in
> the bark, denoting the route the carriages pursue. This done, the

settler's men can proceed back with the teams, and get up their second loadings without any apprehension of losing the road; and thus, in a short period, the track is so beaten.[22]

In this manner, roads radiated out first from Wallis Plains towards Patricks Plains, but did not connect back to Newcastle due to the swamps and marshlands found between it and Wallis Plains. As we have seen, a bridle path existed, but no proper cart road until the later 1820s. To further hinder the overland traveller, few if any bridges existed at the many river and stream crossings. There was no bridge at Wallis Plains until September 1827, meaning anyone arriving there after heavy rain needed to wait for the water to drop or cross by boat.[23]

Further inland, things were worse still. In November 1826, James Greig wrote to a friend in Scotland describing the situation:

The Roads in the County are not yet made so as to communicate from distant places with the Metropole or even with the nearest town with Carts but they are in progress from Newcastle towards my place however there is a good substitute namely a fine River free from any danger, by which the population send their grain or heavy commodity to Newcastle, and sell these or send them to Sydney by water which is seventy two miles [116 kilometres].[24]

The situation had hardly improved seven years later when Robert Scott was asked to give his opinion on the state of the roads to the colonial secretary. Only one main road ran into the valley, connecting Newcastle to Sydney over the mountains, with a branch that led to Wallis Plains and on to Patricks Plains. Scott lamented that 'Nothing can be worse than the engineering of this road—neither a knowledge of the country nor a desire to benefit the Public appear to have actuated the projectors'.[25]

The main road Scott was referring to is today known as the Great North Road, built by convict road gangs from 1826 and connecting the Hunter settlements to Sydney via Wisemans Ferry on the Hawkesbury. Surveyed by Thomas Mitchell, this route was to replace the earlier track forged by Howe and others. It remains one of the engineering marvels of the colonial era, speaking eloquently through the buttressed stone walls, carved culverts and dressed ashlar remains of the skill and hard work of those convicts, masons, overseers and surveyors involved.[26] The road opened for traffic in mid-1831, running from the Wisemans Ferry crossing, via Laguna and Wollombi where it branched north-east towards Wallis Plains. Later extensions from Wollombi to Patricks Plains, Broke and Jerrys Plains took travellers further up the valley. However, as the *Sophia Jane* steamship began running the same year, the road was soon being bypassed, with Robert Scott pointing out in his report that it had 'become comparatively of little value since the introduction of steam navigation'.[27]

The roads, as they came, did bring an increasing sense of permanency. They formed the links of a developing commercial web within the valley and made it easier to take produce down to the wharves at Wallis Plains and Green Hills. Inns were built at strategic crossing points or convenient stopping places, attracting stores, stockyards and other settlers, particularly convicts with a ticket-of-leave or those whose time had recently expired. Coaches also began to appear, making regular runs from the river wharves to the interior.

As those with a ticket-of-leave were restricted in their movements to the police district where it was issued, any work they might seek needed to be near at hand, and these developing communities provided some opportunity. An unknown letter writer in the Hunter in 1832 observed 'that emancipists are generally preferred as employees whether in Town or Country—and keen holding

Tickets of Leave are preferred to all others, owing to the great power the magistrate may exercise over them, and the well-known fact that they have all to gain'.[28]

An increasing number of trades and services became available to people, as shown in the number of workers listed in the Census of 1828. The brothers George and Richard Yeoman, with their young wives, all colonial-born, had a farm of 220 acres (89 hectares) as well as their inn at Wallis Plains. William Wrenshow and Richard Cooper, emancipist sawyers with no land, were both living at Wallis Plains, as was Thomas Wright, former convict stonemason, and James Fallan, a plasterer free by servitude. These men were likely engaged in timber-getting, carpentry and building in the district and in the growing community around Stronarch's store. At Patricks Plains, colonial-born Edward Bailis worked as a blacksmith. The Census showed him as owning two cows and twenty sheep but no land, so it is again likely that he worked around the estates as required, with his livestock acting as a type of living bank account and being agisted on someone else's property.[29]

In Newcastle, Richard and Ann Binder, both convicts sent there during its penal station phase, owned and operated the Australian Inn. When Richard died in 1830, Ann took over the licence and continued to run the hotel. She later moved to Patricks Plains, now Singleton, where she owned and ran the Union Hotel until her own death in 1857. Alexander Phillips, who arrived as a convict in 1818, ran a public house and a bakery in Newcastle. Opportunities also abounded for women to work in domestic service. Charlotte Capp, with a ticket-of-leave, was a housekeeper, with her two children, for Andrew Loder at Patricks Plains; Hannah Chapel, free by servitude, was the housekeeper for Joseph Trimbey, a ticket-of-leave convict originally on the First Fleet in 1788 before being sent to Newcastle in 1818. In Newcastle, Joanna Lane, free by servitude,

worked as the housekeeper for Owen Handshaw, former convict
and now brickmaker.[30]

These men and women represented the beginnings of an
emerging middle class of free, independent workers who were
neither indentured convict labourers nor wealthy landholders. They
were a new group between the master and servant class structures
that had dominated the Hunter Valley for almost 30 years. More
opportunities arose and, by 1841, the year convict transportation
ceased to New South Wales, 293 storekeepers, stock agents, brewers,
publicans, bakers, tailors, schoolteachers, bank managers, butchers,
merchants, dealers and other assorted tradespeople and businesses
were recorded in the valley. Professionals such as doctors, engineers,
solicitors—even a newspaper editor at *The Hunter River Gazette* in
Maitland—added to the numbers. Although comparatively few in
number, with convict numbers in decline they represented a significant demographic in the growing towns and villages.[31] The
short-lived *Hunter River Gazette*, published only between December
1841 and June 1842, represented the first independent voice for
the region. In January 1843, a new paper, *The Maitland Mercury and
Hunter River General Advertiser*, continued where the *Gazette* had left off,
and remains the oldest surviving regional newspaper in New South
Wales and an important regional voice in the Hunter Valley today.

Emancipist Henry Reeve was an example of what could be
achieved in these burgeoning towns. Transported in 1825, he was
assigned to Peter McIntyre at Segenhoe, where he worked primarily as a bullock driver. Being semi-literate and a trusted servant, he
was supported by McIntyre's successor, Hamilton Collins Semphill,
who encouraged him to marry one of the estate's servants, Mary
Grenville. Semphill then took them into his Sydney household,
where both obtained their tickets-of-leave. Returning with Semphill
to Segenhoe and then to Belltrees Estate nearby, Reeve was awarded
his conditional pardon in 1841, after which he and Mary moved to

West Maitland and took ownership of the Albion Inn. Over the next eleven years, until his death in 1852, Reeve established a coaching service, first from his inn to Morpeth, and then to Patricks Plains, where he also ran the mail coach. He built up a sizeable stable of racehorses and ran a livery business and a stud, eventually owning more than 90 horses. In 1846, he established the Maitland Jockey Club, which operated from the Albion Inn, before he purchased the larger Fitzroy Inn close by and relocated his interests there.[32]

Of course, many convicts had been urban or town dwellers prior to their conviction, with large numbers transported from London, Manchester, Liverpool and Dublin.[33] The growing towns, even with their basic public utilities and infrastructure, were familiar places for them. And while they had the potential to further entrench a social stratification wherein the emigrant landholders saw themselves at the top of the hierarchy, followed by colonial-born landholders, down through emancipists to the convicts themselves, they also provided a chance to subvert this hierarchy and provide new pathways to success.[34]

TOWNS GAZETTED AND CONVICT NAMES LOST

As many of the settlements grew organically, the government encouraged others through surveys and land sales. Assistant Surveyor George Boyle White, who held land at Mirannie, was responsible for surveying many of the towns in the Hunter, starting with a survey of Wallis Plains—which became West Maitland— in 1829. This was followed in 1830 with the gazettal of the town of Singleton on the banks of the river at Patricks Plains. As the first street plan was laid down within the grant of Benjamin Singleton, the new town took his name. Singleton was followed by Muscle Brook in 1834, later changed to Muswellbrook; Raymond Terrace at the junction of the Hunter and Williams rivers in 1835;

Scone, on Kingdon Ponds, and Wollombi in 1837; Aberdeen on a portion of the Segenhoe estate in 1838; Murrurundi at the top of the valley in 1839; and Merriwa on its western fringe in 1840. Later still, the village of Denman was set aside on the river opposite Merton, which had for a while looked likely to be the centre of development. The future coalmining town of Cessnock on the road from Wollombi appeared in 1853. Aboriginal people continued to live in and around these settlements as well, although they were increasingly pushed to the margins. Blanket distributions, which continued into the 1850s, recorded 68 people collecting blankets at Singleton in 1856, all using their traditional names as well as an English variant. A young man named Cumboo or Combine, with the English name Billy Goday, was one Singleton survivor who appears on the blanket lists from 1841 until the last list in 1856, by which time he also has a wife.[35] In 1842, Cumboo was the subject of a fine but unfinished portrait by colonial portraitist William Nicholas. The portrait shows a handsome young man with a steady gaze, dressed in quality European clothes. With the exception of Newcastle, which regained its name in 1829, and Wollombi, few if any of the new towns kept their convict names, each erased from the landscape as officialdom took hold. Wallis Plains, Patricks Plains, Green Hills, Invermein and Merton were replaced by Maitland, Singleton, Morpeth, Scone and Denman.

Newcastle, meanwhile, was beginning to rouse itself from its post-penal slumber. In 1825, the government coalmines had been leased for a period of 31 years to the London-based Australian Agricultural Company (A.A. Co.). The A.A. Co. had been established in London the previous year to undertake the 'Cultivation and Improvement of Waste Lands in the Colony of New South Wales', which they did on their vast Port Stephens estate. Their primary focus was the grazing of sheep and cattle, with mining an afterthought, albeit ultimately a profitable one. As part of the lease agreement at Newcastle, no other company or individual was permitted to mine coal without the permission of the Colonial Office, effectively handing the company a monopoly on the industry and making Newcastle a company town.[36]

The company, under the direction of engineer John Henderson, leased 500 acres (202 hectares) on the edge of Dangar's Newcastle town grid for their mines and wharves, and took over the running of the former government mines (which they soon after closed) and had the convict miners transferred to their supervision. Henderson returned to England in 1827, returning two years later with the new director, Sir Edward Parry. Following new negotiations, Parry was able to secure a further 1500 acres (607 hectares) of coal land for the company and began preparations to start the mines. The A.A. Co. came to dominate the development of Newcastle in these crucial years, with the majority of the population either directly or indirectly employed by or associated with the work on the mines. Newcastle had essentially been transformed from one type of company town, that of the government-operated penal station, to another, that of privately operated extractive industries.

Although mining did not actually begin until 1831, the company's use of steam engines and other new technologies meant that production increased year on year. A railway built in 1831 to take the coal from the pitheads to the ships on the harbour was the first built in Australia, predating passenger trains by 24 years.[37] This did not reduce the reliance on manual labourers for the work in the mines. As late as 1843, there were still 183 workers in the mines themselves, 120 convicts and 63 free miners including 37 migrant colliers from Scotland and Wales.[38]

Although the A.A. Co. business was booming by 1837, its monopoly on coal and its large land grant that encircled the town meant that Newcastle was still small. It was also still a very male-dominated place, just as it had been during the convict period.

The opening of the Newcastle Female Factory in 1831, for female convicts—first from the factory at Parramatta—to be held prior to assignment to households and farms in the district, made little difference in the ratios.

It was increasing calls for the break-up of the A.A. Co. monopoly and the cessation of convict transportation that would transform Newcastle's future.[39] As coal prices increased and more steamships and steam engines came into use, a number of colonial business-men began to challenge the A.A. Co. with proposals for new mines. The first to go into production was located on Reverend Threlkeld's Ebenezer estate at Lake Macquarie, with the first cargo shipped to Sydney in 1841.

In June 1846, Newcastle was declared a Free Warehousing Port, allowing goods and produce to be exported directly from Newcastle without having to go through Sydney.[40] The following year, more new mines began to open in competition with the A.A. Co., and its monopoly was discontinued. Part of its coal estate on the western edge of the confined city was subsequently opened for residential subdivision. For Newcastle and the Hunter, this was a turning point, ushering in a dramatic increase in the amount of ships sailing to and from the port, and a rapid expansion of the harbour facilities. For the farmers and producers inland, it became increasingly cost-effective to get their produce to Newcastle for export rather than resorting to the small river ports at Morpeth and Maitland. This was accentuated with the opening of the first section of a new railway between Newcastle and Maitland in 1857, allowing goods to be shipped direct to the harbour, bypassing the old river ports altogether. Newcastle re-emerged as the Hunter's primary urban centre, setting the pattern for the development of the region that continues to the present day.

EPILOGUE

In 1902, *The Singleton Argus* ran the obituary of local man Phillip Kelly, who had died aged 85. Kelly, originally a native of London, had been a resident of the Singleton area for 60 years and had left a wife, seven sons and two daughters, including my grandmother, Sarah. Kelly was respected by all who knew him and was an unofficial local historian, known for his many anecdotes and interesting reminiscences of the history of the town. The obituary did not mention that Phillip Kelly had been a convict, assigned to Robert Scott at Glendon, nor that his 60 years in the district referred to the time after his sentence of seven years had expired, rather than after he had actually arrived as a fifteen-year-old in 1834.[1]

It is hardly surprising that Kelly's obituary did not mention his convict past. A previous conviction was not deemed something worth reminding people of, be it as a colonial convict or a later prisoner, and Kelly had worked hard to establish himself in the community. He died at a time when convicts were being excised from the written histories of the Australian colonial past, despite their experience still being very much in living memory. It is likely that, as Kelly was a long-term resident of a small country town, many of Singleton's residents, particularly the older townsfolk, knew that he had been transported, as was the case for many of the families in Singleton and across the other towns in the valley. It was no secret in our family; my grandfather could remember the scars on his father's back from the floggings he received as a convict.

Kelly and his convict colleagues were part of what historian Tom Griffiths has called the suggestive silences of Australian history, where convict and Aboriginal histories, especially concerning cruelty or violence, were left out or glossed over as a footnote in the history of progress and development.[2] This was as much the case in the Hunter Valley as anywhere else. This dissolution of the convict memory obscured the true importance of their contribution to the character and development of the Hunter Valley and to its later success as an agricultural and industrial region.

As we have seen, those convict men and women lived on; many had families and moved into the fledgling towns and villages to take up a trade, open a hotel or start a business. Around half of those male convicts who remained in the area married, many to convict women or to women in the next generation of arrivals. Phillip Kelly, for example, married Bridget McGarry, a refugee from Ireland's famine, in September 1850. After Bridget died in the late 1850s, he remarried in 1861 to another recent arrival, Cecilia Sweeney, nineteen years his junior. Both lived on in Singleton into the first years of the twentieth century.

Thomas Dunn, the constable ambushed at Fal Brook in 1835, arrived with a life sentence in 1822. He was in the very first wave of convict workers into the Hunter after the closure of the penal station. Like Kelly, he also married and settled in the district, taking fellow convict Rose McGarry (no relation to Bridget McGarry) as his wife in April 1832. Thomas and Rose represent the other line of my family tree. Rose had arrived on the *Edward* in 1829, sentenced to seven years. Sent first to the Parramatta Female Factory, her involvement in a riot there saw her among the first women sent to the Newcastle Female Factory in 1831. Married the following year to Dunn, as the wife of a convict constable she saw the potential for violence on the frontier firsthand. She probably nursed Dunn after the savage beating, tending his cuts and bruises. But they too survived, moving about the valley until they settled close to Singleton, where they stayed.

These two families were like hundreds of others around them, trying to build lives and set down roots. Their success built families who stayed in the Hunter, setting the foundations for the valley as we know it today.

ACKNOWLEDGEMENTS

What a curious thing it is to write a book: a solitary pursuit supported by so many. Like many Australian histories, this book began its life as a PhD thesis. Its transformation from there to here is thanks in no small part to the following people.

Way back when it all started, and then all the time since, I have been generously supported with advice, encouragement and sound direction by two mentors, now both esteemed colleagues and friends—Sharon Veale and Grace Karskens. Both have continued to inspire and help me through the challenge of bringing this story to life in a new form. Sharon gave me the push I needed to commence this journey. Grace's work on colonial Sydney, convict workers, Aboriginal history and the Australian environment has shifted the perspectives of many historians, me included, to allow a more full, more complex and more interesting view of our history.

I am indebted to the librarians and staff of the State Library of New South Wales whose help with the vast collections held by the library was invaluable. During the writing of this book, I was privileged to have been the C.H. Currey Fellow at the library and a Visiting Fellow, both under the library's generous fellowship program. Amongst the many who helped me, special thanks is due to Mitchell Librarian Richard Neville, to Rachel Franks, Andy Carr, Melissa Brooks, Kirsten Thorpe, Melissa Jackson, Ronald Briggs, Jessica Harris, Cathy Perkins and Joy Lai. Linda Brainwood, picture researcher extraordinaire, more than once guided me through picture research difficulties.

John Maynard and Ray Kelly have both helped me understand better the intricacies of the Aboriginal history and languages of the Hunter Valley, as did Laurie Perry in Singleton. Their generosity and patience with my questions and queries are much appreciated.

I have thrown ideas and questions at many friends and colleagues in Sydney, Newcastle and the Hunter Valley. Thank you, Lyndall Ryan, Nancy Cushing and Julie McIntyre, for your help on Newcastle and the Hunter; thanks also to Paul Irish, Michael Bennett and Stephen Gapps for your advice on Aboriginal history, interactions and frontier fighting. Also to Peter Hobbins, Laila Ellmoos, Margo Beasley, Tanya Evans, Ian Hoskins, Chris Cunneen, Beverly Kingston, Terry Kass, Carol Liston, Matthew Kelly, Jim Casey, and the multitude of other historians, archaeologists, friends and specialists I have consulted, asked questions of or simply talked things over with in the course of researching and writing *The Convict Valley*.

I would particularly like to acknowledge Elizabeth Weiss at Allen & Unwin. I was first introduced to Elizabeth via Babette Smith, a fellow historian of the colonial and convict past who encouraged me to pitch the idea. I was delighted when Elizabeth agreed to my proposal and I have benefitted enormously from her expertise. Thanks also to Courtney Lick for the editing and production.

Thank you to Cecilie Knowles, graphics extraordinaire. Your maps make the words make sense. And to Stuart Sutherland, who asked more direct questions over beers at the pub than I cared to answer, but which made me think harder on the book's subject than almost any other interrogation.

This book would not have been possible without the love and support of my family, particularly my mother Ruth, and the endless stories and tales of our family from my late father Mick. Both are descended from first generation Hunter Valley convicts and are proof that convicts stayed on and made lives in the Hunter. Thank you also to my siblings Jane, Fran, Catherine and Peter, who have been as enthusiastic about the project as I have.

The biggest thank you is for Lisa Murray, fellow historian, confidant and beautiful partner; your encouragement, advice, love and support—even as you had your own book to write, job to hold down and me to deal with—made the whole thing possible.

NOTES

CHAPTER ONE: THE VALLEY

1 D.J. Ryan, 'The discovery and first settlement of Newcastle and genesis of the coal industry', *Journal of the Royal Australian Historical Society (JRAHS)*, 1923, vol. IX, part V, p. 230.

2 B. Nashar, *The Geology of the Hunter Valley*, Sydney: The Jacaranda Press, 1964, p. 44.

3 T.W. Edgeworth David and F.B Guthrie, 'The flood silt of the Hunter and Hawkesbury rivers', *Journal and Proceedings of the Royal Society of NSW*, 1904, vol. 38, p. 195.

4 *Hunter, Karuah and Manning Catchments: State of the Rivers and Estuaries Report*, Sydney: NSW Department of Land and Water Conservation, 2000, p. 14.

5 Edgeworth David and Guthrie, 'The flood silt of the Hunter and Hawkesbury rivers', p. 199.

6 M. Kovac and J.W. Lawrie, *Soil Landscapes of Singleton: 1:250 000 Sheet*, Sydney: Soil Conservation Service of NSW, 1991, pp. 23–4; S.K. McInnes-Clark, *Soil Landscapes of the Murrurundi 1:100 000 Sheet*, Gosford: Department of Land and Water Conservation, 2002, p. 10.

7 *Upper Hunter Aboriginal Heritage Baseline Study prepared for Upper Hunter Aboriginal Heritage Trust*, prepared by Environmental Resources Management (ERM) Australia, October 2004, p. 53; M. Koettig, 'Regional Study of Heritage Significance. Central Lowlands, Hunter Valley Electricity Commission Holdings', *A Report to the Electricity Commission in Three Volumes: Assessment of Aboriginal Sites*, vol. 3, 1990, p. 24. See also ERM, *Upper Hunter Aboriginal Heritage Baseline Study*, p. 68. Dates in the range of 20,000 to 35,000 years

ago are within the period of the Last Glacial Maximum, the last ice age. See V. Attenbrow, *Sydney's Aboriginal Past: Investigating the archaeological and historical records*, 2nd edn, Sydney: UNSW Press, 2010, pp. 152–3 for a discussion of this period and its impact on Aboriginal occupation patterns.

8 ERM, *Upper Hunter Aboriginal Heritage Baseline Study*, p. 52.

9 H. Brayshaw, *Aborigines of the Hunter Valley: A study of colonial records*, Scone: Scone and Upper Hunter Historical Society, Bicentennial Publication No. 4, 1988, p. 153.

10 J. Maynard, 'Muloobinbah (Newcastle) and Aboriginal industrial presence: past and present', *JRAHS*, December 2001, vol. 87, part 2, p. 250.

11 W. Scott, *Recollections: The blacks of Port Stephens*, prepared by Gordon Bennett, Dungog, 1929, pp. 19–20.

12 N. Gunson (ed.), *Australian Reminiscences and Papers of L.E. Threlkeld: Missionary to the Aborigines 1824–1859*, two volumes, Canberra: Australian Institute of Aboriginal Studies, 1974, p. 54.

13 Maynard, 'Muloobinbah (Newcastle) and Aboriginal industrial presence', p. 250.

14 Bill Gammage, *The Biggest Estate on Earth: How Aborigines made Australia*, Sydney: Allen & Unwin, 2011, p. 157.

15 D.B. Rose, *Nourishing Terrains: Australian Aboriginal views of landscape and wilderness*, Canberra: Australian Heritage Commission, 1996, p. 63.

16 Gammage, *The Biggest Estate on Earth*, pp. 157–77.

17 Gammage, *The Biggest Estate on Earth*, p. 169.

18 D.R. Moore, 'Results of an archaeological survey of the Hunter River Valley, New South Wales, Australia: Part 2: Problems of the lower Hunter and contacts with the Hawkesbury Valley', *Records of the Australian Museum*, February 1981, vol. 33, no. 6–9, p. 422.

19 Moore, 'Results of an archaeological survey of the Hunter River Valley', p. 422. Chert is also classified as indurated mudstone, which occurs extensively through the Permian coal seams of the upper valley and can be obtained from river pebbles. See Philip Hughes, *NSW National Parks and Wildlife Service, Hunter Valley Region Archaeology Project Stage 1*, vol. 1, prepared by ANU Archaeological Consultancies, November 1984.

20 Brayshaw, *Aborigines of the Hunter Valley*, p. 41.

21 Moore, 'Results of an archaeological survey of the Hunter River Valley', p. 389.

22 J. Miller, *Koori: A will to win*, Sydney: Angus & Robertson, 1985, p. 1.

23 Gunson (ed.), *Australian Reminiscences*, p. 65.

24 W.J. Needham, *Burragurra: Where the spirit walked—The Aboriginal relics of the Cessnock–Wollombi region in the Hunter Valley of NSW*, Cessnock: Author, 1981, p. 10.

25 M. Thomas, *The Many Worlds of R.H. Mathews: In search of an Australian anthropologist*, Sydney: Allen & Unwin, 2012, p. 237.

CHAPTER TWO: FIRST CONTACT

1 Captain Cook's Journals, National Library of Australia, <http://southseas. nla.gov.au/journals/cook/17700510.html>.

2 W. Tench, *Sydney's First Four Years: being a reprint of a narrative of the expedition to Botany Bay and a complete account of the settlement at Port Jackson*, Sydney: Angus & Robertson, 1961, p. 181. Also D. Collins, *An Account of the English Colony in New South Wales*, vol. 1, London: T. Cadell and W. Davies, 1798, p. 136.

3 Collins, *An Account of the English Colony in New South Wales*, vol. 1, p. 426.

4 Collins, *An Account of the English Colony in New South Wales*, vol. 1, pp. 425–6.

5 J. Fraser (ed.), *An Australian Language as Spoken by the Awabakal, the People of Awaba or Lake Macquarie Being an Account of their Language, Traditions and Customs by L.E. Threlkeld*, Sydney: Government Printer, 1892, p. 49.

6 Collins, *An Account of the English Colony in New South Wales*, vol. 1, pp. 484–5.

7 Ryan, 'The discovery and first settlement of Newcastle', p. 230.

8 Ryan, 'The discovery and first settlement of Newcastle', p. 230.

9 Brayshaw, *Aborigines of the Hunter Valley*, p. 41.

10 J. Maynard, *Callaghan, The University of Newcastle: Whose traditional land?*, research paper for Department of Aboriginal Studies and The University of Newcastle, 2000, p. 13.

11 P. Irish, *Hidden in Plain View: The Aboriginal people of coastal Sydney*, Sydney: NewSouth Publishing, 2017, p. 25.

12 *Historical Records of Australia (HRA)*, series I, vol. III, note 66, p. 772.

13 G.P. Walsh, 'Hacking, Henry (1750–1831)', *Australian Dictionary of Biography*, vol. 1, Melbourne: Melbourne University Press, 1966, pp. 497–8.

14 D. Collins, *An Account of the English Colony in New South Wales*, vol. 2, London: T. Cadell and W. Davies, 1802, p. 204.

15 Collins, *An Account of the English Colony in New South Wales*, vol. 2, p. 205.

16 Collins, *An Account of the English Colony in New South Wales*, vol. 1, p. 81.

17 Lieutenant Colonel Paterson to Governor King (King's Papers), *Historical Records of New South Wales (HRNSW), Hunter and King*, 1800–1802, vol. IV, Sydney: Government Printer, 1896, p. 416.

18 G. Karskens, *The Colony: A history of early Sydney*, Sydney: Allen & Unwin, 2009, p. 285.

19 T. Flannery (ed.), *Terra Australis: Matthew Flinders' great adventures in the circumnavigation of Australia*, Melbourne: Text Publishing, 2005, p. 34.

20 M. Dunn, 'Aboriginal guides in the Hunter Valley, New South Wales', in T. Shellam, M. Nugent, S. Kinoshi and A. Cadzow (eds), *Brokers and Boundaries: Colonial exploration in Indigenous territory*, Canberra: ANU Press, 2016, p. 63; H. Reynolds, *Black Pioneers: How Aboriginal and Islander People helped build Australia*, Ringwood: Penguin, 2000, p. 34.

21 K.H. Clouten, *Reid's Mistake: The story of Lake Macquarie from its discovery until 1890*, Lake Macquarie: Lake Macquarie Shire Council, 1967, p. 9. In an unfortunate first, the *Martha* is also the first-known Australian-built ship to be wrecked on the New South Wales coast. Returning from Reids Mistake with a load of coal in August 1800, she was driven ashore near Little Manly, north of Sydney Harbour.

22 J. Grant, *The Narrative of a Voyage of Discovery performed in His Majesty's Vessel The Lady Nelson, of sixty tons burthern, with sliding keel in the years 1800, 1801 and 1802 to New South Wales*, facsimile edition, Adelaide: Libraries Board of South Australia, 1973, p. 151.

23 Surgeon Harris to Governor King (King's Papers), 25 June 1801, *HRNSW*, vol. IV, p. 417.

24 Lieutenant Colonel Paterson's Journal, 1801–1802, *HRA*, series I, vol. III, 1915, Library Committee of the Commonwealth Parliament, Canberra, p. 176. Freshwater Bay was the name given to an inlet on the western side of what is now Stockton, most likely Fullerton Cove. 'Where the rivers meet' is the junction of the Hunter and Williams rivers near present-day Raymond Terrace.

25 Harris to Governor King, 25 June 1801, *HRNSW*, vol. IV, p. 417.

26 Paterson to Governor King, 25 June 1801, *HRNSW*, vol. IV, p. 415.

27 Letter received by Sir Joseph Banks from Charles Francis Greville, April 1802, including excerpt from Ensign Barrallier to Greville c. 1802, Banks Papers, series 23.25, State Library of New South Wales (SLNSW).

28 Lieutenant Grant's Journal at Hunter River, 1801–1802, *HRA*, series I, vol. III, p. 174.

29 Paterson to Governor King, *HRNSW*, vol. IV, p. 415; Grant, *The Narrative of a Voyage of Discovery*, p. 153.

30 Grant, *The Narrative of a Voyage of Discovery*, pp. 154–5.

31 Gammage, *The Biggest Estate on Earth*, pp. 199–213; B. Pascoe, *Dark Emu Black Seeds: Agriculture or accident?*, Broome: Magabala Books, 2014, pp. 53–8.

32 J. Grant, Remarks, &c., on board his Majesty's armed surveying vessel, Lady Nelson, in Hunter River, 1801, *HRNSW*, vol. 4, pp. 404–9.

33 Grant, *The Narrative of a Voyage of Discovery*, p. 158.

34 L.E. Threlkeld, *An Australian Grammar, Comprehending the Principals and Natural Rules of the Language Spoken by the Aborigines in the Vicinity of Hunter's River, Lake Macquarie &c*, Sydney: Stephens & Stokes, 1834, p. xii.

35 Grant, *The Narrative of a Voyage of Discovery*, p. 165.

36 R. Neville, *Mr JW Lewin: Painter & Naturalist*, Sydney: NewSouth Publishing, 2012, pp. 69–71.

37 Grant, *The Narrative of a Voyage of Discovery*, p. 159.

38 Grant, Remarks, &c., pp. 404–9.

39 Orders regulating coal and timber trade, *HRA*, series 1, vol. III, p. 257.

40 Governor King to the Duke of Portland, 21 August 1801, *HRNSW*, vol. 4, p. 476.

41 W.A. Wood, *Dawn in the Valley: The early history of the Hunter Valley settlement*, Sydney: Wentworth Books, 1972, p. 1.

42 Mason to Governor King, 21 November 1801, *HRNSW*, vol. 4, p. 627.

43 Mason to Governor King, 24 October 1801, *HRNSW*, vol. 4, p. 597.

44 Ryan, 'The discovery and first settlement of Newcastle', p. 258.

45 Observation by Surveyor Grimes on Hunters River, *HRA*, series 1, vol. III, pp. 413–15.

46 *HRA*, series I, vol. III, note 71, p. 774.

47 J.F. Atchinson, 'Australian place-names and cartographers', *Cartography*, March 1982, vol. 12, no. 3, p. 151.

48 Maynard, 'Muloobinbah', pp. 248–9; G. Albrecht, *Rediscovering the Coquun: Towards an environmental history of the Hunter River*, Newcastle: The University of Newcastle Cultural Collections, 2000, pp. 1–4.

49 Mason to Governor King, 21 November 1801, *HRNSW*, vol. 4, p. 627.

50 Brayshaw, *Aborigines of the Hunter Valley*, p. 60; Attenbrow, *Sydney's Aboriginal Past*, p. 87. Letter received by Sir Joseph Banks from Charles Francis Greville, April 1802, including excerpt from Ensign Barrallier to Greville c. 1802, Banks Papers, Series 23.25, SLNSW.
51 Ryan, 'The discovery and first settlement of Newcastle', p. 257.

CHAPTER THREE: A CONVICT OUTPOST

1   Karskens, *The Colony*, p. 295.
2   Instructions of Governor Philip Gidley King to Lieutenant Charles Menzies on establishment of the settlement at Newcastle, 15 March 1804, Philip Gidley King Letterbooks (3) 1788–1808, SLNSW, MLMSS 582.
3   *The Sydney Gazette (SG)*, 1 April 1804, p. 2. The others accompanying Menzies included former Sergeant of the Marines Isaac Knight as superintendent of convicts, John Tucker as storekeeper and James Mileham as surgeon.
4   J.W. Turner (ed.), *Newcastle as a Convict Settlement: The evidence before J.T. Bigge in 1819–1821*, Newcastle History Monographs No. 7, Newcastle: Newcastle Regional Public Library, 1973, pp. 13, 53.
5   Turner (ed.), *Newcastle as a Convict Settlement*, p. 142.
6   King to Menzies, *HRA*, series 1, vol. V, pp. 412–17.
7   Robert Brown Correspondence, *Diary of a Journey to Australia 1801–04*, 13 October 1804, Australian Joint Copying Project, SLNSW, M2494.
8   King to Menzies, 15 March 1804, Philip Gidley King Letterbooks (3) 1788–1808, SLNSW, MLMSS 582.
9   J.W. Turner, *Coal Mining in Newcastle 1801–1900*, Newcastle History Monographs No. 9, Newcastle: Newcastle Regional Public Library, 1982, p. 19.
10 D. Roberts and D. Garland, 'The forgotten commandant: James Wallis and the Newcastle penal settlement, 1816–1818', *Australian Historical Studies*, 2010, vol. 41, no. 1, p. 9; G. Karskens, *The Rocks: Life in early Sydney*, Melbourne: Melbourne University Press, 1997, p. 166.
11 King to Menzies, 12 November 1804, Philip Gidley King Letterbooks (3) 1788–1808, SLNSW, MLMSS 582.
12 Turner, *Coal Mining in Newcastle*, p. 17
13 Turner, *Coal Mining in Newcastle*, p. 18.
14 Brown, *Diary of a Journey to Australia*, 16 October 1804.
15 Thompson to Campbell, 24 July 1815, CS, New South Wales State Archives (NSWSA), NRS 937 [4/1805].

16 Patrick Riley, convict carpenter at Newcastle, noted in evidence to Bigge in January 1820 that the timbers being harvested in the Hunter Valley were cedar (*Toona ciliata*), rosewood (*Dysoxylum fraserianum*), flooded gum (*Eucalyptus grandis*), ironbark (*E. sideroxylon* and *E. paniculata*), spotted gum (*Corymbia maculata*), pine (brush cypress, *Callitris macleayana*), beefwood (*Stenocarpus salignus*), honeysuckle red (*Banksia serrata*) and white (*B. integrifolia*), paperbark (*Melaleuca quinquenervia*) as well as mangrove used for wheelwork (*Avicennia marina*), stringybark (*E. sparsifolia*) and Sydney blue gum (*E. saligna*). Turner (ed.), *Newcastle as a Convict Settlement*, p. 168.

17 Sergeant John Evans, Superintendent of Government Works, evidence to Bigge, 18 January 1819, in Turner (ed.), *Newcastle as a Convict Settlement*, p. 91.

18 J.W. Turner, *Manufacturing in Newcastle 1801–1900*, Newcastle History Monographs No. 8, Newcastle: Newcastle Regional Public Library, 1980, p. 15.

19 Menzies to King, 1 July 1804, *HRA*, series I, vol. V, p. 415.

20 Menzies to King, 1 July 1804, *HRA*, series I, vol. V, p. 416.

21 Menzies to King, 1 July 1804, *HRA*, series I, vol. V, p. 416.

22 *SG*, 29 July 1804, p. 3.

23 *SG*, 18 November 1804, p. 3; *HRNSW*, vol. V, King 1803, 1804, 1805, pp. 482–3.

24 Menzies to King, 28 November 1804, *HRA*, series I, vol. V, p. 425.

25 S. Gapps, *The Sydney Wars: Conflict in the early colony 1788–1817*, Sydney: NewSouth Publishing, 2018, p. 149.

26 King to Menzies, 24 November 1804, Philip Gidley King Letterbooks (3) 1788–1808, SLNSW, MLMSS 582.

27 Purcell to Campbell, 21 July 1810, 4/1804; Thomas Thompson to Campbell 21 June 1814, 4/3493; Thomas Thompson to Campbell, 12 January 1816, CS Special Bundles–Newcastle, NSWSA, NRS 898 [4/3494].

28 Campbell to Thompson, 1 August 1815, CS, NSWSA, NRS 898 [4/3494].

29 Turner, *Manufacturing in Newcastle*, p. 16; Turner, *Coal Mining in Newcastle*, p. 17.

30 Turner, *Manufacturing in Newcastle*, p. 18.

31 Turner (ed.), *Newcastle as a Convict Settlement*, p. 59.

32 King to Menzies, 7 June 1804, Philip Gidley King Letterbooks (3) 1788–1808, SLNSW, MLMSS 582.

33 King to Menzies, 24 September 1804, Philip Gidley King Letterbooks (3) 1788–1808, SLNSW, MLMSS 582.

34 Lachlan Macquarie, *Journal of a Tour to and from Newcastle*, 27 July 1818–9 August 1818, SLNSW, A781, p. 13.

35 King to Hobart, 14 August 1804, *HRA*, series I, vol. V, pp. 111–15.

36 Turner (ed.), *Newcastle as a Convict Settlement*, pp. 228–53.

37 *SG*, 9 October 1804, p. 4.

38 Menzies to King 1 July 1804, *HRA*, series I, vol. V, pp. 412–17.

39 Menzies to King, *HRA*, series I, vol. V, 30 April 1805, p. 420.

40 *SG*, 8 March 1807, p. 2; CS Special Bundles–Newcastle, NSWSA, NRS 898 [4/1804], p. 6a; [4/1805], p. 135; [4/1806], p. 44; [4/1806], p. 76; [4/1758], p. 145.

41 Campbell to Wallis, 31 August 1816, CS, NSWSA, NRS 897 [4/3495].

42 CS Special Bundles–Newcastle, NSWSA, NRS 898. For the years 1810–1825, there were only six confirmed reports of Aboriginal men spearing runaway convicts from Newcastle.

43 *Album of Original Drawings by Captain James Wallis and Joseph Lycett*, c. 1817–18, SLNSW, SAFE/PXE 1072.

44 *SG*, 6 December 1820, p. 2; *SG*, 23 December 1820, p. 4.

45 Court of Criminal Jurisdiction Case Papers Nov/Dec 1820, Part II, NSWSA, SZ792 COD452B; Return of Prisoners Punished at Newcastle, 31 October 1820, CS Special Bundles–Newcastle, NSWSA, NRS 898 [4/1718].

46 M. Dunn, 'Exploring connections: Bungaree and connections in the colonial Hunter Valley', in G. Dooley and D. Clode (eds), *The First Wave: Exploring early coastal contact history in Australia*, Adelaide: Wakefield Press, 2019, p. 238.

47 Wallis to Campbell, 14 May 1817, CS, NSWSA, NRS 897 [4/1806].

48 E. Braggett, '150 years of continuous education: Newcastle East Public School', *The Education Gazette*, 2 May 1966, p. 104.

49 Turner, *Coal Mining in Newcastle*, p. 19.

50 J. McPhee (ed.), *Joseph Lycett: Convict artist*, Sydney: Historic Houses Trust of New South Wales, p. 95.

51 E. Ellis, *Rare & Curious: The secret history of Governor Macquarie's collectors' chest*, Melbourne: The Miegunyah Press, 2010, pp. 132–7; J. Maynard, *True Light and Shade: An Aboriginal perspective of Joseph Lycett's art*, Canberra: NLA Publishing, 2014, pp. 8–10.

52 Maynard, *True Light and Shade*, p. 6.

53 E.C. Close, *New South Wales Sketchbook: Sea voyage, Sydney, Illawarra, Newcastle, Morpeth 1817–1840*, SLNSW, PXA1187; E.C. Close, *Sketchbook of scenes of Sydney, Broken Bay, Newcastle and region, New South Wales*, 1817–40 NLA Pic Drawer 8631.

54   J.H. Vaux, *The Memoirs of James Hardy Vaux including his Vocabulary of the Flash Language*, edited by Noel McLachlan, London: Heinemann, 1967.

55   Government and General Orders, 24 December 1819, CS, NSWSA, NRS 897 [SZ759].

56   Farrell to Bligh, 29 January 1810, CS, NSWSA, NRS 897 [4/1804].

57   Purcell to Campbell, 9 July 1811, CS, NSWSA, NRS 897 [4/1804].

58   Purcell to Campbell, 9 July 1811, CS, NSWSA, NRS 897 [4/1804].

59   Threlkeld, *An Australian Grammar*, p. 82.

60   C. Hunter, *Bound for Wallis Plains: Maitland's convict settlers*, Maitland: Maitland City Council, 2012, p. 19.

61   M. Sainty and K.A. Johnson, *Census of New South Wales November 1828*, facsimile edition, Sydney: Library of Australian History, 1980, p. 360.

62   Macquarie, *Journal of a Tour to and from Newcastle*, 27 July 1818–9 August 1818, SLNSW, A781.

63   Campbell to Thompson, 4 August 1814, CS, NSWSA, NRS 897 [4/3493].

64   Hunter, *Bound for Wallis Plains*, p. 27.

65   Hunter, *Bound for Wallis Plains*, pp. 24, 38.

66   Lawson to Campbell, 3 April 1816, CS, NSWSA, NRS 897 [ML1/51].

67   19 March 1819, CS Special Bundles–Newcastle, NSWSA, NRS 898 [4/1807].

68   Roberts and Garland, 'The forgotten commandant', p. 20.

69   3 April 1816, CS Special Bundles–Newcastle, NSWSA, NRS 898 [4/1806]. Davis appears to have recovered his farm, as he is listed in the 1825 muster as having a conditional pardon, married with three convicts assigned to him, and in the 1828 Census as having 320 acres (129 hectares), four horses and 25 sheep on a property at Wallis Plains. Sainty and Johnson, *Census of New South Wales, November 1828*, pp. 117, 427.

70   15 November 1815, CS Special Bundles–Newcastle, NSWSA, NRS 898 [4/1805].

71   Turner (ed.), *Newcastle as a Convict Settlement*, pp. 75, 95.

72   Howe to Macquarie, 17 November 1819, CS, NSWSA, NRS 897 [4/1743].

73   18 December 1821, CS Special Bundles–Newcastle, NSWSA, NRS 898 [4/1807].

74   See L. Ford and D. Roberts, 'New South Wales penal settlements and the transformation of secondary punishments in the nineteenth-century British Empire', *Journal of Colonialism and Colonial History*, Winter 2014, vol. 15, no. 3, pp. 1–8.

CHAPTER FOUR: AS FINE A COUNTRY AS IMAGINATION CAN FORM

1 A. Macqueen, *Somewhat Perilous: The journeys of Singleton, Parr, Howe, Myles & Blaxland in the northern Blue Mountains*, Wentworth Falls: Author, 2004, pp. 24–30.

2 Macqueen, *Somewhat Perilous*, p. 34.

3 *Journal and Station Book of a trip to the north and westward (Hawkesbury Valley)*, probably by William Parr, 30 October–29 November 1817: 7 November 1817, 10 November 1817, CS, NSWSA, NRS 897 [2/3623].

4 Parr, *Journal and Station Book*, 12 November 1817.

5 Parr, *Journal and Station Book*, 14 November 1817.

6 Parr, *Journal and Station Book*, 18 November 1817.

7 Parr, *Journal and Station Book*, 17 November 1817.

8 Gammage, *The Biggest Estate on Earth*, p. 169.

9 Parr, *Journal and Station Book*, 21 November 1817.

10 Parr, *Journal and Station Book*, 22 November 1817.

11 Benjamin Singleton, *Journal*, 29 April 1818, CS, NSWSA, NRS 897 [4/1740].

12 Gapps, *The Sydney Wars*, p. 218.

13 Singleton, *Journal*, 5 May 1818.

14 Singleton, *Journal*, 6 May 1818.

15 Singleton, *Journal*, 6 May 1818.

16 T.M. Perry, *Australia's First Frontier: The spread and settlement of New South Wales 1788–1829*, Melbourne: Melbourne University Press, 1963, p. 31.

17 *SG*, 3 June 1804, p. 3.

18 N. Grey, 'Howe, John (1774–1852)', *Australian Dictionary of Biography*, National Centre of Biography, Australian National University, <http://adb.anu.edu.au/biography/howe-john-2205/text2855>.

19 John Howe to Governor Macquarie, 17 November 1819, CS, NSWSA, NRS 897 [4/1743].

20 Macqueen, *Somewhat Perilous*, p. 102.

21 Gapps, *The Sydney Wars*, p. 247.

22 William Cox to Governor Macquarie, 19 July 1816, Documents relating to Australian Aborigines 1816–1853, Sir William Dixson Collection, SLNSW, DLADD 81, pp. 187–196.

23 *SG*, 27 July 1816, p. 1.

24 Gapps, *The Sydney Wars*, p. 236.

25 *SG*, 2 November 1816, p. 1.

26 William Cox to Governor Macquarie, 15 November 1816, Documents relating to Australian Aborigines 1816–1853, Sir William Dixson Collection, SLNSW, DLADD 81, pp. 187–96.

27 H. Reynolds, *Black Pioneers: How Aboriginal and Islander people helped build Australia*, Ringwood: Penguin Books, 2000, p. 25.

28 *Journal of John Howe of Expedition from Windsor to the Hunter River in 1819*, 1 November 1819, NSW Surveyor General Field Books, NSWSA, NRS 13889 [2/8093].

29 Howe, *Journal*, 4 November 1819.

30 Howe, *Journal*, 5 November 1819.

31 Howe to Macquarie, 17 November 1819, CS, NSWSA, NRS 897 [4/1743].

32 Howe, *Journal*, 5 November 1819.

33 Howe, *Journal*, 7 November 1819.

34 Howe, *Journal*, 11 November 1819.

35 Howe to Macquarie, 17 November 1819, CS, NSWSA, NRS 897 [4/1743].

36 Howe to Macquarie, 27 December 1819, CS, NSWSA, NRS 897 [4/1743].

37 *SG*, 15 January 1820, p. 1.

38 Howe to Macquarie, 5 February 1820, CS, NSWSA, NRS 897 [4/1744].

39 Bigge Appendices, Bonwick Transcript [hereafter BT], Box 2, SLNSW, p. 734. Howe was later reimbursed £76 14s 6d for expenses incurred on the expedition: *SG*, 29 July 1820, p. 29.

40 Howe's party consisted of himself, Aboriginal guides Myles and Mullaboy, free men George Loder, Benjamin Singleton, Daniel Phillips; volunteers Andrew Loder (younger brother of George), Thomas Dargin, Phillip Thorley; ticket-of-leave holder Jeremiah Butler; and convicts Charles Berry, Robert Bridle, Nicholas Connelly, James House, Samuel Marshall and Frederick Rhodes: CS, NSWSA, NRS 897 [4/1747]. In May 1820, Howe was reappointed chief constable at Windsor, George Loder was reappointed as the gaoler and pound-keeper, and both Jeremiah Butler and James House were appointed as town constables: *SG*, 27 May 1820, p. 1.

41 Howe to Macquarie, 21 March 1820, CS, NSWSA, NRS 897 [4/1744]. Howe kept no known journal during this expedition.

42 Macquarie to Howe, 18 September 1820, CS, NSWSA, NRS 897 [CY1449 C330].

43 Collins, *An Account of the English Colony*, vol.1, appendix XII, p. 610.

44 T. Shellam, *Shaking Hands on the Frontier: Negotiating the Aboriginal world at King George's Sound*, Perth: University of Western Australia Press, 2009, pp. 139–141.

Shellam has shown the value of new information for guides in her work on the King Ya-Nup people of south-west Western Australia in the 1830s.

45 Macquarie to Earl Bathurst, 8 March 1819, *HRA*, series 1, vol. 10, p. 44.

CHAPTER FIVE: THE LAND RUSH

1 Turner (ed.), *Newcastle as a Convict Settlement*, pp. 225–6.

2 Morisset to Macquarie, 6 July 1820, CS, NSWSA, NRS 897 [4/1807].

3 Wood, *Dawn in the Valley*, p. 14.

4 Campbell to Morisset, 16 October 1820, CS, NSWSA, NRS 937 [4/3502].

5 Wood, *Dawn in the Valley*, p. 16.

6 John Marquett Blaxland, *Journal 14 February–31 August 1821*, SLNSW, SAFE/C128.

7 Morisset to Campbell, 25 November 1821, CS, NSWSA, NRS 897 [4/1807].

8 *SG*, 29 December 1821; 25 January 1822. Morisset to Campbell, 18 December 1821, CS, NSWSA, NRS 897 [4/1807]. The underlining was Morisset's emphasis.

9 Macquarie had previously toured to Newcastle in 1812 and 1818.

10 Macquarie University, *Journeys in Time 1809–1822*, The Journals of Lachlan & Elizabeth Macquarie, <www.mq.edu.au/macquarie-archive/journeys/1821/1821b.html>.

11 Dunn, 'Exploring connections', p. 238.

12 Wood, *Dawn in the Valley*, p. 18.

13 Morisset to Goulburn, 18 December 1821, CS, NSWSA, NRS 897 [4/1807].

14 *SG*, 24 November 1821, p. 1.

15 J. Ritchie (ed.), *The Evidence to the Bigge Reports: New South Wales under Governor Macquarie, Volume 1: Oral Evidence*, Melbourne: Heinemann, 1971, pp. xi–xii.

16 J.T. Bigge, *Report of Inquiry into the State of the Colony of New South Wales*, vol. 1, London: House of Commons, 1822, p. 155.

17 Karskens, *The Colony*, p. 227.

18 Bigge, *Report of Inquiry into the State of the Colony*, p. 161.

19 Bigge, *Report of Inquiry into the State of the Colony*, p. 173.

20 Morisset to Goulburn, 28 February 1822, CS, NSWSA, NRS 897 [4/1808].

21 Wood, *Dawn in the Valley*, p. 20.

22 L. Ford, *Settler Sovereignty: Jurisdiction and indigenous people in America and Australia, 1788–1836*, Cambridge, MA: Harvard University Press, 2010, p. 124.

23 B. Kercher, *An Unruly Child: A history of law in Australia*, Sydney: Allen & Unwin, 1995, p. 44.

24 Roberts and Garland, 'The forgotten commandant', p. 9.

25 Close to Goulburn, 30 December 1823, CS, NSWSA, NRS 897 [4/1809].

26 Close to Goulburn, 6 December 1823, CS, NSWSA, NRS 897 [4/1809].

27 Instructions to Dangar, 1 March 1822, CS, NSWSA, NRS 897 [4/1808].

28 D. Byrne, 'Affective Afterlives: Public history, archaeology and the material turn', in P. Ashton and A. Trapeznik (eds), *What is Public History Globally? Working with the past in the present*, Sydney: Bloomsbury Academic, 2019, p. 181; J. Gascoigne, 'Joseph Banks, mapping and the geographies of natural knowledge', in M. Ogborn and C. Withers (eds), *Georgian Geographies: Essays on space, place and landscape in the eighteenth century*, Manchester: Manchester University Press, 2004, p. 154.

29 H. Dangar, Surveyor's Field Book 193, 1822, NSWSA, NRS 13889 [2/4837].

30 H. Dangar, Letters to the Surveyor General, 28 March 1822, NSWSA, NRS 13716 [2/1526.1].

31 G. Karskens, 'The settler evolution: Space, place and memory in early colonial Australia', *Journal of the Association of the Study of Australian Literature*, 2013, vol. 13, no. 2, p. 7.

32 Dangar, Surveyor's Field Book 195, 1822–3, NSWSA, NRS 13889 [2/4839]. Dangar's descriptions of the Wallis Plains and Paterson River settlers appear throughout the field book between pages 24 and 54.

33 Hunter, *Bound for Wallis Plains*, p. 29.

34 *The Australian*, 28 February 1834, p. 3.

35 J. Bingle, *Past and Present Records of Newcastle, New South Wales*, Newcastle: Bailey, Son and Harwood, 1873, p. 13.

36 Dangar, Letters to Surveyor General, 21 August 1822, NSWSA, NRS 13716 [2/1526.1].

37 Wood, *Dawn in the Valley*, pp. 21–40.

38 Noel Butlin Archives Centre, *In Service of the Company: Letters of Sir Edward Parry Commissioner of the Australian Agricultural Company Volume 1. December 1829– June 1832*, Canberra: ANU EPRESS, 2005, p. vi.

39 Perry, *Australia's First Frontier*, Table 1, p. 130.

40 Perry, *Australia's First Frontier*, p. 131; J. Boyce, *Van Diemen's Land*, Melbourne: Black Inc., 2009, p. 148.

41 Mudie to Goulburn, 25 January 1823, CS, NSWSA, NRS 897 [4/1809].

42 Mudie to Goulburn, 25 January 1823, CS, NSWSA, NRS 897 [4/1809].

43 Mudie to Goulburn 25 January 1823, CS, NSWSA, NRS 897 [4/1809].
    Note the underlining is as per the original letter.

44 *SG*, 21 December 1821.

45 Morisset to Goulburn, 30 October 1822, CS, NSWSA, NRS 897 [4/1808].

46 Morisset to Goulburn, 12 November 1822, CS, NSWSA, NRS 897 [4/1808];
    25 February 1823, CS, NSWSA, NRS 897 [4/1809].

47 Mudie to Goulburn, 25 January 1823, CS, NSWSA, NRS 897 [4/1809].

48 Morisset to Goulburn, 25 February 1823, CS, NSWSA, NRS 897 [4/1809].

49 This figure is derived from an examination of 24 passes issued between May
    1823 and September 1824, as recorded in CS, NSWSA, NRS 937 [4/3508];
    [4/3509]; [4/3510]; [4/3512].

50 Anon, *Hunter Valley Manuscript 1832*, The University of Newcastle Cultural
    Collections.

51 *Portion of the Journal of Robert Scott, 14–17 October 1823 describing a voyage from
    Hunter River to Sydney*, SLNSW, A2266, Item 6.

52 J. Hirst, *Freedom on the Fatal Shore: Australia's first colony*, Melbourne: Black Inc.,
    2008, p. 141.

53 Wood, *Dawn in the Valley*, p. 26. T.V. Blomfield, *Memoirs of the Blomfield Family:
    being letters written by the late Captain TV Blomfield and his wife to relatives in England*,
    Armidale: Craigie and Hipgrave, 1926, p. 33.

54 Wood, *Dawn in the Valley*, pp. 24–6.

55 H. Dangar, *Index and Directory to the Map of the Country Bordering upon the River
    Hunter, the lands of the Australian Agricultural Company; with the ground plan and
    allotments of King's Town, New South Wales*, London: British Library Historical
    Print Collection, 1828, pp. 8–9; Sainty and Johnson, *Census of New South
    Wales 1828*.

56 Permit to travel for Joseph Pennington, 17 May 1825, CS, NSWSA, NRS
    937 [4/3508]; Close to Goulburn, 29 September 1823, CS, NSWSA, NRS
    897 [4/1809].

57 Depositions regarding enquiry into illegal private logging, 5 October 1822,
    CS, NSWSA, NRS 897 [4/1808].

58 Morisset to Goulburn, 25 June 1823, CS, NSWSA, NRS 897 [4/1809].

59 Harris to Goulburn, 11 February 1824, CS, NSWSA, NRS 897 [4/1810].

60 Close to Brisbane, 11 December 1823, CS, NSWSA, NRS 897 [4/1809].

61 McIntyre to Governor Brisbane, 3 September 1825, CS, NSWSA, NRS 897 [4/1813].

62 Blomfield, *Memoirs*, p. 33.

CHAPTER SIX: WORKING ON THE FRONTIER

1 G. Macdonald, 'Master narratives and the dispossession of the Wiradjuri', *Aboriginal History*, 1998, vol. 22, p. 167.

2 Reynolds, *Black Pioneers*, p. 7.

3 H. Reynolds, *The Other Side of the Frontier: Aboriginal resistance to the European invasion of Australia*, Sydney: UNSW Press, 2006, p. 144; Report of the Committee on Immigration: replies to circular letter on Aborigines, SLNSW, ZA611.

4 Bingle, *Past and Present Records of Newcastle*, p. 14.

5 Helenus did not arrive in time to secure a position and returned to New South Wales in 1823, joining Robert at Glendon. Robert Scott, letter to his mother Augusta, 14 May 1822, Scott Family Correspondence, SLNSW, A2263.

6 Anonymous diary of a servant of the Scott family, 8 August 1821–March 1824, SLNSW, MLMSS 7808.

7 Blanket Returns 1834, Patersons Plains, CS, NSWSA, NRS 906 [4/6666B].

8 I. Clendinnen, *Dancing with Strangers*, Melbourne: Text Publishing, 2003, p. 103.

9 S. Konishi, *The Aboriginal Male in the Enlightenment World*, London: Pickering and Chatto, 2012, p. 124.

10 Anonymous diary of a servant, p. 20.

11 R. White, *The Middle Ground: Indians, empires and republics in the Great Lakes Region 1650–1815*, New York, NY: Cambridge University Press, 1991, p. 52.

12 Anonymous diary of a servant, p. 56.

13 Rose, *Nourishing Terrains*, p. 8; Gammage, *The Biggest Estate on Earth*, p. 139.

14 Anonymous diary of a servant, p. 61.

15 Journal of Robert Scott, 15 October 1823, Scott Family Correspondence, SLNSW, A2266.

16 E. Rolls, *A Million Wild Acres*, Melbourne: Penguin Books, 1984, p. 60.

17 Surveyor General Letters Received 1822–55, NSWSA, NRS 13716; Dangar, Surveyor's Field Book 221, 1824, NSWSA, NRS 13889.

18 R. Dawson, *The Present State of Australia: a description of the country, its advantages and prospects, with reference to emigration; and a particular account of the manners, customs and conditions of its Aboriginal inhabitants*, London: Smith, Elder & Co, 1831, p. 8.

19 Dangar, *Index and Directory*, p. v.

20 J. Atkinson, *An Account of the State of Agriculture and Grazing in New South Wales*, London: J. Cross, 1826, p. 137.

21 R. Oldfield, 'Account of the Aborigines of N.S.W., Sydney', *The South Asian Register*, 2 January 1828, p. 107.

22 Lieut. H.W. Breton, *Excursions in New South Wales, Western Australia and Van Diemen's Land during the years 1830, 1831, 1832 and 1833*, London: Richard Bently, 1833, p. 213.

23 Lieut. G.P. Malcolm, 50th (Queens Own) Regiment of Foot, 'Account of six week tour in the District of Hunter River, October 9, 1834', SLNSW, MSS 5312, p. 8.

24 G. Blyton, 'Harry Brown (c. 1819–1854): Contribution of an Aboriginal guide in Australian exploration', *Aboriginal History Journal*, 2015, vol. 39, pp. 63–80.

25 M.L. Pratt, *Imperial Eyes: Travel writing and transculturation*, 2nd edn, New York, NY: Routledge, 2007, p. 8.

26 Pratt, *Imperial Eyes*, p. 8.

27 R. Castle and J. Hagan, 'Settlers and the State: The creation of an Aboriginal workforce in Australia', *Aboriginal History*, 1998, vol. 22, p. 24.

28 R. Harrison, *Shared Landscapes: Archaeology of attachment and the pastoral industry in New South Wales*, Sydney: UNSW Press, 2004, p. 6.

29 Clouten, *Reid's Mistake*, pp. 24–6.

30 Evidence of Major Morisset to J.T. Bigge, 17 January 1820, BT, Box 1, SLNSW, p. 479.

31 Karskens, *The Colony*, pp. 456–60.

32 P. Cunningham, *Two Years in New South Wales Comprising Sketches of the Actual State of Society in that Colony*, vol. 2, London: Henry Colburn, 1827, p. 193.

33 J. McIntyre, *First Vintage: Wine in colonial New South Wales*, Sydney: UNSW Press, 2012, pp. 202–3.

34 George Wyndham, *Diary 1830–1840*, 21 June 1833 SLNSW, B1313; *A History of Aboriginal Sydney*, <www.historyofaboriginalsydney.edu.au/north-west/working-land-%E2%80%93-more-early-family-history-gavi-duncan>.

35 Wyndham, *Diary 1830–1840*, 25 February 1833, SLNSW, B1313.

36 J. McIntyre and J. Germov, *Hunter Wine: A history*, Sydney: NewSouth Publishing, 2018, p. 62.

37 A. Harris, *Settlers and Convicts: Recollections of sixteen years' labour in the Australian backwoods by an emigrant mechanic*, Melbourne: Melbourne University Press, 1977, p. 160.

38 Harris, *Settlers and Convicts*, p. 233.

39 Harris, *Settlers and Convicts*, p. 232.

40 E.J. Eyre, *Autobiographical Narrative of Residence and Exploration in Australia 1832–1841*, SLNSW, A1806, pp. 50–1.

41 Helenus Scott, letter to his mother, 16 April 1827, Scott Family Correspondence, SLNSW, A2264.

42 Helenus Scott, letter to his mother, 16 April 1827, Scott Family Correspondence, SLNSW, A2264.

43 Cunningham, *Two Years in New South Wales*, vol. 2, p. 189; Gunson (ed.), *Australian Reminiscences*, p. 96.

44 Harris, *Settlers and Convicts*, p. 232.

45 Dawson, *The Present State of Australia*, p. 9.

46 D. Bairstow, 'With the best will in the world: Some records of early white contact with the Gampignal on the Australian Agricultural Company's estate at Port Stephens', *Aboriginal History*, 1993, vol. 17, no. 1, p. 10. Dawson acted as Commissioner from the establishment of the A.A. Co. run at Port Stephens in 1825 until 1828.

47 George Wyndham, *Evidence to Select Committee of the Legislative Council of NSW on Immigration Response to Circular on Aboriginal Labourers, Australian Aboriginals: Reports on Employment and Civilisation*, July 1832–July 1841, SLNSW, A611, pp. 97–100.

48 Phillip Parker King, *Evidence to Select Committee of the Legislative Council of NSW on Immigration Response to Circular on Aboriginal Labourers, Australian Aboriginals: Reports on Employment and Civilisation*, July 1832–July 1841, SLNSW, A611, pp. 123–31.

49 W. Stevens, *Memoirs of William Stevens*, 1897, SLNSW, MSS 6156 1(1), p. 4.

50 Correspondence of Helenus Scott 1821–1879, Letter Sarannah to Helenus, 3 June 1855, Scott Family Correspondence, SLNSW, A2264.

51 *The Maitland Mercury and Hunter River General Advertiser*, 2 December 1848, p. 2.

52 *Bells Life in Sydney and Sporting Reviewer*, 19 August 1848, p. 2.

CHAPTER SEVEN: LIVING ON COUNTRY

1   *SG*, 4 August 1825, p. 3. William Powditch, a merchant who later established the first store at Wallis Plains, was nearly wrecked in a whaleboat rowed by Aboriginal men that was swept onto a reef at the entrance to the harbour known as the Oyster Banks.

2   Gunson (ed.), *Australian Reminiscences*, p. 97.

3   J.F. Campbell, 'The genesis of rural settlement on the Hunter', *JRAHS*, 1926, vol. XII, part II, p. 111.

4   'Account of a trip to Hunter's River', *The Australian*, 31 January 1827, p. 3.

5   Gunson (ed.), *Australian Reminiscences*, p. 144.

6   J. Backhouse, *A Narrative of a Visit to the Australian Colonies*, London: Hamilton, Adams and Co, 1843, p. 389.

7   G.F. Davidson, *Trade and Travel in the Far East; or recollections of twenty-one years passed in Java, Singapore, Australia and China*, London: Madden and Malcolm, 1846, p. 144.

8   Reynolds, *The Other Side of the Frontier*, p. 194.

9   'Account of a trip to Hunter's River', *The Australian*, 7 February 1827, p. 2.

10   *The Maitland Daily Mercury*, 20 August 1895, p. 4; H. Brayshaw, *Looking for the Bora Ground in the Wallaby Scrub near Bulga*, March 2003, p. 2, <https://hunterlivinghistories.com/wp-content/uploads/2015/01/bulga-bora-ground-by-helen-brayshaw.pdf>; A.N. Eather, *The History of Bulga 1820–1921* (manuscript), Percy Haslam Collection, The University of Newcastle Cultural Collections, A5410x; W.J. Enright, 'The initiation ceremonies of the Aborigines of Port Stephens', *Journal of the Royal Society of NSW*, 1899, vol. 33, pp. 115–24.

11   Robert Scott to Colonial Secretary, 30 November 1833, Supreme Court Miscellaneous Correspondence relating to Aborigines, NSWSA COD [294A 5]. One of the two Aboriginal men attacked, known as Joe Priest, was in possession of a musket given to him by George Wyndham, which was stolen by the convict runaway.

12   *MM*, 3 June 1843, p. 2.

13   F.D. McCarthy, 'The Elourea industry of Singleton, Hunter River, New South Wales', *Records of the Australian Museum*, 1943, vol. 21, no. 4, p. 228.

14   'Letters from local magistrates and settlers in response to a directive from the Governor to take a count of Aborigines in their districts, name the tribes and the chiefs if possible', CS, NSWSA, NRS 905 [4/2045]–[29/7059], [27/3054], [27/4011]. In comparison, there were approximately 3118

settlers living in the Hunter at the same time (author analysis of 1828 Census).

15 Alexander McLeod to Alexander McLeay, 17 April 1827, 'Letters from local magistrates and settlers in response to a directive from the Governor to take a count of Aborigines in their districts, name the tribes and the chiefs if possible', CS, NSWSA, NRS 905 [4/2045]–[27/4011].

16 CS Special Bundles, List of Blanket Returns 1838, NSWSA, NRS 906 [4/1133.3].

17 Breton, *Excursions in New South Wales*, p. 90.

18 Stevens, *Memoirs*, p. 3.

19 Albrecht, *Rediscovering the Coquun*, p. 3.

20 Atchison, 'Australian place-names and cartographers', p. 151.

21 T. Bonyhady and T. Griffiths, *Words for Country: Landscape & language in Australia*, Sydney: UNSW Press, 2002, p. 2.

22 *The Australian*, 28 February 1834, p3; Threlkeld, *An Australian Grammar*, p. 91.

23 B.T. Dowd and A. Fink, ' "Harlequin of the Hunter": Major James Mudie of Castle Forbes (Part I)', *JRAHS*, December 1968, vol. 54, part 4, p. 383; Wood, *Dawn in the Valley*, p. 281; Breton, *Excursions in New South Wales*, p. 96.

24 Letters from Susan Caswell and her daughter Emily to Catherine Jackson 1829–1851, Caswell Family Papers, SLNSW, Ac147.

25 Houston Mitchell to Thomas Mitchell, 9 April 1831, Papers of Sir T.L. Mitchell, vol. 3: 1830–1839, SLNSW, CYA292.

26 Houston Mitchell to Thomas Mitchell, 18 April 1830, 30 May 1830, SLNSW CYA 292, pp. 17, 32; *The Sydney Herald (SH)*, 8 August 1831, p. 3; *SH*, 5 February 1835, p. 1.

27 T. Griffiths, *Hunters and Collectors: The antiquarian imagination in Australia*, Melbourne: Cambridge University Press, 1996, p. 223.

28 Helenus Scott, letter to his mother, October 1824, Scott Family Correspondence, SLNSW, A2264.

29 Jane Dickson, 'Notes with news cuttings 1838–1877', SLNSW, MSS 1972.

30 Dickson, 'Notes with news cuttings 1838–1877'.

31 J.D. Lang, *An Historical and Statistical Account of New South Wales both as a Penal Settlement and as a British Colony*, vol. II, London: Cochrane and McCrone, 1834, p. 114.

32 Lang, *An Historical and Statistical Account of New South Wales*, p. 115.

33 Breton, *Excursions in New South Wales*, p. 127.

34 *Report of Commission Appointed to Enquire into and Report Respecting Floods in the District of the Hunter River*, Votes and Proceedings NSW Legislative Assembly 1870/71, vol. 4, Minutes of Evidence.

35 Alexander Munro evidence, *Report of Commission Appointed to Enquire into and Report Respecting Floods in the District of the Hunter River*, p. 59.

36 John Wyndham evidence, *Report of Commission Appointed to Enquire into and Report Respecting Floods in the District of the Hunter River*, p. 122.

37 Helenus Scott to Augusta Scott, 8 May 1824, Scott Family Correspondence, SLNSW, A2264.

38 Dowd and Fink, ' "Harlequin of the Hunter" (Part I)', p. 380; Breton, *Excursions in New South Wales*, p. 120.

39 J.D. Emberg and B.T. Emberg (eds), *The Uncensored Story of Martin Cash the Australian bushranger as Told to James Lester Burke*, Launceston: Regal Publications, 1991, p. 10.

40 Letters from Susan Caswell and her daughter Emily to Catherine Jackson 1829–1851, Caswell Family Papers, SLNSW, Ac147.

41 Ellis, *Rare & Curious*, pp. 70, 233–40.

42 Blaxland, *Journal 14 February–31 August 1821*.

43 Helenus Scott to Patrick Scott, 26 December 1825, Scott Family Correspondence, SLNSW, A2264.

44 C.M. Wright, *Memories of Far-off Days: Reminiscences of Mrs Charlotte Wright including copies of correspondence 1827–1898*, 1927, SLNSW, MSS 4273, p. 20.

45 Brayshaw, *Aborigines of the Hunter Valley*, p. 67.

46 Mary Ann to George Wyndham, 3 August 1835, Letters to George and Margaret Wyndham, SLNSW, MSS 190/2, p. 110.

47 H. Reynolds, *With the White People: The crucial role of Aborigines in the exploration and development of Australia*, Ringwood: Penguin Books, 1990, p. 97.

48 Macdonald, 'Master narratives', p. 167; Harrison, *Shared Landscapes*, p. 20.

CHAPTER EIGHT: RESISTANCE AND REPRISALS

1 'Murder by the Native Blacks', *The Australian*, 10 November 1825, p. 3.

2 Examples of these animals as food items have been recorded in archaeological deposits in the middle and upper parts of the Hunter Valley. See Moore, 'Results of an archaeological survey of the Hunter River Valley', p. 401; Brayshaw, *Aborigines of the Hunter Valley*, p. 75.

3 Perry, *Australia's First Frontier*, Tables 2–6, pp. 131–2; C. Baxter (ed.), *General Muster List of New South Wales 1823, 1824, 1825*, Sydney: Society of Australian Genealogists, 1999; Sainty and Johnson, *Census of New South Wales 1828*.

4 Morisset to Goulburn, 28 July 1822, CS, NSWSA, NRS 897 [4/1808].

5 *Account of Maize due by settlers on the Banks of the Hunters River*, CS, NSWSA, NRS 897 [4/1809].

6 Gapps, *The Sydney Wars*, pp. 143–4.

7 Helenus Scott to Augusta Scott, 8 May 1824, Scott Family Correspondence, SLNSW, A2264.

8 J. Connor, *The Australian Frontier Wars: 1788–1838*, Sydney: UNSW Press, 2002, p. 40.

9 Deposition of John Fawcett, 9 November 1824, CS, NSWSA, NRS 897 [4/1811].

10 T.A. Coghlan, *Labour and Industry in Australia: From the first settlement in 1788 to the establishment of the Commonwealth in 1901*, vol. 1, Melbourne: Macmillan, 1969, pp. 257–60; 499–500.

11 Robert Scott to John Earl, August 1824, Supreme Court Miscellaneous Correspondence Relating to Aborigines, NSWSA, NRS 13696 COD294A [5/1161].

12 W.B. Ranken, *The Rankens of Bathurst*, Sydney: Townsend & Co, 1916, p. 20.

13 Report of Magistrates Mr Scott and Mr McLeod to Colonial Secretary, 3 October 1826, Governor's Despatches, vol. 8, SLNSW, A1197.

14 Karskens, *The Colony*, pp. 468, 505; Gapps, *The Sydney Wars*, p. 218.

15 James Greig to his brother, 11 November 1826, SLNSW, MLDOC 2316.

16 James Greig to Andrew Kettie, 11 November 1826, SLNSW, MLDOC 2316.

17 Report of Magistrates Mr Scott and Mr McLeod to Colonial Secretary, 3 October 1826, Governor's Despatches, vol. 8, SLNSW, A1197; Gunson (ed.), *Australian Reminiscences*, p. 91.

18 Cunningham, *Two Years in New South Wales*, vol. 1, p. 197. It is worth noting that the magistrate's report did not identify the persons involved, although names of men involved in later attacks were made known. Cunningham's source for the name is unknown.

19 Reynolds, *The Other Side of the Frontier*, p. 105.

20 Cunningham, *Two Years in New South Wales*, vol. 1, p. 197.

21 Cunningham, *Two Years in New South Wales*, vol. 1, p. 198; R. Milliss, *Waterloo Creek: The Australia Day massacre of 1838, George Gipps and the British conquest of New South Wales*, Ringwood: McPhee Gribble, 1992, p. 55.

22 George Bowman to Scott, 5 January 1839, Indigenous Peoples File: Correspondence on Black Natives, Upper Hunter 1826, Singleton District Historical Society.

23 George Bowman to Scott, 5 January 1839, Singleton District Historical Society.

24 William Ogilvie to Captain Francis Allman, 17 May 1826, CS, NSWSA, NRS 905 [4/1894, 29/3534].

25 William Ogilvie to Captain Francis Allman, 17 May 1826, CS, NSWSA, NRS 905 [4/1894, 29/3534].

26 William Ogilvie to Captain Francis Allman, 17 May 1826, CS, NSWSA, NRS 905 [4/1894, 29/3534].

27 Connor, *The Australian Frontier Wars*, p. 62.

28 Wood, *Dawn in the Valley*, p. 116.

29 Gunson (ed.), *Australian Reminiscences*, p. 93.

30 *The Australian*, 28 June 1826, p. 3.

31 Deposition of William Salisbury, 9 May 1827; Depositions of Nathaniel Lowe re: Murder of a Native Jackey Jackey otherwise called Commandant 1827, Indigenous Colonial Court Cases, NSWSA [T24A, SC 27/56]; *The Australian*, 23 May 1827, pp. 3–4; Decisions of the superior courts of New South Wales 1788–1899, Macquarie University Law School, <www.law. mq.edu.au/research/colonial_case_law/nsw/cases/case_index/1827/r_v_ lowe>.

32 Deposition of Mr John Lanarch, 6 October 1826, Re: Aboriginal Outrages 1826, Governor's Despatches, vol. 8, SLNSW, A1197.

33 Deposition of Mr James Glennie, 6 October 1826, Re: Aboriginal Outrages 1826, Governor's Despatches, vol. 8, SLNSW, A1197.

34 Deposition of Sergeant Lewis Moore, 6 October 1826, Re: Aboriginal Outrages 1826, Governor's Despatches, vol. 8, SLNSW, A1197.

35 Deposition of Lieutenant Nathaniel Lowe, 6 October 1826, Re: Aboriginal Outrages 1826, Governor's Despatches, vol. 8, SLNSW, A1197.

36 Milliss, *Waterloo Creek*, p. 55.

37 Gunson (ed.), *Australian Reminiscences*, p. 92.

38 Wood, *Dawn in the Valley*, p. 122.

39 Foley to Condamine, 22 September 1826, SLNSW Governor's Despatches, vol. 8, SLNSW, A1197, p. 372.

40 Mary Bundock Memoir, Papers of the Bundock Family of Wynagarie, Richmond River, SLNSW, A6939, p. 7.

41 Cunningham, *Two Years in New South Wales*, vol. 1, p. 199.

42 *The Australian*, 9 September 1826, p. 3; Cunningham, *Two Years in New South Wales*, vol. 1, p. 199.

43 Deposition of John Woodbury, 30 September 1826, Governor's Despatches, vol. 8, SLNSW, A1197, p. 357.

44 Deposition of John Woodbury, 29 August 1826, CS, Letters Received, NSWSA, NRS905 [5/7951, 26/5653].

45 Deposition of John Woodbury, 29 August 1826; Report of Robert Scott, Governor's Despatches, vol. 8, SLNSW, A1197, pp. 352–7, 344.

46 Deposition of John Woodbury, 29 August 1826, CS, Letters Received, NSWSA, NRS905 [5/7951, 26/5653].

47 Report of Magistrates Mr Scott and Mr McLeod to Colonial Secretary, 3 October 1826, Governor's Despatches, vol. 8, SLNSW, A1197; Captain Foley to Lieutenant Condamine, 22 September 1826, Governor's Despatches, vol. 8, SLNSW, A1197.

48 *The Australian*, 23 September 1826, p. 3.

49 Captain Foley to Lieutenant Condamine, 22 September 1826, Governor's Despatches, vol. 8, SLNSW, A1197.

CHAPTER NINE: A LANDSCAPE OF VIOLENCE

1 L. Ryan, *Tasmanian Aborigines: A History since 1803*, Sydney: Allen & Unwin, 2012, p. 82.

2 Darling to Bathurst, 6 October 1826, Governor's Despatches, vol. 8, SLNSW, A1197, p. 288.

3 Wood, *Dawn in the Valley*, p. 131.

4 *The Australian*, 17 February 1827, p. 2.

5 Gunson (ed.), *Australian Reminiscences*, p. 95.

6 Gunson (ed.), *Australian Reminiscences*, p. 95.

7 Gunson (ed.), *Australian Reminiscences*, p. 95.

8 Gunson (ed.), *Australian Reminiscences*, p. 92.

9 Helenus Scott to Augusta Scott, 25 September 1826, Scott Family Correspondence, SLNSW, A2264.

10 Petition to Governor Darling, 4 September 1826, Governor's Despatches, vol. 8, SLNSW, A1197, p. 219. The signatories to the petition were

Dr J. Bowman (Ravensworth), Peter McIntyre (Segenhoe), A.B. Sparke (Ravensfield, Maitland), Leslie Duguid (Lochinvar), J. Gaggin (Fal Brook), John Cobb (Minimbah), T.W. Winder (Windermere near Lochinvar), David Maziere (farm on site of Dalwood, Branxton), William Ogilvie (Merton), H. Malcolm and John Brown (Bolwarra).

11 Gunson (ed.), *Australian Reminiscences*, p. 91.

12 Darling to Bathurst, 6 October 1826, Governor's Despatches, vol. 8, SLNSW, A1197, p. 336.

13 Breton, *Excursions in New South Wales*, p. 201.

14 G. Blyton and J. Ramsland, 'Mixed-race unions and Indigenous demography in the Hunter Valley of New South Wales, 1788–1850', *JRAHS*, June 2012, vol. 98, part 1, p. 136.

15 Governor Darling–Response to petitioners, 5 September 1826, Governor's Despatches, vol. 8, SLNSW, A1197, p. 223.

16 Allman was the last commandant of the penal station at Newcastle.

17 Ford, *Settler Sovereignty*, p. 123. Five men had been charged with the murder of two Aboriginal boys at the Hawkesbury in 1799. Although found guilty, they were all pardoned. See Karskens, *The Colony*, pp. 467–74.

18 K. Chaves, ' "A solemn judicial farce, the mere mockery of a trial": The acquittal of Lieutenant Lowe, 1827', *Aboriginal History*, 2007, vol. 31, p. 135; Supreme Court, *The King against Nathaniel Lowe*, Information and Depositions, Indigenous Colonial Court Cases, NSWSA, T24A, SC27/56.

19 *R. v. Lowe* (1827), NSWKR4, <www.law.mq.edu.au/research/colonial_case_law/nsw/cases/case_index/1827/r_v_lowe/>.

20 Wood, *Dawn in the Valley*, pp. 117, 240. John McIntyre was later murdered in his bed in 1830 by three of his convict servants.

21 *The Australian*, 18 November 1826, p. 2.

22 Robert Scott to Alex Macleay, August 1824, Supreme Court Miscellaneous Correspondence Relating to Aborigines, NSWSA, NRS 13696, COD 294A [5/1161], p. 90; Letters from local magistrates and settlers in response to a directive from the Governor to take a count of Aborigines in their districts, name the tribes and the chiefs if possible, J. Glennie, Patricks Plains, 4 August 1829, CS, NSWSA [4/2045, 29/6435]. Bit-O-Bread/Birrybirry also appears on a blanket list in 1834 for Patricks Plains, aged 29 years, making him 22 during the period in question; see List of Blankets 1834, CS Special Bundles, NSWSA, NRS 906 [4/6666B, 34/5678], pp. 178–9.

23 George Claris, 25 March 1827, Supreme Court Miscellaneous Correspondence relating to Aborigines, NSWSA, NRS 13696, COD 294A [5/1161], Items 378–867, p. 74.

24 Attenbrow, *Sydney's Aboriginal Past*, p. 60.

25 Samuel Owen, 28 March 1827, Supreme Court Miscellaneous Correspondence relating to Aborigines, NSWSA, NRS 13696, COD 294A [5/1161], Items 378–867, p. 80. The man Jackass is probably Girrogan from Patricks Plains, as both he and Bit-O-Bread appear on the same list in 1834 and, as it was Bit-O-Bread's wife who intervened, it suggests some closer connection.

26 James Glennie, 28 March 1827, Supreme Court Miscellaneous Correspondence relating to Aborigines, NSWSA, NRS 13696, COD 294A [5/1161], Items 378–867, p. 84.

27 Robert Scott to Alexander McLeay, 17 May 1827, 28 March 1827, CS, NSWSA, NRS 905 [4/1932, 27/4692].

28 Robert Scott to Alexander McLeay, 17 May 1827, 28 March 1827, CS, NSWSA, NRS 905 [4/1932, 27/4692].

29 Robert Scott to Alexander McLeay, 17 May 1827, 28 March 1827, CS, NSWSA, NRS 905 [4/1932, 27/4692].

30 H. Reynolds, *Forgotten War*, Sydney: NewSouth Publishing, 2013, p. 86.

31 Darling to Bathurst, 6 October 1826, Governor's Despatches, vol. 8, SLNSW, A1197, p. 336; *The Australian*, 17 February 1827, p. 2.

32 B. Morris, 'Frontier colonialism as a culture of terror', in B. Attwood and J. Arnold (eds), *Power, Knowledge and Aborigines*, Melbourne: La Trobe University Press, 1992, p. 85.

33 Cunningham, *Two Years in New South Wales*, vol. 2, p. 192.

34 Breton, *Excursions in New South Wales*, p. 200.

35 Invermein Court of Petty Sessions: Letter from William Hobbs to Police Magistrate Invermein concerning the Myall Creek Massacre, 9 July 1838, NSWSA, NRS 19437.

36 It was not the first time that Dangar's Liverpool Plains estates had been the scene of bloody murder. In 1833, James Finney, one of his assigned men at Peel River, had been charged with the wilful murder of an Aboriginal man known as Black Jemmy. Accused of stealing sheep, Jemmy had been bound, bayonetted and then drowned. Finney, the only suspect, was found not guilty in the Supreme Court. See Invermein, Bench Books 1833–34, NSWSA, 7/90.

37 L. Ryan, 'A very bad business: Henry Dangar and the Myall Creek massacre', in J. Lydon and L. Ryan (eds), *Remembering the Myall Creek Massacre*, Sydney: NewSouth Publishing, 2018, p. 28.

38 Testimony of Robert Scott, *Aborigines Question: Report from the Committee on the Aborigines Question with Minutes of Evidence*, 12 October 1838, Legislative Council, Extract from Votes and Proceedings No. 23, pp. 15–16.

CHAPTER TEN: CONVICT REVOLT AND RUINED REPUTATIONS

1 *SH*, 23 December 1833, p. 2; *SH*, 30 December 1833, p. 2; *The Sydney Monitor (SM)*, 10 January 1834, p. 2; B.T. Dowd and A. Fink, ' "Harlequin of the Hunter": Major James Mudie of Castle Forbes (Part II)', *JRAHS*, March 1969, vol. 55, part 1, p. 86. Parrot was returned to Castle Forbes, despite having been sent to an iron gang. In February 1834, he was given 25 lashes for insolence and then absconded in April, having been overheard to declare that he wished he had hanged with the rest rather than continue his service at Castle Forbes; see Register of convicts tried before the Bench (Black Books) Singleton, 1833–1839, NSWSA, NRS 3370 [7/3714]; *SG*, 16 December 1833, p. 2.

2 Dowd and Fink, ' "Harlequin of the Hunter" (Part II)', p. 87. See also Supreme Court of New South Wales: Informations and Other Papers 1824–1833, *The King v Anthony Hitchcock (also called Anthony Hath), John Poole, James Riley, David Jones, John Perry, James Ryan*, NSWSA [33/234–236].

3 Lieutenant Charles Steel to Captain Williams, Mounted Police, 20 November 1833, CS, NSWSA [33/7860, 4/2240.5]. At the time, there were only eleven mounted police in the area, with two at the police headquarters at Jerrys Plains, three near the Goulburn River, two chasing runaways, two guarding the Windsor Road, one escorting a prisoner to the lockup in Maitland and one returning with the detachment's pay.

4 *SM*, 16 November 1833, p. 2.

5 Alexander McLeay to Robert Scott, 13 December 1833, Scott Family Correspondence, vol. 4, SLNSW, A2263.

6 Roger Therry, *Reminiscences of Thirty Years of Residence in New South Wales and Victoria*, 2nd edn, London: Sampson Low, Son and Co, 1863, p. 199. The donor was later revealed to be his friend and fellow Irishman, the Reverend John Joseph Therry (no relation), who was a fierce and vocal advocate for the

Irish Catholic convicts in the Colony; see Dowd and Fink, '"Harlequin of the Hunter" (Part II)', p. 89.

7 Therry, *Reminiscences*, p. 169.

8 S.J. Blair, 'The revolt at Castle Forbes: A catalyst to emancipist emigrant confrontation', *JRAHS*, 1978, vol. 64, part 2, p. 101; *SH*, 26 August 1833, p. 2.

9 *SG*, 12 December 1833, p. 2.

10 D. Roberts, 'Masters, magistrates and the management of complaint: The 1833 convict revolt at Castle Forbes and the failure of local governance', *Journal of Australian Colonial History–Colonial Newcastle: Essays on a Nineteenth Century Port and Hinterland*, 2017, vol. 19, p. 59.

11 Roberts, 'Masters, magistrates and the management of complaint', p. 79.

12 Evidence as to the treatment of assigned servants of Messrs Mudie and Lanarch, evidence of Hugh Thompson (d/5), evidence of Henry Russell (d/31), CS, NSWSA, NRS 905 [4/2182.1]; Roberts, 'Masters, magistrates and the management of complaint', p. 77.

13 Emberg and Emberg (eds), *The Uncensored Story of Martin Cash*, p. 8.

14 Harris, *Settlers and Convicts*, p. 231.

15 Evidence as to the treatment of assigned servants of Messrs Mudie and Lanarch, evidence of James Brown (a/103), CS, NSWSA, NRS 905 [4/2182.1]; Register of convicts tried before the Bench (Black Books) Singleton, 1833–1839, NSWSA, NRS 3370 [7/3714], 2 December 1833.

16 Evidence as to the treatment of assigned servants of Messrs Mudie and Lanarch, evidence of James Dodds (b/47), CS, NSWSA, NRS 905 [4/2182.1].

17 Wright, *Memories of Far-off Days*, p. 5.

18 Wood, *Dawn in the Valley*, p. 240.

19 Peter McIntyre to Brisbane, 3 September 1825, CS, NSWSA, NRS 897 [4/1813].

20 Wood, *Dawn in the Valley*, pp. 82–3.

21 R. Scott to Francis Allman, 3 September 1825, Scott Family Correspondence, Robert Scott Letters, SLNSW, A2263.

22 McLeod to Bannister, 15 December 1825, CS, NSWSA, NRS 897 [4/1813].

23 *The Australian*, 22 December 1825, p. 4. Clynch was later shot in an apparent execution by soldiers on Norfolk Island after escaping from the prison in 1829.

24 Anon, *Hunter Valley Manuscript 1832*, The University of Newcastle Cultural Collections.

25 Evidence as to the treatment of assigned servants of Messrs Mudie and Lanarch, evidence of John Lanarch, Part IV, CS, NSWSA, NRS 905 [4/2182.1].

26 Roberts, 'Masters, magistrates and the management of complaint', p. 76.

27 Evidence as to the treatment of assigned servants of Messrs Mudie and Lanarch, evidence of James Harvey (a/27), Peter Ponsonby (a/43) and Henry Brown (a/81), CS, NSWSA, NRS 905 [4/2182.1].

28 Eyre, *Autobiographical Narrative*, p. 45.

29 Magistrates Deposition Books, Hunter Valley, 1834–35, NLA, MS67; Register of convicts tried before the Bench (Black Books) Singleton, 1833–1839, NSWSA, NRS 3370 [7/3714].

30 A. Atkinson, 'Four patterns of convict protest', *Labour History*, 1979, vol. 37, p. 43.

31 Analysis by author of Register of convicts tried before the Bench (Black Books) Singleton, 1833–1839, NSWSA, NRS 3370 [7/3714]. The top six masters sending convicts to the bench were (in order) Robert and Helenus Scott (222), James Mudie and John Lanarch (201), Dr James Bowman (181), Alexander McDougall (87), Captain Robert Lethbridge (84) and James Glennie (67).

32 Evidence as to the treatment of assigned servants of Messrs Mudie and Lanarch, evidence of James Brown (a/5–a/21), CS, NSWSA, NRS 905 [4/2182.1].

33 Singleton to Close, 10 December 1823; Close to Colonial Secretary, 11 December 1823, CS, NSWSA, NRS 897 [4/1809].

34 J. Mudie, *The Felonry of New South Wales (1837)*, Walter Stone (ed.), Melbourne: Lansdowne Press, 1967, p. 7.

35 Mudie to Close, 12 December 1823, CS, NSWSA, NRS 897 [4/1809].

36 Earl to Goulburn, 26 December 1823, CS, NSWSA, NRS 897 [4/1809].

37 Helenus Scott to Augusta Scott, October 1824, Scott Family Correspondence, SLNSW, A2264; Robert Scott to Edward Frederick, from Sydney, 10 April 1822, Scott Family Correspondence, SLNSW, A2263.

38 Houston Mitchell to T.L. Mitchell, 18 April 1830, Papers of Sir Thomas Livingstone Mitchell, SLNSW, CYA292, vol. 3: 1830–1839.

39 Hunter, *Bound for Wallis Plains*, pp. 41–2.

40 H.L. Mitchell to Thomas Mitchell, 30 August 1830, Papers of Sir Thomas Livingstone Mitchell, SLNSW, CYA292, vol. 3: 1830–1839.

41 H.L. Mitchell to Thomas Mitchell, 30 August 1830, Papers of Sir Thomas Livingstone Mitchell, SLNSW, CYA292, vol. 3: 1830–1839.

42 Magistrates Deposition Books, Hunter Valley District, 22 October 1834–16 March 1835, NLA, MS67.

43 Analysis by author of the 1828 census; Perry, *Australia's First Frontier*, Table 11, p. 136.

44 Perry, *Australia's First Frontier*, Table 14, p. 138.

45 Davidson, *Trade and Travel in the Far East*, p. 197.

46 Anon, *Hunter Valley Manuscript 1832*, The University of Newcastle Cultural Collections.

47 Letters to George and Margaret Wyndham, SLNSW, MLMSS 190/1–5, p. 52.

48 Susan Caswell, Letter, 28 April 1835, Caswell Family Papers; letters from Susan Caswell and her daughter Emily to Catherine Jackson 1829–1851, SLNSW, aC147/1.

49 Susan Caswell, Letter, 28 April 1835, Caswell Family Papers; James Grieg letter to Andrew Kettie, 11 November 1826, SLNSW, MLDOC 2316; Blomfield, *Memoirs*, p. 39.

50 Eyre, *Autobiographical Narrative*, p. 45.

51 H.C. Semphill to Colonial Secretary, 26 December 1833, CS, Special Bundles: Invermein Mounted Police 1834 [4/2250.6].

52 Magistrates Deposition Books 1834–1835 Hunter Valley, NLA, MS67.

53 Letter to the Right Honourable His Majesty's Principal Secretary of State for the Colonies, London: from John Bingle Esq, one of His Majesty's Justices of the Peace for the Colony of New South Wales dated Sydney 15 August 1832; accompanied by official correspondence with the colonial Government of that colony, SLNSW, PAM83/472.

54 Wright, *Memories of Far-off Days*, p. 7.

55 Helenus Scott to Augusta Scott, 6 December 1828, Scott Family Correspondence, SLNSW A2264.

56 Mary Singleton to Joseph Sharling, 22 March 1833, Collection of letters and documents relating to Benjamin Singleton and his family, Singleton Local Studies Collection, Singleton Public Library.

57 Cunningham, *Two Years in New South Wales*, vol. 1, p. 79.

58 William Edward Riley, *Journal in New South Wales 1830–31*, SLNSW, A2012.

59 Eyre, *Autobiographical Narrative*, pp. 54–5.

60 H.L. Mitchell to Thomas Mitchell, 13 January 1835, Papers of Sir Thomas Livingstone Mitchell, SLNSW, CYA292, vol 3: 1830–1839.

61 Mary Singleton to Joseph Sharling, 9 February 1824, 22 March 1833; Collection of letters and documents relating to Benjamin Singleton and his family, Singleton Local Studies Collection, Singleton Public Library.

62 Robert Scott to Augusta Scott, 18 December 1825, Scott Family Correspondence, vol. 4, SLNSW, A2263.

63 Wood, *Dawn in the Valley*, pp. 86–92.

64 H.L. Mitchell to Thomas Mitchell, 30 August 1830, Papers of Sir Thomas Livingstone Mitchell, vol 3: 1830–1839, SLNSW, CYA292.

65 Dowd and Fink, ' "Harlequin of the Hunter" (Part II)', p. 106.

CHAPTER ELEVEN: THE CONVICT VALLEY

1 In all there were eleven commandants at Newcastle between 1804 and 1826. Eight managed the penal station exclusively; the last three oversaw its transition and closure. They were: Charles Menzies (1804–5); Charles Throsby (1805–6); William Lawson (1806–10); John Purcell (1810–11); Thomas Skottowe (1811–14); Thomas Thompson (1814–16); James Wallis (1816–18); James Morisset (1818–23); Henry Gillman (1823–4); Thomas Owen (1825); Francis Allman (1825–6).

2 Turner (ed.), *Newcastle as a Convict Settlement*, pp. 225–7; Turner, *Coal Mining in Newcastle*, p. 19.

3 Bingle, *Past and Present Records of Newcastle*, p. 7.

4 Present Distribution of Two Hundred Convicts on the Stores in Government Service at Hunters River, Henry Gillman, 1 January 1824, CS, NSWSA, NRS 897 [4/1810].

5 Dangar, *Index and Directory*, p. 47.

6 J. Windross and J.P. Ralston, *Historical Records of Newcastle 1797–1897*, Newcastle: Federal Printing and Bookbinding Works, 1897, p. 15.

7 'Account of a Trip to Hunter's River', *The Australian*, 31 January 1827, p. 2; Cunningham, *Two Years in New South Wales*, vol. 2, p. 78.

8 *SG*, 29 July 1824, p. 1.

9 *SG*, 31 October 1825, p. 3; *SM*, 24 November 1828, p. 8.

10 Sainty and Johnson, *Census of New South Wales 1828; SG*, 7 November 1828, p. 3.

11 J. Jervis, 'Genesis of settlement at Wallis Plains and Maitland', *JRAHS*, 1940, vol. 26, part II, p. 176.

12 Cunningham, *Two Years in New South Wales*, vol. 1, p. 76; Wood, *Dawn in the Valley*, p. 244; NSW Legislative Assembly, Report on the Prevention of Floods in the Hunter, by the Engineer-in-chief for Harbours and Rivers, 12 January 1869, p. 35.

13 Wood, *Dawn in the Valley*, p. 248.

14 Wood, *Dawn in the Valley*, p. 245; Hunter, *Bound for Wallis Plains*, p. 42.

15 Houston Mitchell to Thomas Mitchell, 18 April 1830, Papers of T.L. Mitchell, vol. 3: 1830–1839, SLNSW, CYA292.

16 Wood, *Dawn in the Valley*, p. 256.

17 *The Australian*, 8 July 1834, p. 4.

18 'Account of Hunter's River: Letter IV', *The Australian*, 10 February 1827, p. 2.

19 Perry, *Australia's First Frontier*, p. 72; *The Australian*, 26 August 1826, p. 2. Population derived from author analysis of 1828 Census.

20 *SG*, 26 July 1831, p. 1.

21 A. Atkinson, *Camden: Farm and village life in early New South Wales*, 2nd edn, Melbourne: Australian Scholarly Publishing, 2008, p. 42.

22 Dangar, *Index and Directory*, p. 59.

23 Jervis, 'Genesis of settlement at Wallis Plains and Maitland', p. 178.

24 James Greig to John Anderson and Andrew Kettie in Scotland 1824–29, SLNSW, MLDOC 2316.

25 Robert Scott, Report on State of Roads 1833, Scott Family Correspondence, SLNSW, A2263, vol. 4.

26 G. Karskens, 'Defiance, deference and diligence: Three views of convicts in New South Wales road gangs', *Australian Historical Archaeology*, 1986, vol. 4, p. 22.

27 Robert Scott, Report on State of Roads 1833, Scott Family Correspondence, SLNSW, A2263, vol. 4.

28 Anon, *Hunter Valley Manuscript 1832*, The University of Newcastle Cultural Collections.

29 Sainty and Johnson, *Census of New South Wales November 1828* (various entries).

30 Sainty and Johnson, *Census of New South Wales November 1828* (various entries).

31 E. Guilford (ed.), *Hunter Valley Directory 1841*, Newcastle: Hunter Valley Publications, 1987, pp. 8–17. In 1841, there were still 1028 male and 146 female convicts in both government service and private assignment in

the Hunter, while over 160 ticket-of-leave holders lived in the towns of East and West Maitland.

32 K. Binney, *Horsemen of the First Frontier (1788–1900) and the Serpent's Legacy*, Neutral Bay: Volcanic Productions, 2005, p. 288.

33 L.L. Robson, *The Convict Settlers of Australia*, Melbourne: Melbourne University Press, 1976, pp. 10–29.

34 R. Waterhouse, *The Vision Splendid: A social and cultural history of rural Australia*, Fremantle: Curtin University Books, 2005, p. 33.

35 Papers relating to Aboriginal people in the Singleton District 1843–1856, SLNSW, Aa 44, Folder 1, Item 1.

36 Turner, *Coal Mining in Newcastle*, p. 27.

37 B.R. Andrews, *Coal, Railways and Mines: The colliery railways of the Newcastle district and the early coal shipping facilities*, vol. 1, Sydney: Iron Horse Press, 2009, p. 15.

38 *Australian Agricultural Company Annual Reports 1831–1834*, A.A. Co. Collection 131/4–20, Noel Butlin Archive, ANU, Canberra.

39 *Australian Agricultural Company Annual Reports 1835–1840*, A.A. Co. Collection 131/4/12–17, Noel Butlin Archive, ANU, Canberra.

40 *The Shipping Gazette and Sydney General Trade List*, 4 July 1846, p. 192.

EPILOGUE

1 *The Singleton Argus*, 19 August 1902, p. 2.

2 T. Griffiths, 'Past Silences: Aborigines and convicts in our history-making', in Penny Russell and Richard White (eds), *Pastiche I: Reflections on 19th century Australia*, Sydney: Allen & Unwin, 1994, p. 17.

BIBLIOGRAPHY

PRIMARY SOURCES—UNPUBLISHED

State Records New South Wales

Colonial Secretary's Correspondence, Copies of Letters sent within the Colony 1 January 1814–30 January 1827, NRS 937, 4/3504–4/3512.

Colonial Secretary's Correspondence, Letters Received, Main Series 1788–1826, NRS 897, 4/1740–4/1750, 4/1807–4/1813.

Colonial Secretary's Correspondence, Letters Received, Main Series 1826–1982, NRS 905, 4/2045, 4/2182.1, 27/3054, 27/4011, 29/7059.

Colonial Secretary's Correspondence, Memorials to the Governor 1810–1822, NRS 899, 4/1835B.

Colonial Secretary's Correspondence, Special Bundles 1794–1825, NRS 898, 2/3623, 4/1718.

Colonial Secretary's Correspondence, Special Bundles 1833–1845, Aborigines: Papers dealing with issue of blankets etc, NRS 906, 4/6666B.

Court of Criminal Jurisdiction, Case Papers November–December 1820 Part II, NRS 1043, SZ792 COD452B.

Howe, John, *Journal of expedition from Windsor to the Hunter River*, in 1819, NSWSA, NRS 13889 [2/8093].

Indigenous Colonial Court Cases: Depositions of Nathaniel Lowe re: Murder of a Native Jackey Jackey otherwise called Commandant 1827, T24A, SC 27/56.

Invermein Court of Petty Sessions, 1838, NRS 19437.

Parr, W., Journal and Station Book of a trip to the north and westward (Hawkesbury River), probably by William Parr 30 October–29 November 1817, 2/3623.

Register of Convict Punishments, Singleton, 1833–1839, 7/3714, R681.

Supreme Court of New South Wales, Miscellaneous Correspondence relating to Aborigines, NRS 13696, COD 294A, 5/1161.

Supreme Court of New South Wales, Reverend Lancelet Threlkeld: Memoranda selected from 24 years of missionary engagements in the South Sea Islands and Australia by LE Threlkeld 1838, NRS 13705, COD 554, 5/1123.

Supreme Court Records, *The King v Anthony Hitchcock (also called Anthony Hath), John Poole, James Riley, David Jones, John Perry, James Ryan*, 13477 [T35], 33/234–236.

Surveyor General, Letters received from Surveyors 1822–1855, NRS 13716, 2/1526.1.

Surveyor General, Surveyors Field Books, NRS 13889, Items 109, 193–196, 208–213, 215, 218–223, 236.

State Library of New South Wales

Anonymous diary of a servant of the Scott Family, 8 August 1821–March 1824, MLMSS 7808.

Banks Papers, Correspondence with various persons concerning Australia and the South Seas, being mainly letters received by Banks 1786–1809, SAFE/Banks Papers/Series 23, Letter 25 Charles Francis Greville.

Bingle, J., Letter to the Right Honourable His Majesty's Principal Secretary of State for the Colonies, London: from John Bingle Esq, one of His Majesty's Justices of the Peace for the Colony of New South Wales dated Sydney 15 August 1832; accompanied by official correspondence with the colonial Government of that colony, PAM83/472.

Blaxland, John Marquett, *Journal 14 February–31 August 1821*, SAFE/C128, Reel 1480.

Bonwick, James, Transcripts of Records in the Public Records Office, London: Bigge, BT1-88, CY 1304.

Bonwick, James, Transcripts of Records in the Public Records Office, London: Bigge-Evidence-General, BT5, CY1494.

Bundock Family, Papers of the Bundock Family of Wynagarie, Richmond River, Notes on early recollections of Richmond River by Mary Bundock, A6939.

Caswell Family Papers, Letters from Susan Caswell and her daughter Emily to Catherine Jackson 1829–1851, Ac147.

Close, E.C., *New South Wales Sketchbook: Sea voyage, Sydney, Illawarra, Newcastle, Morpeth, c. 1817–1840*, PXA 1187.

Dickson, Jane, Notes with news cuttings 1838–1877, MLMSS 1972.

Documents relating to Australian Aborigines 1816–1853, Sir William Dixson Collection, DLADD 81.

Eyre, E.J., *Autobiographical Narrative of residence and exploration in Australia 1832–1841*, A1806.

Governor's Despatches Re: Aboriginal Outrages 1826, Governor's Despatches Volume 8 A1197.

Greig, James, Letters to John Anderson and Andrew Kettie in Scotland 1824–29, MLDOC 2316.

King, Philip Gidley, Letterbooks, 1788–1808, MLMSS 582, CY Reel 3490.

King, Philip Gidley, Letters, Re: Newcastle 1801–1805, MLMSS 582.

Macquarie, Lachlan, *A Voyage and Tour of Inspection from Port Jackson to the Settlements of Port Macquarie and Newcastle*, November 1821, SAFE A785.

Macquarie, Lachlan, *Journal of a Tour to and from Newcastle*, 27 July 1818–9 August 1818, A781, CY Reel 303.

Malcolm, Lieut. G.P., 50th (Queens Own) Regiment of Foot, 'Account of six week tour in the District of Hunter River, October 9, 1834', MLMSS 5312.

Mitchell, Sir Thomas L., Papers, vol. 3: 1830–1839, CYA292.

New South Wales Magistrates Court, Newcastle 1823–1827 Bench Books, MLMSS 2482/4–5 CY367.

Riley, William Edward, *Journal in New South Wales 1830–31*, A2012, CY Reel 424.

Scott Family, Helenus Scott Correspondence, 1821–1879, A2264, CY1587.

Scott, Robert, *Portion of a Journal 14–17 October 1823 describing a voyage from Hunter River to Sydney*, A2266 Item 6.

Stevens, William, *Memoirs of William Stevens*, 1897, MSS 6156 1(1).

Wallis, James, *Album of Original Drawings by Captain James Wallis and Joseph Lycett*, c. 1817–1818, SAFE/PXE 1072.

Wright, C.M., *Memories of Far-off Days: Reminiscences of Mrs Charlotte Wright including copies of correspondence 1827–1898*, 1927, MSS 4273.

Wyndham, George, *Diary 1830–1840*, B1313.

Wyndham, George, Letters to George and Margaret Wyndham, MLMSS 190.

National Library of Australia

Close, E.C., *Sketchbook of scenes of Sydney, Broken Bay, Newcastle and region, New South Wales, 1817–1840*, Pic Drawer 8631.

Magistrates Deposition Books, Hunter Valley, 1834–35, MS67.

White, George Boyle, Extracts from the Diary of GB White, Assistant Surveyor, Singleton 1845–47, MS3217.

Singleton District Historical Society

Indigenous Peoples File: Correspondence on Black Natives, Upper Hunter 1826.

Singleton Public Library: Local Studies

Collection of letters and documents relating to Benjamin Singleton and his family.

The University of Newcastle Cultural Collections

Anon, *Hunter Valley Manuscript 1832*.

Noel Butlin Archive of Business and Labour, ANU Canberra

Australian Agricultural Company Annual Reports 1835–1840, A.A. Co. Collection 131/4/12–17.

PRIMARY SOURCES—PUBLISHED

Atkinson, James, *An Account of the State of Agriculture and Grazing in New South Wales*, London: J. Cross, 1826.

Backhouse, James, *A Narrative of a Visit to the Australian Colonies*, London: Hamilton, Adams and Co, 1843 (1967 reprint).

Bigge, John Thomas, *Report of Inquiry into the State of the Colony of New South Wales*, vol. 1, London: House of Commons, 1822.

Bladen, F.M. (ed.), *Historical Records of New South Wales, Hunter and King, 1800–1802*, vol. 4, Sydney: Government Printer, 1896.

Blomfield, T.V., *Memoirs of the Blomfield Family: being letters written by the late Captain TV Blomfield and his wife to relatives in England*, Armidale: Craigie and Hipgrave, 1926.

Breton, Lieut. H.W., *Excursions in New South Wales, Western Australia and Van Diemen's Land during the years 1830, 1831, 1832, and 1833*, London: Richard Bently, 1833.

Collins, David, *An Account of the English Colony in New South Wales*, vol. I, London: T. Cadell and W. Davies, 1798.

Collins, David, *An Account of the English Colony in New South Wales*, vol. II, London: T. Cadell and W. Davies, 1802.

Cunningham, Peter, *Two Years in New South Wales comprising Sketches of the Actual State of Society in that Colony*, vols. I and II, London: Henry Colburn, 1827.

Dangar, Henry, *Index and Directory to the Map of the Country Bordering upon the River Hunter; the lands of the Australian Agricultural Company; with the ground plan and allotments of King's Town, New South Wales*, London: British Library Historical Print Collection, 1828.

Davidson, G.F., *Trade and Travel in the Far East; or recollections of twenty-one years passed in Java, Singapore, Australia and China*, London: Madden and Malcolm, 1846.

Dawson, Robert, *The Present State of Australia: A description of the country, its advantages and prospects, with reference to emigration; and a particular account of the manners, customs and conditions of its Aboriginal inhabitants*, London: Smith, Elder & Co, 1831.

Grant, James, *The Narrative of a Voyage of Discovery Performed in His Majesty's Vessel The Lady Nelson, of sixty tons burthen, with sliding keel in the years 1800, 1801 and 1802 to New South Wales*, facsimile edition, Adelaide: Libraries Board of South Australia, 1973.

Lang, John Dunmore, *An Historical and Statistical Account of New South Wales both as a Penal Settlement and as a British Colony*, vol. II, London: Cochrane and McCrone, 1834.

Mudie, James, *The Felonry of New South Wales*, Walter Stone (ed.), Melbourne: Lansdowne Press, 1967.

New South Wales Legislative Assembly, *Floods in the Hunter Progress Report of Commission Appointed to Enquire into and Report Respecting Floods in the District of the Hunter River*, Sydney: Government Printer, 1870.

New South Wales Legislative Assembly, *Report of Commission Appointed to Enquire into and Report Respecting Floods in the District of the Hunter River*, New South Wales Parliamentary Papers, vol. 4, 1870/71.

New South Wales Legislative Assembly, *Report on the Prevention of Floods in the Hunter by the Engineer-in-Chief for Harbours and Rivers*, Sydney: Government Printer, 12 January 1869.

New South Wales Legislative Council, *Aborigines Question: Report from the Committee on the Aborigines Question with Minutes of Evidence*, Sydney: Government Printer, 12 October 1838, Legislative Council, Extract from Votes and Proceedings No. 23.

New South Wales Legislative Council, *Evidence to Select Committee of the Legislative Council of New South Wales on Immigration; Response to Circular on Aboriginal Labourers, Australian Aboriginals: Reports on Employment and Civilisation*, Sydney: Government Printer, July 1832–July 1841.

Tench, W., *Sydney's First Four Years: Being a reprint of a narrative of the expedition to Botany Bay and a complete account of the settlement at Port Jackson*, Sydney: Angus & Robertson, 1961.

Therry, Roger, *Reminiscences of Thirty Years of Residence in New South Wales and Victoria*, 2nd edn, London: Sampson Low, Son and Co, 1863.

Threlkeld, L.E., *An Australian Grammar, Comprehending the Principals and Natural Rules of the Language Spoken by the Aborigines in the Vicinity of Hunter's River, Lake Macquarie &c.*, Sydney: Stephens & Stokes, 1834.

Watson, Frederick (ed.), *Historic Records of Australia*, series 1, vols III–X, Canberra: Library Committee of the Commonwealth Parliament, 1915.

SECONDARY SOURCES—PUBLISHED

Books, chapters and reports

Andrews, B.R., *Coal, Railways and Mines: The colliery railways of the Newcastle District and the early coal shipping facilities*, vol. 1, Sydney: Iron Horse Press, 2009.

Atkinson, Alan, *Camden: Farm and village life in early New South Wales*, Melbourne: Australian Scholarly Publishing, 2008.

Attenbrow, Val, *Sydney's Aboriginal Past: Investigating the archaeological and historical records*, 2nd edn, Sydney: UNSW Press, 2010.

Baxter, Carol (ed.), *General Muster List of New South Wales 1823, 1824, 1825*, Sydney: Society of Australian Genealogists, 1999.

Bingle, J., *Past and Present Records of Newcastle, New South Wales*, Newcastle: Bailey, Son and Harwood, 1873.

Binney, Keith, *Horsemen of the First Frontier (1788–1900) and the Serpent's Legacy*, Neutral Bay: Volcanic Productions, 2005.

Bonyhady, Tim and Griffiths, Tom, *Words for Country: Landscape and language in Australia*, Sydney: UNSW Press, 2002.

Boyce, James, *Van Diemen's Land*, Melbourne: Black Inc., 2009.

Brayshaw, Helen, *Aborigines of the Hunter Valley: A study of colonial records*, Scone: Scone and Upper Hunter Historical Society, 1986.

Byrne, D., 'Affective Afterlives: Public history, archaeology and the material turn', in P. Ashton and A. Trapeznik (eds), *What is Public History Globally? Working with the past in the present*, Sydney: Bloomsbury Academic, 2019.

Clendinnen, Inga, *Dancing with Strangers*, Melbourne: Text Publishing, 2003.

Clouten, K.H., *Reid's Mistake: The story of Lake Macquarie from its discovery until 1890*, Speers Point, NSW: Lake Macquarie Shire Council, 1988.

Coghlan, T.A., *Labour and Industry in Australia: From the first settlement in 1788 to the establishment of the Commonwealth in 1901*, vol. 1, Melbourne: Macmillan, 1969.

Connor, John, *The Australian Frontier Wars: 1788–1838*, Sydney: UNSW Press, 2002.

Department of Land and Water Conservation, *Hunter, Karuah, Manning Catchments: State of the Rivers and Estuaries Report*, Sydney: Department of Land and Water Conservation, 2000.

Dunn, M., 'Aboriginal guides in the Hunter Valley, New South Wales', in T. Shellam, M. Nugent, S. Kinoshi and A. Cadzow (eds), *Brokers and Boundaries: Colonial exploration in Indigenous territory*, Canberra: ANU Press, 2016.

Dunn, M., 'Exploring connections: Bungaree and connections in the colonial Hunter Valley', in G. Dooley and D. Clode (eds), *The First Wave: Exploring early coastal contact history in Australia*, Adelaide: Wakefield Press, 2019.

Eather, A.N., *The History of Bulga 1820–1921*, Percy Haslam Collection, The University of Newcastle Cultural Collections.

Ellis, Elizabeth, *Rare & Curious: The secret history of Governor Macquarie's collectors' chest*, Melbourne: The Miegunyah Press, 2010.

Emberg, J.D. and Emberg, B.T. (eds), *The Uncensored Story of Martin Cash the Australian Bushranger as Told to James Lester Burke*, Launceston: Regal Publications, 1991.

Flannery, Tim (ed.), *Terra Australis: Matthew Flinders' great adventures in the circumnavigation of Australia*, Melbourne: Text Publishing, 2000.

Ford, Lisa, *Settler Sovereignty: Jurisdiction and Indigenous people in America and Australia, 1788–1836*, Cambridge, MA: Harvard University Press, 2010.

Fraser, John (ed.), *An Australian Language as Spoken by the Awabakal, The People of Awaba or Lake Macquarie Being an Account of their Language, Traditions and Customs by L.E. Threlkeld*, Sydney: Government Printer, 1892.

Gammage, Bill, *The Biggest Estate on Earth: How Aborigines made Australia*, Sydney: Allen & Unwin, 2011.

Gapps, S., *The Sydney Wars: Conflict in the early colony 1788–1817*, Sydney: NewSouth Publishing, 2018.

Gascoigne, John, 'Joseph Banks, mapping and the geographies of natural knowledge', in Miles Ogborn and Charles Withers (eds), *Georgian Geographies: Essays on space, place and landscape in the eighteenth century*, Manchester: Manchester University Press, 2004.

Griffiths, Tom, *Hunters and Collectors: The antiquarian imagination in Australia*, Melbourne: Cambridge University Press, 1996.

Griffiths, Tom, 'Past Silences: Aborigines and convicts in our history-making', in Penny Russell and Richard White (eds), *Pastiche I: Reflections on 19th century Australia*, Sydney: Allen & Unwin, 1994.

Guilford, E. (ed.), *Hunter Valley Directory 1841*, Newcastle: Hunter Valley Publications, 1987.

Gunson, Neil (ed.), *Australian Reminiscences and Papers of L.E. Threlkeld: Missionary to the Aborigines 1824–1859*, vols I and II, Canberra: Australian Institute of Aboriginal Studies, 1974.

Harris, Alexander, *Settlers and Convicts: Recollections of sixteen years' labour in the Australian backwoods by an emigrant mechanic*, Melbourne: Melbourne University Press, 1977.

Harrison, Rodney, *Shared Landscapes: Archaeologies of attachment and the pastoral industry in New South Wales*, Sydney: UNSW Press, 2004.

Haslam, Percy, *Aboriginal Dreamtime of the Hunter Region: The Percy Haslam Collection*, The University of Newcastle Cultural Collections.

Hirst, John, *Freedom on the Fatal Shore*, Melbourne: Black Inc., 2008.

Hunter, Cynthia, *Bound for Wallis Plains: Maitland's convict settlers*, Maitland: Maitland City Council, 2012.

Irish, P., *Hidden in Plain View: The Aboriginal people of coastal Sydney*, Sydney: NewSouth Publishing, 2017.

Karskens, Grace, *The Colony: A history of early Sydney*, Sydney: Allen & Unwin, 2009.

Karskens, Grace, *The Rocks: Life in early Sydney*, Melbourne: Melbourne University Press, 1997.

Kercher, Bruce, *An Unruly Child: A history of law in Australia*, Sydney: Allen & Unwin, 1995.

Konishi, Shino, *The Aboriginal Male in the Enlightenment World*, London: Pickering and Chatto, 2012.

Macqueen, Andy, *Somewhat Perilous: The journeys of Singleton, Parr, Howe, Myles &* *Blaxland in the northern Blue Mountains*, Wentworth Falls: Author, 2004.

Maynard, John, *Callaghan, The University of Newcastle: Whose traditional land?*, research paper for Department of Aboriginal Studies and University of Newcastle, 2000.

Maynard, John, *True Light and Shade: An Aboriginal perspective of Joseph Lycett's art*, Canberra: NLA Publishing, 2014.

McIntyre, Julie, *First Vintage: Wine in colonial New South Wales*, Sydney: UNSW Press, 2012.

McIntyre, J. and Germov, J., *Hunter Wine: A history*, Sydney: NewSouth Publishing, 2018.

McPhee, John (ed.), *Joseph Lycett: Convict artist*, Sydney: Historic Houses Trust of New South Wales, 2006.

Miller, James, *Koori: A will to win*, Sydney: Angus & Robertson, 1985.

Millis, Roger, *Waterloo Creek: The Australia Day massacre of 1838, George Gipps and the British conquest of New South Wales*, Ringwood: McPhee Gribble, 1992.

Morris, B., 'Frontier colonialism as a culture of terror', in B. Attwood and J. Arnold (eds), *Power, Knowledge and Aborigines*, Melbourne: La Trobe University Press, 1992.

Nashar, Beryl, *The Geology of the Hunter Valley*, Sydney: The Jacaranda Press, 1964.

Needham, William J., *Burragurra: Where Spirit walked—The Aboriginal relics of the Cessnock–Wollombi region in the Hunter Valley of NSW*, Cessnock: Author, 1981.

Neville, Richard, *Mr J.W. Lewin: Painter and naturalist*, Sydney: NewSouth Publishing, 2012.

Pascoe, B., *Dark Emu Black Seeds: Agriculture or accident?*, Broome: Magabala Books, 2014.

Perry, Thomas Melville, *Australia's First Frontier: The spread of settlement in New South Wales 1788–1829*, Melbourne: Melbourne University Press, 1963.

Pike, Douglas (ed.), *Australian Dictionary of Biography*, vols 1 and 2, 1788–1850, Melbourne: Melbourne University Press, 1967.

Pratt, Mary Louise, *Imperial Eyes: Travel writing and transculturation*, 2nd edn, New York, NY: Routledge, 2007.

Reynolds, Henry, *Black Pioneers: How Aboriginal and Islander People helped build Australia*, Ringwood: Penguin Books, 2000.

Reynolds, Henry, *Forgotten War*, Sydney: NewSouth Publishing, 2013.

Reynolds, Henry, *The Other Side of the Frontier: Aboriginal resistance to the European invasion of Australia*, Sydney: UNSW Press, 2006.

Reynolds, Henry, *With the White People: The crucial role of Aborigines in the exploration and development of Australia*, Ringwood: Penguin Books, 1990.

Ritchie, J. (ed.), *The Evidence to the Bigge reports: New South Wales under Governor Macquarie, Vol. 1: Oral Evidence*, Melbourne: Heinemann, 1971.

Robson, Leslie Lloyd, *The Convict Settlers of Australia*, Melbourne: Melbourne University Press, 1976.

Rolls, Eric, *A Million Wild Acres*, Ringwood: Penguin Books, 1984.

Rose, Deborah Bird, *Nourishing Terrains: Australian Aboriginal views of landscape and wilderness*, Canberra: Australian Heritage Commission, 1996.

Ryan, Lyndall, '"A very bad business": Henry Dangar and the Myall Creek massacre', in J. Lydon and L. Ryan (eds), *Remembering the Myall Creek Massacre*, Sydney: NewSouth Publishing, 2018.

Ryan, Lyndall, *Tasmanian Aborigines: A history since 1803*, Sydney: Allen & Unwin, 2012.

Sainty, Malcolm and Johnson, Keith (eds), *Census of New South Wales November 1828*, facsimile edition, Sydney: Library of Australian History, 1980.

Scott, W., *Recollections: The blacks of Port Stephens*, prepared by Gordon Bennett, Dungog, 1929.

Shellam, Tiffany, *Shaking Hands on the Fringe: Negotiating the Aboriginal world at King George's Sound*, Perth: University of Western Australia Press, 2009.

Thomas, Martin, *The Many Worlds of R.H. Mathews: In search of an Australian anthropologist*, Sydney: Allen & Unwin, 2011.

Turner, J.W., *Coal Mining in Newcastle 1801–1900*, Newcastle History Monographs No. 9, Newcastle: Newcastle Regional Public Library, 1982.

Turner, J.W., *Manufacturing in Newcastle 1801–1900*, Newcastle History Monographs No. 8, Newcastle: Newcastle Regional Public Library, 1980.

Turner, J.W. (ed.), *Newcastle as a Convict Settlement: The evidence before J.T. Bigge in 1819–1821*, Newcastle History Monographs No. 7, Newcastle: Newcastle Regional Public Library, 1973.

Vaux, J.H., *The Memoirs of James Hardy Vaux including his Vocabulary of the Flash Language*, Noel McLachlan (ed.), London: Heinemann, 1967.

Waterhouse, R., *The Vision Splendid: A social and cultural history of rural Australia*, Fremantle: Curtin University Books, 2005.

White, R., *The Middle Ground: Indians, empires and republics in the Great Lakes Region 1650–1815*, New York, NY: Cambridge University Press, 1991.

Windross, J. and Ralston, J.P., *Historical Records of Newcastle 1797–1897*, Newcastle: Federal Printing and Bookbinding Works, 1897.

Wood, W.A., *Dawn in the Valley: The story of settlement in the Hunter River valley to 1833*, Sydney: Wentworth Books, 1972.

Journal articles

Atchison, J.F., 'Australian place-names and cartographers', *Cartography*, March 1982, vol. 12, no. 3, pp. 151–5.

Atkinson, Alan, 'Four patterns of convict protest', *Labour History*, 1979, vol. 37, pp. 28–51.

Bairstow, D., 'With the best will in the world: Some records of early white contact with the Gampignal on the Australian Agricultural Company's estate at Port Stephens', *Aboriginal History*, 1993, vol. 17, no. 1, pp. 4–16.

Blair, Sandra, 'The revolt at Castle Forbes: A catalyst to emancipist emigrant confrontation', *Journal of the Royal Australian Historical Society*, September 1978, vol. 64, part 2, pp. 89–107.

Blyton, Greg, 'Harry Brown (c. 1819–1854): Contribution of an Aboriginal guide in Australian exploration', *Aboriginal History Journal*, 2015, vol. 39, pp. 63–82.

Blyton, Greg and Ramsland, John, 'Mixed-race unions and Indigenous demography in the Hunter Valley of New South Wales, 1788–1850', *Journal of the Royal Australian Historical Society*, June 2012, vol. 98, part 1, pp. 125–48.

Braggett, Edwin, '150 Years of continuous education: Newcastle East Public School', *The Education Gazette*, 2 May 1966, pp. 103–10.

Campbell, J.F., 'The genesis of rural settlement on the Hunter', *Journal of the Royal Australian Historical Society*, 1926, vol. XII, part II, pp. 73–112.

Castle, R. and Hagan, J., 'Settlers and the state: The creation of an Aboriginal workforce in Australia', *Aboriginal History*, 1998, vol. 22, pp. 24–35.

Chaves, K., '"A solemn judicial farce, the mere mockery of a trial": The acquittal of Lieutenant Lowe, 1827', *Aboriginal History*, 2007, vol. 31, pp. 122–40.

Dowd, Bernard and Fink, Averil, '"Harlequin of the Hunter": Major James Mudie of Castle Forbes (Part I)', *Journal of the Royal Australian Historical Society*, December 1968, vol. 54, part 4, pp. 368–86.

Dowd, Bernard T. and Fink, Averil, ' "Harlequin of the Hunter": Major James Mudie of Castle Forbes (Part II)', *Journal of the Royal Australian Historical Society*, March 1969, vol. 55, part 1, pp. 83–110.

Edgeworth David, T.W. and Guthrie, F.B., 'The flood silt of the Hunter and Hawkesbury Rivers', *Journal and Proceedings of the Royal Society of New South Wales*, 1904, vol. 38, pp. 191–202.

Enright, W.J., 'The initiation ceremonies of the Aborigines of Port Stephens', *Journal of the Royal Society of New South Wales*, 1899, vol. 33, pp. 115–24.

Ford, Lisa and Roberts, David, 'New South Wales penal settlements and the transformation of secondary punishments in the nineteenth-century British Empire', *Journal of Colonialism and Colonial History*, Winter 2014, vol. 15, no. 3, pp. 1–8.

Jervis, James, 'Genesis of settlement at Wallis Plains and Maitland', *Journal of the Royal Australian Historical Society*, 1940, vol. 26, part II, pp. 165–86.

Karskens, Grace, 'Defiance, deference and diligence: Three views of convicts in New South Wales road gangs', *Australian Historical Archaeology*, 1986, vol. 4, pp. 17–28.

Karskens, Grace, 'The settler evolution: Space, place and memory in early colonial Australia', *Journal of the Association of the Study of Australian Literature*, 2013, vol. 13, no. 2, pp. 1–21.

Macdonald, G., 'Master narratives and the dispossession of the Wiradjuri', *Aboriginal History*, 1998, vol. 22, pp. 162–79.

Maynard, John, 'Muloobinbah (Newcastle) and Aboriginal industrial presence: past and present', *Journal of the Royal Australian Historical Society*, December 2001, vol. 87, part 2, pp. 248–65.

McCarthy, F. and Davidson, F.A., 'The Elouera industry of Singleton, Hunter River, New South Wales', *Records of the Australian Museum*, 1943, vol. 21, no. 4, pp. 210–30.

Moore, David R., 'Results of an archaeological survey of the Hunter River Valley, New South Wales, Australia: Part 2: Problems of the lower Hunter and contacts with the Hawkesbury Valley', *Records of the Australian Museum*, February 1981, vol. 33, no. 6–9, pp. 388–426.

Oldfield, Dr Roger, 'Account of the Aborigines of New South Wales, Sydney', *The South Asian Register*, January 1828, pp. 101–15.

Roberts, David, 'Masters, magistrates and the management of complaint: The 1833 convict revolt at Castle Forbes and the failure of local governance', *Journal of Australian Colonial History–Colonial Newcastle: Essays on a Nineteenth Century Port and Hinterland*, 2017, vol. 19, pp. 57–94.

Roberts, David A. and Garland, D., 'The forgotten commandant: James Wallis and the Newcastle penal settlement, 1816–1818', *Australian Historical Studies*, March 2010, vol. 41, no. 1, pp. 5–24.

Ryan, D.J., 'The discovery and first settlement of Newcastle and genesis of the coal industry', *The Royal Australian Historical Society Journal and Proceedings*, 1923, vol. IX, part V, pp. 225–59.

UNPUBLISHED REPORTS

Environmental Resources Management (ERM) Australia, *Upper Hunter Aboriginal Heritage Baseline Study prepared for Upper Hunter Aboriginal Heritage Trust*, October 2004.

Hughes, Philip, *NSW National Parks and Wildlife Service, Hunter Valley Region Archaeology Project Stage 1*, vol. 1, prepared by ANU Archaeological Consultancies, November 1984.

Koettig, M., 'Regional Study of Heritage Significance. Central Lowlands, Hunter Valley Electricity Commission Holdings', *A Report to the Electricity Commission in Three Volumes: Assessment of Aboriginal Sites*, vol. 3, 1990.

WEBSITES

A History of Aboriginal Sydney, Oral History Project, <www.historyofaboriginal sydney.edu.au/north-west/working-land-%E2%80%93-more-early-family-history-gavi-duncan>.

Decisions of the Superior Courts of New South Wales 1788–1899, <www.law.mq.edu.au/research/colonial_case_law/nsw/cases/case_index/1827/r_v_lowe/>.

Miromaa Aboriginal Language & Technology Centre, <www.acra.org.au/>.

Rock paintings in the Upper Hunter, <www.workingwithatsi.info/content/rock paintings1.htm>.

The Lachlan & Elizabeth Macquarie Archive, <www.mq.edu.au/macquarie-archive/lema>.

NEWSPAPERS

The Australian
The Maitland Mercury and Hunter River General Advertiser
The Shipping Gazetteer and Sydney General Trade List
The Singleton Argus
The Sydney Gazette and NSW Advertiser
The Sydney Herald
The Sydney Monitor

INDEX